Rhetorical Narratology

Rhetorical

Narratology

Michael Kearns

University of Nebraska Press
Lincoln and London

Figure 3 is reprinted from Seymour B. Chatman, *Story and Discourse: Narrative Structure in Fiction and Film* (Ithaca: Cornell UP, 1978).
© 1978 Cornell University Press. Used by permission of Cornell University Press.

Figure 8 is reprinted from Susan S. Lanser, *The Narrative Act* (Princeton: Princeton UP, 1981). Used by permission of the author.

Library of Congress Cataloging-
in-Publication Data
Kearns, Michael S., 1947–
Rhetorical narratology / Michael Kearns.
p.   cm.—(Stages ; v. 16)
Includes bibliographical references
and index.
ISBN 0-8032-2742-6 (cl.: alk. paper)
1. Discourse analysis, Narrative.
2. Narration (Rhetoric)
3. Speech acts (Linguistics)   I. Title.
II. Series: Stages (Series) ; v. 16.
P302.7.K4   1999
808'.001'4—dc21   99-10618
CIP

Contents

Figures

Preface

My goal in *Rhetorical Narratology* is to provide a coherent synthesis of the rhetorical and structuralist approaches to narrative, grounded in speech-act theory. I ask such questions as, What are the essential elements of the narrative act? and How does an audience's recognition that a text is a narrative influence how that audience interacts with the narrative? I describe myself as a strong contextualist: the answers to these questions must begin with a consideration of the dominant role played by context in every linguistic interaction. I see no way that any textual element can guarantee a text's being taken as a narrative, but if the context directs an audience to that end, many texts that we might at first think of as nonnarrative may actually be taken as narrative. "Taken as"—this phrase is crucial to my *rhetorical*-narratological project.

Because I argue for the primary role of context, it seems fair to provide my readers with one (My narrating self is trying to establish some common ground with my narrating audience.) by briefly telling the story of how this book came to be written. (Can I prove myself here a competent narrator?) About four years ago, I designed a senior-level course in narrative theory. In addition to selecting several novels, including Henry James's *The Portrait of a Lady* and Charles Dickens's *Bleak House,* I assigned three theoretical books: one that I felt was a pretty good survey of narratology (As narrator, I'm taking a bit of a risk: will my actual readers feel that I'm breaking a contract by not naming a name?), Wayne Booth's *The Rhetoric of Fiction,* and Gérard Genette's *Narrative Discourse.* Needless to say (More common ground.), I spent most of the semester trying to explain Genette's analytical categories and Booth's concept of rhetoric; the survey wasn't much help, nor was I able to profit from other, similar texts.

So, with hubris equal to that of any teenager (I'm playing the role of the self-reflexive narrator here.), I decided to write the book I'd needed for that course. Originally, I was just trying to summarize what I felt were some of the best ideas and approaches, especially from Booth and Genette. But the more I got into the project, the more I realized that my almost intuitive privileging of these two books was leading me to an argument—that narratology needed to take a strong *rhetorical* turn, without losing the technical orientation that had done so much to deepen the study of narrative during the past thirty or so years. (Ideological function: I'm explicitly asserting a theme here, and of course I'm also at last making explicit my narrative's plot.) I found myself returning repeatedly to Mary Louise Pratt's *Toward a Speech Act Theory of Literary Discourse*, Susan S. Lanser's *The Narrative Act*, James Phelan's *Reading People, Reading Plots*; these were giving me, often indirectly, a clearer sense of how Genette's brilliant discussions of structural devices correlate with actual or possible reactions of readers, and how Booth's key concepts such as "implied author" necessarily follow from speech-act theory and must be incorporated in any "rhetorical narratology" worthy of the name. Without these books, I couldn't have written my own. (All narrators know that readers like a little modesty; the trick is to make it sound honest.)

Equally important in this process were my students—not only those in that narrative-theory course, but also a group of graduate students, including some high-school teachers, who worked with me one summer on narrative and who had the fearful privilege of using an earlier draft of this book as our only critical text. They asked the hard questions, especially, time and again, "How can I apply this in my eleventh-grade (or tenth, or twelfth) classroom?" There were also some intrepid souls who paid me the highest compliment by trying to apply my approach in other courses and in master's theses.

The point to this part of my narrative (Every narrative must have a point; in the best of all modernist worlds, the point need not be spelled out.) is that, first and last, I've thought of myself as writing for students and teachers of narrative. I don't naturally incline toward theory, and I didn't set out to write a theoretical book—like Esther Summerson, I had "usefulness" as my goal. But creative writers are not the only ones who have to follow where their subjects lead them; I felt compelled to theorize in order to preserve essential insights from speech-act theory. (Here I put myself in the company of all "driven" narrators. Good company?) Like Esther, who wonders, Why me? and whose reasons for telling her story are never made clear, I hope I've managed to leave those theoretical issues a little clearer than I found them.

My second point (Multiple points for a short narrative? Yes, that's risky.) is that my choice of exemplary narrative texts probably says more about me than I'm aware of—not only about what I've read but about my values. I try to live by the Golden Rule; I value books that value life, that make me feel I'm keeping good company or at least that reinforce my preference for and understanding of "good company." (Another risk—I truly want these points to be taken seriously, whereas these interpolated comments are somewhat tongue-in-cheek. Can I get away with such discrepant registers in a short narrative?) I probably tend to see affirmation of life where other readers might not, for example, in Alain Robbe-Grillet's *In the Labyrinth*—proof, perhaps, that a life spent in the ivory tower doesn't have to make a person irredeemably cynical. This tendency has led me, I'm sure, occasionally to describe plots and themes in ways that some of my readers will take issue with. On the other hand, I've been as fair to my examples as any flawed human can be. Probably there are places where my voice overwhelms the voices in these narratives, although I've done my best to listen to and respect them. (Begging the good will of my readers—do I go too far?)

Especially during the past two years, other actual-world plots were threatening this fragile verbal world I was trying to craft. There were more days than I care to remember when both the writing and the living seemed to cost too much. (Are the narrating and authorial voices merging in a way that will make my readers uncomfortable? Well, perhaps, but this is serious—as much about the story of this book as are the other points.) I often felt like one of Henry James's characters, very much needing "saved." But I was luckier than many of them; there were people near me who were up to the job. And so, as inadequate as these two words are, "Thank you" to those who were there, before all to my daughters, Monika Leah and Shannon Alexandra, whose stories have been my life.

Rhetorical Narratology

1

Introduction to Rhetorical Narratology and Speech-Act Theory

Rhetorical and Narratological Approaches to Narrative

In one of the final paragraphs of Henry James's *The Portrait of a Lady*, Isabel flees the terrifyingly seductive embrace of Caspar Goodwood, running across the lawn and to the door of Gardencourt. "Here only she paused. She looked all about her; she listened a little; then she put her hand on the latch. She had not known where to turn; but she knew now. There was a very straight path" (644). Two days later Caspar learns that she has left for Rome. It would be easy to assume that the "path" to Rome, back to her equally terrifying husband, was the one she had discovered in that moment of pause, with her hand on the latch. To read the ending this way, however, to take it as validating Isabel's choice to lock herself up once again, invites (perhaps even requires) us to take that sentence about what she knew as having behind it the authority of the narrating voice. Yet that voice has expressed a limitation only a page earlier: "I know not whether she believed everything [Caspar] said" (James, *Portrait* 643). Suppose, then, that we take "she knew now" as Isabel's desperate attempt to convince herself that she finally has the answer. Whatever heroism or optimism we may have seen in the ending can suddenly vanish, replaced by something much darker. Instead of being a fully conscious return to a life she after all did choose, Isabel's action may be yet another of her romantic excesses.

Over the past thirty years, narratology has offered students of literature the tools to pose this kind of question, starting with the fundamental distinction between *story* and *discourse*. Seymour Chatman explains: "the story is the *what* in a narrative that is depicted, discourse the *how*" (*Story and Discourse* 19). Other terms that foreground this distinction, although their meanings are not entirely parallel, are *fabula/sjuzhet* from the Russian formalists and *histoire/discours* from the French structuralists (Martin 108, fig. 5a). In the example at hand, either reading of the ending suits the plot conflicts that have been present throughout the story of Isabel Archer, although many readers of the novel, including academics, fall into James's probably too-subtle trap and read "she knew now" as having authorial sanction. By directing our attention to discourse elements—here, the use of "transposed (indirect) inner speech" (as Genette terms it in *Narrative Discourse*)—narratology brings to light the possibility that Isabel's certainty is not shared by the narrating voice.

Narratology cannot choose between these possibilities, however—only the reader can do so, and the reader's choice will result from many factors, some located within the text but others extrinsic, factors that traditionally have fallen within the domain of rhetoric. To my knowledge there is no theory that combines these two fields—that draws on narratology's tools for analyzing texts and rhetoric's tools for analyzing the interplay between texts and contexts in order better to understand how audiences experience narratives. To fill this gap I'm proposing a rhetorical narratology that is grounded in speech-act theory and thus considers narrative from the perspective of the socially constituted actions it performs: narrative as "doing" as well as "saying." Speech-act theory provides the means for describing, and occasionally for explaining, how narratives and audiences interact. It also justifies my strong-contextualist position: I insist that the right context can cause almost any text to be taken as a narrative and that there are no textual elements that guarantee such a reception. Rhetorical narratology recognizes story elements, but because this speech-act theoretical basis foregrounds the interaction between reader and text, I give more prominence to discourse elements. Hence I treat narrative as a type of discourse rather than a genre, identified by the functions it serves and the kinds of situations in which it occurs. My strong-contextualist position also allows for more rigor than can be found in what Ingeborg Hoesterey has recently named "critical narratology," which blends relatively structuralist narratology with recent "philosophical, political, and psychoanalytical positions" (4). "Eclectic narratology" might be a better name for this blend, and while the best criticism may often be eclectic, students and teachers of narrative need a way to approach their topic systematically.

I intend rhetorical narratology to meet this need by consistently granting to *context* the determination of what will count as a narrative text and the basic expectations governing how an audience will process such a text, expectations I discuss as "ur-conventions." Within my contextualist framework, the most interesting and powerful features are what I term the *audience* and *voice* positions: the roles that are theoretically available within any narrative to readers (and other audiences) and that can be inferred by an audience. Together these sets of roles determine how an audience will take the narrative as being transmitted and where authority will lie within the interaction between audience and narrative. Context, the ur-conventions, and the positions of voice and audience, I will show, are primarily characteristics of the type of discourse *use* that is termed *narrative*, rather than features of texts. Several of them are likely to be invoked by textual features (the *extratextual voice* and the *narratee*, discussed in chapter 3), but such invoking can only happen within a context in which "narrating" has already been determined to be the discourse type—the way this particular text is recognized as intended to be used. Throughout this book I will advocate the strong version of this position: nothing *in* a text can guarantee that it will be taken as a narrative, whereas extratextual features can cause an audience to at least consider the possibility that an informative or persuasive discourse is a narrative. I advocate this version partly to stimulate further empirical research: a study might demonstrate that a certain density or variety of "narrative" features in a text *can* guarantee that it will be received as a narrative. But until such research is conducted, I will remain on the side of speech-act theorists, for whom context holds the power. I also advocate the strong version because I believe that authorial reading—the belief, shared by audience and author, that a narrative text exists to move the audience in some way—governs the interaction between narrative texts and their audiences.

In order better to establish the need for a rhetorical narratology, I want briefly to review the history of narratology as a named field of academic inquiry, focusing on two points: that it has been mainly concerned with the technical analysis of narrative texts and that it has not given enough attention to the contexts within which audiences encounter these texts. Tzvetan Todorov is credited with having created the French term *narratologie* in 1969, defining it as "the science of narrative" (Jefferson 91). Gérard Genette used the French term in 1972; one early instance of the English *narratology* was in Robert Scholes's *Structuralism in Literature* (1974). The best short description, from M. H. Abrams, captures the field's governing purpose and methodology. Abrams writes that narratology's "general undertaking is to determine the rules, or codes of composition, that are manifested by the diverse forms of plot, and also to formulate the 'grammar' of narrative in terms of structures and narrative formulae that recur in many stories, whatever the differences in the narrated subject matters" (123–24). To determine this "grammar," the narratologist "deals especially with the identification of structural elements and their diverse modes of combination, with recurrent narrative devices, and with the analysis of the kinds of discourse by which a narrative gets told." Equally important is what narratologists do not do: treat narrative mimetically, "as a fictional representation of life." Narrative is to be studied "as a systematic formal construction."

As Abrams's description makes clear, narratology's most direct ancestors are formalism and structuralism: both emphasize rigorous analysis, and the latter especially seeks principles that connect broad areas of human action. Narratology has aimed at such breadth by studying all narratives, not just fictitious ones, and the field has achieved a great deal in terms of elaborating the characteristic features of texts taken as narrative and explaining how they function. Surveying this work, Gerald Prince points out that narratology has contributed a great deal to our understanding of narrative discourse (including point of view, narrator, and temporal relations), story (causality, chronology, minimal constituents), characters and settings, fictional worlds, and conventions ("Narrative Studies" 271–74).

However, narratology has not achieved the ideal held by some of its earliest practitioners: using the study of narrative as a means of achieving a comprehensive grasp of human endeavors. "The initial excitements and fairly rapid disappointments of narratology must have had to do with the early high claims of universality" is the assessment offered by Christine Brooke-Rose (283). Nevertheless, according to Mieke Bal, narratology has contributed some important concepts and analytical tools to disciplines outside its natural realms of literature and anthropology ("The Point" 730). Jackson Barry gives three reasons for this extension: (1) "the gradual establishment of narratology as an autonomous field distinct from literary theory as a part of literary criticism, historiography, or sociolinguistics" (297); (2) the movement away from any notion of "truth" and "the deconstruction of scientific reporting with such literary tools as point of view, figuration, etc." (297); and (3) "the appearance of strong claims for narrative as a particular, essential, and basic cognitive instrument" (298). The psychologist, the historian, even the cosmologist may approach critical issues in their fields from a perspective to which narratology has contributed.

These articles by Barry, Bal, Brooke-Rose, and Prince were published in 1990 as part of a ten-year retrospective on the 1979 narratology conference held at Tel Aviv University, a conference whose papers helped inaugurate the influential journal *Poetics Today* and gave additional visibility to the then-still-new discipline of narratology. While Prince, as befits one of the field's main systematizers, seems interested in adding to narratology's tool kit, the others articulate the limitations of these tools. One reason for these limitations is that the field has participated in what has been called "the linguistic turn" in much recent critical theory: "a move away from concrete experience to abstract patterns" (Petrey 48). This move has caused an explanatory gap between the analytical tools and the phenomena they describe: the actual human experience of narrative. As Wayne Booth wrote in the afterword to the second edition of *The Rhetoric of Fiction*: "the search for greater precision has often led to an impoverishment of the issues—as is so often the case in efforts to make humanistic study more scientific" (422).

An excellent example of Booth's point is Genette's elaborate taxonomy of "narrative *anachronies* . . . the various types of discordance between the two orderings of story and narrative" (*Narrative Discourse* 35–36). On the one hand, a narrative's deviations from a strictly linear ordering of events are true to the human experience of time, and the different types of deviations (such as flashback and flash-forward, in ordinary terms) affect readers differently. On the other hand, this taxonomy says nothing about how important anachronies may be in a particular novel, how they may operate in the time-bound process of reading. To put the point in a practical light, students can be taught the scheme, just as they can be taught the main types of poetic feet. But they must also be led to understand that no "prolepsis" (Genette's term for flash-forward) is important in itself, that the personal, textual, rhetorical, and cultural contexts have much to do with whatever value the element carries. Genette has shown himself sensitive to this issue, concluding *Narrative Discourse* with the "hope, that all this technology—prolepses, analepses . . . the metadiegetic, etc. . . . tomorrow will seem positively rustic, and will go to join other packaging, the detritus of Poetics" (263). The "technology" is important for understanding texts that are being taken as narrative, but it can't explain why texts *are* taken this way—hence my strong contextualism.

Narratologists have not been scrapping their tools, but they have taken some steps toward placing these tools within the larger realm of rhetoric. Prince, one of the leading proponents of a structuralist approach, remarks in his seminal work *Narratology* that it is less illuminating to define a narrative, as he does, as "the representation of *at least two* real or fictive events in a time sequence, neither of which presupposes or entails the other" (4), than to keep this rhetorical point in mind: "a text constitutes a narrative if and only if it is processed as such a representation" (163). And twenty years ago Jonathan Culler, in *Structuralist Poetics*, wrote that any approach to narrative "must take account of the process of reading so that . . . it provides some explanation of the way in which plots are built up from the actions and incidents that the reader encounters" (219). The approach must also "expli-

cate the structural intuitions of readers by studying their formal expectations" (223).

In spite of these rhetorical inclinations, the books normally used as
texts in courses in narrative theory still tend toward a structuralist approach: *Narrative Discourse* (Genette), *Narrative Fiction* (Rimmon-
Kenan), *Narratology: Introduction to the Theory of Narrative* (Bal),
Story and Discourse (Chatman), and *Narratology: The Form and Functioning of Narrative* (Prince). The most recent of these to appear in English, Mieke Bal's *Narratology*, was published in 1985 and was reprinted three times through 1994, but it actually derives from the
structuralist work of the 1960s and 1970s. *Narrative Fiction* has been
reprinted four times, *Narrative Discourse* five. Yet none of these has
been revised to clarify confusions within the "instruments" (such as
the practical distinction between *narratee* and *narrative audience*), let
alone to foreground rhetorical considerations. Genette has provided a
witty and thoughtful response to his critics in *Narrative Discourse Revisited* (translation published in 1988), but he does not bring to the
forefront the rhetorical turn. The same is true of Seymour Chatman's
Coming to Terms: The Rhetoric of Narrative in Fiction and Film
(1990). Chatman's title suggests the kind of rhetorical narratology I'm
discussing, but he does not explain how rhetorical effects are to be
analyzed or what methods can be used to link a narrative's elements,
objectively described, with the way it moves (or fails to move) an
audience.

The limitations of these texts are symptomatic of the continuing
and unfortunate separation between the fields of rhetoric and literature. The hefty anthology *Contemporary Literary Criticism* contains
only one selection from contemporary rhetoric, reprinting Kenneth
Burke's famous essay "Literature as Equipment for Living" in its section on "Rhetoric and Reader Response." None of the selections offers
anything like a theoretical overview of the rhetorical approach; in
their introduction to this section, Robert Con Davis and Ronald Schleifer discuss rhetoric in its Aristotelian sense (emphasizing figures and
tropes) and in what they feel is a broader sense (looking at how texts affect readers), but there is no consideration of rhetoric as a theory of discourse (68). David Richter's anthology *Falling into Theory* is limited in
the same way: part 3 ("How We Read—Interpretive Communities and
Literary Meaning") ignores the issue of how discourse *functions*. Richter has used the phrase "rhetorical narratology" in his anthology *Nar-
rative/Theory* with exactly my meaning: "rhetorical narratology is
concerned with what [narrative] *does* or how it *works*" (ix), and "[t]he
rhetorical narratologist starts with the premise that the narrative is
from the outset an act of communication between author and reader"

[margin annotation: structuralist narratology]

(94). However, he does not develop the approach (nor would one expect him to in an anthology), and his selections illustrate my point that *rhetorical* narratology has never been given a solid basis in rhetorical or discourse theory. Terry Eagleton calls for a "reinvention of rhetoric" but does not reference such important contemporary works as James Kinneavy's *A Theory of Discourse: The Aims of Discourse*; neither does Wayne Booth in *The Rhetoric of Fiction* or *The Company We Keep*, although he does use Kenneth Burke a few times to illustrate specific points. (Anneliese Watt remarks on the lack of critical attention to Burke's comments on narrative, but her study is peripheral to my interest here.) Nor, for that matter, do the most influential practitioners of speech-act theory in the literary arena, Mary Louise Pratt and Susan S. Lanser. Yet this particular link would seem obvious and natural, given Kinneavy's discussion of literature as one of the four "aims" of discourse, the purpose of which is to call attention to itself (39). I'll return shortly to Kinneavy; for now, I want simply to emphasize his placement of "aims" under the heading of "pragmatics," an orientation that is shared by speech-act theorists and by literary critics who have adopted the speech-act approach.

Robert Scholes has actually termed Genette a rhetorician (*Structuralism* 161), even though the main impact of his work has been on the "technology" of analysis. *Narrative Discourse* in fact remains the single best book on narratology, a book that, when combined with Wayne Booth's famous *The Rhetoric of Fiction*, anchors the whole field. That such a pairing is necessary, however, signals Genette's limitations, whereas if literary theory had taken a slightly different course, Genette might now be honored as an early practitioner of another recent turn in literary studies, the rhetorical. Eagleton, for instance, advocates such a turn in the concluding chapter of his *Literary Theory: An Introduction* (1983), calling for a "reinvention of rhetoric" along the lines of " 'discourse theory' or 'cultural studies' " (210). And if the rhetorical elements of Genette's *Narrative Discourse* had been taken up as vigorously as have been the more formalist and structuralist elements, his influence might have helped move the rhetorical analysis of narrative to a more technical level. He might also have helped sensitize theorists of narrative to their underlying unspoken assumptions. *The Rhetoric of Fiction*, to take one example, has long been recognized as valuing plurality, complexity, and stable irony. These values, which it shares with many other systematic approaches such as Wolfgang Iser's *The Act of Reading*, are not intrinsically superior to others, as is demonstrated by recent studies of, for instance, the novel of sentiment in nineteenth-century America.

This mild criticism of Booth's work is related to a more general problem noted by Mark Turner, that the whole field of English studies pays too much attention to the odd, the unusual, the ambiguous—qualities that are recognized by and processed in our conscious minds. This criticism is not especially applicable to Genette because he consistently explains the norms that are challenged by his major example, Proust. On the other hand, he does not discriminate between the rhetorical effects of following and deviating from conventions. Turner insists that until we understand the cognitive basis against which ambiguous or unusual features stand out, we really can't claim to understand these departures from it; he could also have noted that concentrating on such features leads theorists to overlook the role of context. According to Turner, "acts of language and literature" are "for the most part . . . acts of the unconscious mind," based on "conceptual connections" revealed in "our patterns of reading and writing" (*Reading Minds* 43, 149). Turner may be overstating the problem in one respect: readers can experience ambiguity, for instance, even when they aren't aware of the background against which the experience is set. But his basic point is still valid: reading is partially a rule-governed activity, and these rules (or codes and conventions, as they're usually called) are established by context and influence readers at the preconscious level as well as at the conscious. In chapter 2 I consider at greater length this distinction, and in chapter 5 I sketch a "script" that organizes some of what readers of fictional narratives do both consciously and preconsciously.

The rhetorical narratology I develop in the following chapters addresses Turner's critique by applying fundamental concepts from speech-act theory (such as the transactional nature of all human language, the principles of relevance, the cooperative principle, and markedness) to draw together the strengths of rhetoric and narratology. Rhetoric has always been interested in the interaction between text and audience as that interaction occurs in specific contexts and through time (rather than in some timeless, arhetorical realm). This interest contributed a great deal to the success of Booth's *The Rhetoric of Fiction*, which took as one of its main tasks the dismantling of critical prescriptions generated by Henry James and codified in Percy Lubbock's *The Craft of Fiction* (first published in 1921). Booth carefully demonstrated that there was nothing intrinsically superior about the "General Rules" he took to task, for instance, "All authors should be objective." He showed that the rhetorical question is always the crucial one: how well does a given technique suit the purpose that a reader infers from the text? This is the point of two of his main chapters, "The Uses of Reliable Commentary" and "The Uses of Authorial Silence." Like many other people who teach narrative, I frequently return to

Booth. I doubt that I could have conceived of rhetorical narratology had not that book (or one like it) been written. Almost single-handedly, Booth sparked a revolution in the study of narrative by emphasizing such concepts as *voice* and *implied author*, but he also carried on the formalist concentration on these as textual features rather than considering, theoretically, how they are or might be perceived by readers.

Chatman provides one example of the necessary further step in his essay "The 'Rhetoric' of 'Fiction.'" He points out that the interactions between texts and readers involve an element of "suasion" that defines the way any text is to be taken. (Here and throughout, when I use the word *text*, I mean the physically transmitted document that exists independently of its performance. I realize that some theorists question whether this independence is possible, but practically speaking, the distinction works—text is the set of pages we all read, the set of spoken words or gestures a tape recorder or camera would capture.) A "novel's narrative technique," Chatman says, "functions to suade us of the text's right to be considered *as* fictional narrative, of its existence as a nonarbitrary and noncontingent utterance, one which has its own force, autonomy, its own right to be taken seriously as a legitimate member of the recognizable class of texts which we call narrative fiction" ("The 'Rhetoric'" 46). Considered as rhetorical, "end-oriented discourse," the novel also suades readers "toward the investigation of some view of how things are in the real world" (55). Most theorists today would agree with Chatman's first assertion, and most would also agree that narrative, whether novelistic or not, has a particular relationship to the actual world, although the nature of that relationship is still disputed. The most radically postmodern narrative will still have a *point* (as I explain later), even if the point is that no actual world can be known independently of linguistic constructions.

Speech-Act Theory and Rhetorical Narratology

With rhetorical narratology I intend to give narratology's rhetorical turn a strong push by keeping at the center of the inquiry the question, How do the elements of narrative actually work on readers? and by approaching this question by means of speech-act theory. Chatman has criticized what he terms "contextualist narratology" as having much less to offer the study of narrative than its proponents claim; he finds "little evidence" that the contextualist approach provides "greater explanatory power" than a structuralist or text-centered narratology ("What Can We Learn" 312). His critique unfortunately hinges on some oversimplifications of the theory of speech acts that underlies contextualism, especially on his claim that the theory has no interest in textual structures and insists on regarding narrative as an "interchange ... between Real Authors and Real Readers" (315). Chatman plays down the speech-act theorists' commitment to understanding the shared conventions by which any text is produced and received, but this commitment is essential to rhetorical narratology, which treats any narrative as a speech act produced and received within, although not wholly determined by, a rule-governed context. Because, as Henry Shaw notes, whatever laws may govern narrative are probably subordinate to "broader cultural presuppositions" (113), Chatman's antagonism toward speech-act theory, which attempts to mediate between text and context on the basis of such presuppositions, is not justified. In fact, Chatman's own earlier insistence on the role of "cultural codes" speaks against this criticism (*Story and Discourse* 149). A similarly limited critique comes from Wallace Martin: "though speech-act theorists may explain meaning in discourse, they do not explain what one needs to know in order to understand the meaning of any third-personal fictional narrative," for example (185). This critique may hold for the theory's seminal philosophical treatises, such as J. L. Austin's *How to Do Things with Words*, but not for later studies. Susan S. Lanser, in *The Narrative Act*, describes quite clearly the framework within which a third-person narrator will be constructed (the ways in which this narrator may differ from the narrative's extrafictional voice, for example, and the axes of contact, status, and stance on which the voice can position itself). The narrator of *The Portrait of a Lady* communicates in a different way than does the narrator of *Emma*, and both have a different kind of existence than does the third-person narrating voice of a biography. In the following chapters I show how the theory illuminates these and other differences.

Speech-act theory in fact provides the basis for my strong-contextualist position, hence for a truly "rhetorical" narratology. This theory has been defined as nothing less than "an account of the conditions of intelligibility, of what it means to mean in a community, of the procedures which must be instituted before one can even be said to be understood" (Fish 1024). For the speech-act theorist, the meanings of most interest are those that exist within a community, and no utterance can be said to be understood unless it is viewed within a context in which some action or effect is possible. As such a theorist, I would say that Martin's critique is not well formulated because it seems to presume that such a thing as "the meaning of a third-person fictional narrative" exists, when in fact the interesting questions have to do with how a reader decides to begin with the assumption that a text is a fictional narrative and how that decision then shapes the reader's transaction with the narrative. Whereas an earlier generation of linguistic critics would search the deep structure of a narrative's sentences for clues to modality (the speaker's attitude toward her utterance and her addressee) (Fowler 13), the speech-act theorist looks outside of these sentences. The theory explains that the force of any utterance is determined by the conventions surrounding that utterance as well as by those the utterance invokes (Petrey 12). This is the reason that the same string of words can have two entirely different effects. Sandy Petrey provides an excellent example: "[t]he constitution is suspended" in a newspaper article compared to the same sentence in a government decree (12). Speech-act theory emphasizes the "social process" rather than the text's "formal structure," as do other linguistic theories (3); this is not to say that the theory ignores such structures, only that it does not specify a text's "meaning" on that basis. Whereas a formalist might try to explain the simple declarative statement "X is suspended" as a form of a decree, "Let X be suspended," the speech-act theorist looks at the situational contexts in which this utterance takes place and asks what conventions and expectations operate in each, because these, like the label "Romance" on the shelf where a book is found, principally determine how the utterance is going to be taken, what illocutionary force it will have.

Petrey's reference to social process drives home the fact that speech-act theory tends to look at surfaces, as it were—at actual utterances, the contexts (especially social) for those utterances, and the effects of the utterances, rather than at deep structures analogous to those postulated by transformational-generative grammar. I've already indicated that in spite of this tendency, and even though it is not cognitivist in orientation, the theory addresses the problem with literary theory pointed out by Mark Turner by specifying conventions that condition discourse transactions at the preconscious level. Similarly, the theory is mutually supportive with the so-called connectionist models of cognition developed by researchers in artificial intelligence. These models eschew computation-like processing rules in favor of probabilistically weighted associations; they attach a great deal of importance to humans' ability to match patterns, create models, and manipulate environments for purposes (among others) of representation (Williams 556–57). Unlike the formulas used by structuralist narratologists to generate narratives, formulas that can work with only a few elements, connectionist models hold out some hope of explaining how humans actually generate and respond to narratives that involve tens of hours to receive, such as novels and histories. (Here I'm extrapolating from points made by Williams [562–63].) Both the traditional "mentalistic" approach to cognitivism and the new connectionist approach deserve further exploration by narratologists, always within a framework that regards discovered or hypothesized structures as used by human beings for particular ends (Beaugrande 418–19).

The speech-act theorist's interest in context leads to the crucial distinction between *locution* (what is said), *illocution* (very roughly, what is meant), and *perlocution* (the effect of an utterance on its audience). Most important for rhetorical narratology are the first two components of the speech act, which can effectively, albeit approximately, be characterized by the title of the book in which John Searle analyzes and classifies illocutionary acts, *Expression and Meaning*. (As this title suggests, speech-act theorists have tended to pay relatively less attention to perlocution; this is an aspect deserving considerable empirical research, by narratologists as well as by speech-act theorists more generally.) Meaning, for Searle, is primarily determined by the use to which an utterance is put. The ability of language to act on its users cannot be explained on the basis of the users' "mastery of those rules which constitute linguistic competence"; there must also exist "an extra-linguistic institution" within which both speaker and hearer have a definite place (18). Depending on the utterance, such an institution might be a church, an initiation ceremony, or a classroom. To these obvious examples, I would add any context associated with "literature," such as that section of a bookstore. Searle writes, "If we adopt illocutionary point as the basic notion on which to classify uses of language, then there are a rather limited number of basic things we do with language: we tell people how things are, we try to get them to do things, we commit ourselves to doing things, we express our feelings and attitudes and we bring about changes through our utterances. Often, we do more than one of these at once in the same utterance" (29). Searle's taxonomy is based on what he terms "the direction of fit" between words and world—how the "propositional content" of an illocution "is supposed to relate to the world" (4)—and on the "sincerity condition," the psychological state expressed by the utterance (12). Briefly, the categories are as follows:

> *Assertives*: words to world (that is, the words of the locution are supposed to match the world); psychological state of belief that something is the case. Example: I state or hypothesize that something is so.
> *Directives*: world to words; state of want, wish, desire. Example: I order or invite you to do something.
> *Commissives*: world to words; state of intention. Example: I promise or guarantee something.
> *Expressives*: "[t]he illocutionary point of this class is to express the psychological state specified in the sincerity condition about a state of affairs spe-

cified in the propositional content" (Searle 15). Hence, no direction of fit; the sincerity condition is determined by the proposition. Example: I congratulate you/thank you/apologize to you.
Declarations: both world to words and words to world, no sincerity condition. Example: a judge says, "I pronounce you guilty"; an umpire says, "You're out." (Searle 12–19)

This taxonomy highlights the contextualist approach of speech-act theory. Both the "direction of fit" and the "sincerity condition" have to do with how utterances are taken by audiences and with how speakers operate on the basis of expectations regarding such "taking." The fundamental principles here are what Dan Sperber and Dierdre Wilson term "Relevance," which I'll discuss shortly, only noting here that Relevance assumes that all parties involved in a communication expect rationality. Without a shared concept of what is rational, we probably could not communicate with each other, although our linguistic behaviors often are not rational.

Two items in Searle's list match up nicely with two of Kinneavy's aims of discourse: reference (assertives) and persuasion (directives). Kinneavy's other two aims, literature and expression, do not match well, a point that draws attention to an interesting methodological difference between these theorists: Searle emphasizes the producer of the discourse, while Kinneavy allows for intentionality to be attached to the discourse itself. Both methods are useful; together they accurately reflect the reality of any linguistic interaction, in which sometimes the speaker is more prominent, sometimes the text, and sometimes the receiver.

In another essay in this book, "The Logical Status of Fictional Discourse," Searle argues that the author of a work of fiction is only pretending to perform illocutionary acts, hence is not committed to the truth of the locutions but is to be understood as "invoking the horizontal conventions that suspend the normal illocutionary commitments of the utterances" (68). The "normal" commitments have to do with the "vertical" fit between words and world that obtains in the "serious" illocutionary act (66). Searle's use of "pretend" has come under heavy fire, but it is important to remember, first, that in this essay he is appropriately tentative about his choice of words, and, second, that the verb "contain[s] the concept of intention built into it." Furthermore, the whole issue of pretending can be finessed by concentrating on Searle's explanation that an author of a fictional work invokes conventions suspending the "normal" commitment. The end result, for Searle, is most important: "[t]here is no textual property, syntactical or semantic, that will identify a text as a work of fiction. What makes it a work of fiction is, so to speak, the illocutionary stance that the author takes toward it" (65). This is the essence of the strong-contextualist position.

Searle carries out the same line of reasoning for a type of text—*display*—that is crucial to rhetorical narratology. For this type of text, according to Searle, a "horizontal convention" is invoked such that, while the illocutionary acts seem to be, as with fiction, mainly of the assertive type (including "statements, assertions, descriptions, characterizations, identifications, explanations, and numerous others" [65 n.5]), the speaker is not committed to their truth. Yet the speaker's (author's) lack of commitment to the "truth" of such assertions seems beside the point. Instead of this method of defining display text by the negative (not intended as truth), it makes more sense to describe it as a *use* of language, determined by context more than by the attitude taken by the speaker. This attitude is relevant but will not always be known, and other aspects of the situational context may cause a text to be received differently than it was intended (for example, someone might pick up a biography that had been mistakenly shelved as fiction). Following Kinneavy, I contend that *aim* is the most important aspect of any verbal transaction, but I combine two of his uses—expressive and literature—into one, *display*, that demonstrates the leading characteristics of "calling attention to," no matter whether the object of the attention is the text or the speaker. While these two do stand as logically discrete categories, distinguishing between the two is not always possible, nor is it really necessary—both are types of display.

In designating display as a fundamental use of language, I am building on Mary Louise Pratt's ground-breaking application of speech-act theory to literature, *Toward a Speech Act Theory of Literary Discourse.* According to Pratt, "speech act theory provides a way of talking about utterances not only in terms of their surface grammatical properties but also in terms of the context in which they are made, the intentions, attitudes, and expectations of the participants, the relationships existing between participants, and generally, the unspoken rules and conventions that are understood to be in play when an utterance is made and received" (86). Pratt's "not only . . . but also" construction demonstrates the fallacy of Chatman's critique. Speech-act theory actually has quite a bit to say about such things as the "surface grammatical properties" of utterances (for instance, in classifying types of illocutions), but its more pressing concern is to redress the imbalance between text and reader fostered by formalist and structuralist approaches. Speech-act theory reminds us that "literature is a context" like any other (Pratt, *Toward a Speech Act Theory* 99), with rules and conventions that both writers and readers know to be in place.

Because they treat literature as a context, speech-act theorists do not attempt to define literature intrinsically, as a specific kind of language or as dependent on a certain level of fictionality. Instead, according to Pratt, "many if not all literary works fall into the class whose primary point is thought-producing, representative or world-describing," a class Pratt terms "display texts" (*Toward a Speech Act Theory* 143). At first glance this description suggests that a display text might belong in the category of what Searle terms "assertives." However, Pratt states that in contrast to "informing assertions," display texts assert something that is "tellable": "states of affairs that are held to be unusual, contrary to expectations, or otherwise problematic; informing assertions may do so, but they do not have to, and it is not their point to do so" (136). Thus there is also an "expressive" component to a display. Two key points must be made about this distinction between informing assertions and display texts. First, the *locutionary* content of a display text is ideally going to be created and received in a context that fosters an audience's recognition of the text's "tellability." One such context is literature, by definition; a text placed within this context will be assumed to have this "thought-producing" purpose. Second, as Kinneavy helps us understand, the verb rather than the noun sense of *display* is most important here. A speaker or a text is actively asserting that a state of affairs is tellable, attempting to create a context that will result in the audience's active validation of and participation in the display. Pratt continues:

In making an assertion whose relevance is tellability, a speaker is not only reporting but also verbally *displaying* a state of affairs, inviting his addressee(s) to join him in contemplating it, evaluating it, and responding to it. His point is to produce in his hearers not only belief but also an imaginative and affective involvement in the state of affairs he is representing and an evaluative stance toward it. He intends them to share his wonder, amusement, terror, or admiration of the event. Ultimately, it would seem, what he is after is an *interpretation* of the problematic event, an assignment of meaning and value supported by the consensus of himself and his hearers. (136)

This description implies that a display text may simultaneously involve the illocutionary acts of asserting, directing, and expressing. The description also emphasizes the rhetorical nature of display. The speaker has a purpose: to elicit a particular response in the audience. The audience recognizes the purposeful nature of the display and can either go along with or reject the purpose.

"News" provides an interesting example of both the display purpose and the informing purpose. By convention, a news "event" is unusual or problematic. A news "text" is the report of this event. But this text can be presented strictly to inform (likely in a newspaper article) or in a way that calls on an audience to interpret the event (as a segment of *60 Minutes*). These are two different uses: assertive and display. Moreover, audiences approach the two contexts expecting to encounter these uses. Similarly, that form of text we term the *footnote*, which in an academic text usually exists only to inform, in a different setting can be used as display. In Manuel Puig's *The Kiss of the Spider Woman*, the only way most of my students can make sense of the terribly obtrusive and obtuse footnotes is by assuming that Puig intends the information they present to be taken as irrelevant. As display elements, in this context, these footnote texts can be taken as making the point that academic explanations of human behavior miss the point. The lengthy affidavit near the end of Melville's novella "Benito Cereno" functions the same way.

These examples illustrate the validity of Kinneavy's emphasis on *use*. As a strong contextualist, I will treat display as a separate category of illocutionary act that, in written texts, is likely to occur within certain extralinguistic institutions such as the economic and social system of literary publication; as an act, it is more prominent than either asserting or informing. The most important felicity condition of the display act is that the act's recipient accept the locution, the text, *as a display*; the sincerity condition is that the act is intended as display; there is no controlling expectation regarding either the degree or the direction of the fit between words and world. Alternatively, we might simply speak of the illocutionary *force* of a display act as involving both the speaker and the audience in the kinds of activities described by Pratt: contemplating, evaluating, responding. Robert de Beaugrande puts the point in a somewhat different and useful way. He defines literature as a "communicative domain" governed by an "alternativity" schema that "control[s] the selection and application of other schemas" and "shifts the routine boundary between automatic versus attentional processing" ("Schemas" 58–59). I take up later the whole vexed issue of codes, schemas, scripts, frames, and so on; here I want to stress that Beaugrande is not saying that a literary fiction intrinsically carries a marker stating "fictional," but that "[w]e can increase attention and thereby alter processing of *any* text by registering it as one among several alternative ways of organizing worlds and discourses" ("Schemas" 59). A text so registered is a display text, different from an informing text in the way it will be processed. In fact, Beaugrande's definition allows us to consider the *60 Minutes* version of an event as literature, just as we would treat a Molly Ivins essay on the same event: the event itself is relatively less important than is this particular display of it.

I want to emphasize that a display text is established to be such mainly by what discourse theorists refer to as the *situational context*: the immediate conditions surrounding the reception of the individual text, including the physical details of the text and the audience's motivation for receiving the text. Kinneavy defines *cultural context*, albeit somewhat loosely, as that context "the nature and conventions of which make the situational context permissible and meaningful" (24). The cultural context often operates unconsciously, according to Kinneavy; the situational context is most important in informative discourse (95). I extend these points about cultural and situational contexts to all discourse aims. (Because I see the situational context as more significant than the cultural for determining the *use* of most texts, and because this is the context to which I most often refer, I will usually just use the term *context* to mean situational context; if I mean cultural context, I will always attach the adjective.) Chatman strongly criticizes the approach via tellability and display, accusing speech-act theorists of "*de*contextualizing" texts in answering the question, "What is it that a text does to induce the audience to regard it as display and not information?" ("What Can We Learn" 321–24). But this oversimplifies. A text can "do" many different things, for instance, announce "romance" in the title. But compare two titles: *The Blithedale Romance* and *The Clinton Romance*. I suspect that my readers will recognize the former as a fictional work by Hawthorne whose purposes include display. The latter, my own creation, probably evokes an expectation of political history. Yet the presence of the word *romance* in the latter is also likely to "induce" an audience to expect at least some display; it does so, however, not because of any characteristic demonstrably in the word but because of what the word is conventionally taken to suggest when present in a title. A second problem with Chatman's critique is the failure to take up Pratt's essential point that a display text exists within a situational context in which the audience knows that interpretation is a valid and expected response. True, at times Pratt foregrounds the intention of the speaker and thus seems to decontextualize the text from the context of its reception. But more often she rigorously preserves the focus on the entire context within which the text exists.

This situational context is governed, according to Pratt, by Paul Grice's concept of the cooperative principle (CP): the participants in any speech situation assume that they are cooperating in the situation—that they share the same goals—unless the assumption becomes untenable. In the case of literary texts, the audience recognizes that one of these goals is to take the text as a particular *use* of language (Pratt, *Toward a Speech Act Theory* xiii). Nothing in the literary text itself, Pratt insists, marks it as literary. She strongly disagrees with theorists who hold what she terms the "poetic language fallacy," that "literature is linguistically autonomous, that is, possessed of intrinsic linguistic properties which distinguish it from all other kinds of discourse" (xii). According to Pratt, readers assume that "the writer is trying to communicate *something*" when they encounter a *display* text, and readers automatically draw on the awareness that a text becomes public in our culture because publishers and editors have accepted it, validated it, *as* such a text (169). Thus,

> given his knowledge of how literary works come into being, the reader is entitled to assume, among other things, that he and the writer are in agreement about the "purpose of the exchange"; that the writer was aware of the appropriateness conditions for the literary speech situation and for the genre he has selected; that he believes this version of the text successfully accomplishes his purpose and is "worth it" to us; and that at least some readers agree with him, notably the publishers, and perhaps the professor who assigned the book or the friend who recommended it. (173)

The "purpose" of such an exchange includes the reader's recognition that the text is meant to be taken as a display: calling attention to either the text itself or its producer or both. In other words, the "something" that the writer is trying to communicate includes not only a what but a how: how to take the text.

The assumptions described by Pratt allow a reader to recognize that when a voice in a literary work violates one of the four sets of "maxims" for conversation that Grice sets out, the violation is "in accord with the 'accepted purpose or direction of the exchange' in which [the reader] and the author are engaged" (*Toward a Speech Act Theory* 198–99). Grice lists the "maxims" as follows:

QUANTITY
Make your contribution as informative as is required (for the current purposes of the exchange).
Do not make your contribution more informative than is required.
QUALITY
Do not say what you believe to be false.
Do not say that for which you lack adequate evidence.
RELATION
Be relevant.
MANNER
Avoid obscurity of expression.
Avoid ambiguity.
Be brief (avoid unnecessary prolixity).
Be orderly. (26–27)

Grice does not intend this list to be exhaustive; he recognizes that not all conversation serves the purpose of "maximally effective exchange of information" but can serve, for instance, to influence someone else's actions (28).

These maxims establish a basic set of expectations that readers will apply to narrating voices. (Other applications will be developed in the following chapters.) Literary narrative is full of narrating voices that violate some or all of these maxims: Ishmael, Tristram Shandy, Beckett's Unnamable, for example. Because readers understand "the accepted purpose or direction of the exchange" to be display, they don't "opt out" of the exchange (unless they're not in the mood for display).

When readers of literary narrative make this adjustment that enables them to continue reading, they are applying what Sperber and Wilson term the "principle of relevance," which is nothing less than "the single general factor which determines the course of human information processing" ("Loose Talk" 544). Sperber and Wilson show that

humans automatically aim at maximal relevance, i.e. maximal cognitive effect for minimal processing effort. . . . [This principle] determines which information is attended to, which background assumptions are retrieved from memory and used as context, which inferences are drawn. Subjectively, of course, it seems that it is particular interests, transient or long-term, which guide our thoughts and determine the relevance of new information. We claim that interests are simply by-products of our cognitive history, some topics in our memory are richer in information and, either temporarily or permanently, more accessible than others, so that information relating to them is likely to produce greater effect for less effort, i.e., be more relevant as defined. . . .

The principle of relevance differs from every other principle, maxim, convention or presumption proposed in modern pragmatics in that it is not something that people have to know, let alone learn, in order to communicate effectively; it is not something that they obey or might disobey: it is an exceptionless generalization about human communicative behaviour. ("Loose Talk" 544)

The principle of relevance provides an explanation for Pratt's point that "our ability to produce and interpret [fictive speech acts] must be viewed as part of our normal linguistic and cognitive competence" (*Toward a Speech Act Theory* 200); we do not learn separate rules for handling fictive acts. Relevance thus described is much broader than the term as explained by Ross Chambers: "the relevance 'we' perceive in a story is at one and the same time the story's way of defining 'us,' and roles such as 'storyteller' and 'hearer' are slots without which a story cannot exist (it would literally be pointless) but which equally the story gives substance to by coming into existence as an event" (22). Chambers is correct in stressing the transaction among text, reader,

and context, but he consistently attributes to texts the power to produce "their appropriate reading situation" (24). As Ian Reid notes,
Chambers "appears after all to remain nostalgically attached to the
structuralist notion that texts are treatable as self-contained semiotic
systems" (33). This attribution conflicts with his occasional references
to speech-act theory but follows his metaphorical rendering of narrative authority as seduction, an approach that limits the potential reach
of his theory compared to that of Sperber and Wilson.

The processing of fictive speech acts is identical to the processing of
metaphor and irony. Sperber and Wilson explain:

> Metaphor and a variety of related tropes . . . are simply creative exploitations of
> a perfectly general dimension of language use. The search for optimal rele-
> vance leads the speaker to adopt, on different occasions, a more or a less faith-
> ful interpretation of her thoughts. The result in some cases is literalness, in
> others metaphor. Metaphor thus requires no special interpretive abilities or
> procedures: it is a natural outcome of some very general abilities and pro-
> cedures used in verbal communication. (*Relevance* 237)

The same is true for irony: neither the classical definition (saying the
opposite of what you mean) nor Grice's updating can explain "why a
speaker who could, by hypothesis, have expressed her intended message directly should decide instead to say the opposite of what she
meant. It cannot be too strongly emphasised [*sic*] what a bizarre practice this would be" (240). Nor does either accounting explain what
moves a listener to take an utterance as ironic. According to Sperber
and Wilson, the listener actually must recognize that the ironic utterance "echoes" an opinion the source of which is identified in the utterance, and that "the speaker's attitude to the opinion echoed is one of
rejection or disapproval" (*Relevance* 240).

In the second edition of *Relevance*, Sperber and Wilson refine their discussion of relevance, distinguishing between "the First (or Cognitive)
Principle of Relevance" and the second "Communicative Principle,"
which operates because of the assumption that "the First Principle
does indeed make the cognitive behavior of another human predictable enough to guide communication" (260–61, 263). Throughout the
rest of this book I'll be referring to these as the cognitive and communicative principles, as Sperber and Wilson define them. Just as the
principles themselves make possible human communication, a basic
understanding of their role is essential for any discussion of how narratives "do" as well as "say." Together, they define the conditions under
which any audience in any instance of linguistic communication will
determine implicatures and recognize marked cases. An implicature
is "a proposition emerging from something that is said, but not actu-

ally stated by the words uttered, nor logically derivable from them. It must therefore be a product of the relationship between utterance and context" (Fowler 106). For example, a professor of philosophy writes a letter recommending one of her students for a graduate program. The letter states that the student "has good handwriting." In the context "letters of recommendation for graduate school," this statement fails to fulfill the maxim of quantity or of relevance or both, a failure that *implicates* to the selection committee the proposition that Sam is not a good student. (This example's original source is Grice; my use of it is adapted from Steven Davis [8].) Bach and Harnish draw on Grice to explain that there are two basic conditions under which an audience may recognize that implicature is present. First, a speaker may fail to fulfill a maxim: "one may quietly and unostentatiously *violate* a maxim"; there may be a *clash* between two maxims; "the speaker may *flout* a maxim—he may blatantly fail to fulfill it" (167–69). The example of the letter demonstrates *violation*. Second, the context itself can give rise to a "*generalized* conversational implicature." One of Grice's examples of generalized conversational implicature, quoted by Bach and Harnish, is this: " 'X is meeting a woman this evening' implicates 'the woman is not his sister, mother, wife, or close platonic friend' " (170). An important distinction between these two conditions has to do with the level of intentionality an audience is likely to attribute to the sender. Failures to fulfill a maxim convey a definite intentionality, whereas the generalized implicature may do so but need not. This distinction, on which I will presently elaborate, explains why only *flouting* counts as implicature in the literary speech situation.

The concept of *markedness* has been of interest to linguists who concentrate on phonology and grammar. However, as described by Michael Shapiro, markedness is actually present in all domains of language, from the production of sounds to the interpretation of discourse (16–18). It is based on the fact that every element of a linguistic system "is built on an opposition of two logical contradictories: the presence of an attribute ('markedness') in contraposition to its absence ('unmarkedness')" (Shapiro 17, quoting Jakobson). The unmarked member is broader in scope; this "asymmetric character" gives rise to an "evaluative superstructure defined by the two polar values, marked and unmarked" (18). According to Shapiro, the asymmetry "is clearly rooted in biological and neurophysiological isomorphisms, namely the structure of the genetic code and the lateralization of the brain" (18). A striking example of the "evaluative superstructure" is the tendency (in the English language) to take "man" as designating humankind, while "woman" is the "marked" subset (16). The important point in Shapiro's explanation is that markedness establishes an asymmetry; he does not mean that "man" and "woman" are "logical contradictories" but rather that the marked term, "woman," is taken as denoting a *limited* class, compared to the unmarked term, "man."

Like implicature, markedness is a general principle whose operation depends on particular circumstances. In the past, literary language has often been treated as a marked type, but as Kinneavy and others have argued, such language is a *use*, no different in value from expressive or referential discourse. The same holds true for display texts: they will be processed differently from other types of texts, but there is no intrinsic evaluative superstructure creating a hierarchy of types. All are equally governed by the principle of relevance: maximum cognitive effect with minimum effort. Marking becomes important within each discourse aim—for instance, within that mode of literature we term "the novel."

Markedness seems closely tied to literacy: the more linguistic forms and uses a person internalizes, the more the types of marking that person will recognize. This phenomenon is clearly demonstrated in the realm of grammar. Reviewing a great deal of research, Patrick Hartwell writes that the "intuitive grammar" of "literate adults seems profoundly affected by the acquisition of literacy" (241). Such adults recognize and are sensitive to certain forms that only appear in print or that are more prominent in print. The notorious difficulty that many basic writers have in distinguishing between the plural *s* on nouns and the third-person singular *s* on verbs, on the one hand, and, on the other hand, the *'s* to signal possession is an excellent example. For most individuals with substantial print literacy, correct use of the *'s* has become part of their intuitive grammar; misuse is automatically noticed (marked). Hartwell also points out that a "broad range of cross-cultural studies suggests that metalinguistic awareness is a defining feature of print literacy" (249). This suggestion helps explain why practiced readers so easily accept the violation of the Gricean maxims that frequently occurs in literary narratives. These readers have learned what they need to do with such narratives in order to accommodate the principle of relevance.

Speech-Act Theory and Literary Narrative

While rhetorical narratology, like its structuralist forebear, is not limited to literary narratives, that particular use of language allows me to further develop the concepts of relevance, display, and marking. Pratt specifies how the novel genre operates as a context: "the initial hypothesis of the novel reader is that the fictional speech act will take the form of a narrative display text" (*Toward a Speech Act Theory* 205).

If the novel's "fictional speech situation reproduces the speech situation obtaining in real world narrative display texts," then we call this the "unmarked case" (205). Pratt gives a superb description of this speech situation:

a speaker [narrator] addresses to an Audience a narrative utterance whose point is display and whose relevance is tellability; the speaker observes the CP and maxims as specified for such utterances; that is, he knows the story, provides all the relevant information, evaluates adequately, and succeeds in making our Audience-ship worth it. In the unmarked case, the speaker in addition observes all the rules governing written discourse at the time of the work's composition. By written discourse, I mean here discourse composed in writing and intended for publication, that is, addressed to an Audience whose exact size and membership are unspecified in advance. These would include rules governing grammar, style, text presentation, subject matter, and so on. Again, we are struck by the fact that the mayor of Casterbridge uses dialect words but not by the fact that Jane Eyre does not. (205)

In the unmarked case, "the reader's position with respect to the speaker is the same as his position with respect to the author except that in the speaker's world the utterance is true and in the author's world it is not" (208).

Deviations from this unmarked case, usually in the form of the author "flouting" a conversational maxim, count as implicatures, signaling that "there is something [for the reader] to discover" (208; 210, quoting Michael Riffaterre). In fact, Pratt argues that flouting is "the only kind of intentional nonfulfillment possible in the literary speech situation," and that "[i]n literary works, intentionally failing to observe a maxim always counts as flouting" ("Literary Cooperation" 382–83). In every instance of the literary speech act, "the writer is understood to be *seeking out* an audience," hence any violation of the conversational maxims will count as flouting; readers will understand that the writer's breaking of the rules "was in accord with his communicative intent" (391). Recognition of flouting within this context leads the reader to "calculate all the implicatures necessary to maintain" the assumption that "the author is observing the CP for display texts" (409). Implicatures, that is, are not intrinsic to the text but are determined or "calculated" by readers in order to preserve the CP.

Such flouting is found in many avant-garde novels of the twentieth century, in which the author apparently tries to stay one step ahead of the reader's process of interpreting implicatures. Pratt notes that these novels show a "radically decreasing conformity to the unmarked case for novels and a concomitant radical increase in the number and difficulty of implicatures required to make sense of the given text" (211). Discussing the French "new novel," she aptly characterizes the apparently expected response of the reader: "not '*then* what *happened*?' but '*now* what's he going to *say*?'" (214). Even though a reader may adopt the expectation of being surprised at every turn of a page, even though a reader expects to see the maxims violated, there is no way for a reader to predict the type of violation or its extent. Perhaps a reader whose sole experience with *narrative* (not just novels) was of the new-novel sort might not react to violations by assuming "Here is something to discover," but most of us have been conditioned by a lifetime of expecting that, in general, storytellers will be relevant, fully informative, and so forth. The unmarked case has been determined by our culture, ultimately. This conditioning explains why a reader will feel the need to determine implicatures whenever the narrating voice of a more traditional novel violates one of Grice's maxims. The narrator who is wordy, who gives either more or less information than seems appropriate, who digresses, or who seems not to be telling the truth will be taken by the reader as implicating the intention of the author that the reader recognize that "there is something to discover"—but only because the principle of relevance dictates that in this situational context such a recognition is appropriate.

Pratt's use of markedness distinctions is pragmatic, not technical: an unmarked case is one that goes unnoticed. This is the use I'll adopt, consistent with my strong-contextualist position. Past-tense narration provides a good example: as long as a story begun in past tense remains in past tense, no one notices the verb tenses. Marking, of course, always depends on the situational and cultural contexts. Colloquial speech allows relatively indiscriminate movement between past and present tenses when telling a story. When my younger daughter narrates a playground incident, I notice (mark) her tense shifts, because my intuitive grammar has been shaped by standard *written* English. Her older sister does not mark the shifts—at least not yet. Pratt's example of the new novel is also helpful here. This type of narrative definitely qualifies as display, but the point of the display is often self-referential, the problematic event about which the speaker is attempting to elicit readers' "wonder, amusement, terror, or admiration" being the act of narrating rather than the ostensible story. There is nothing in the description of narrative display text that predicts the marking of this kind of display, but because novels typically focus on stories other than those having to do with the telling of stories, readers may be uncertain about, and notice, the narrating itself: "*Now* what's he going to *say*?" Were the new novel to become the norm for literary narrative, later generations of readers might feel similarly unsettled by something as traditional as *Great Expectations*. (Because of the occasional lack of sentence-to-sentence cohesion in new novels, they might always remain more difficult to process at the sentence level, although whether or not that difficulty would carry over into interpretation is not at all clear.)

The new novel may also ostensibly violate the CP either by not providing all relevant information or by providing apparently irrelevant information. A reader who approaches Robbe-Grillet's *In the Labyrinth* in a facilitating context (say, a college English course) will be able to assume the CP at a different level, recognizing for instance that the concept of "relevance" is being thematized. A reader who picks up the same novel expecting to while away the hours with a good story will feel cheated. As a pragmatics of language, speech-act theory attempts to identify the background (the conventionally unmarked cases) against which variations will be noticed (marked). Rhetorical narratology relies on this same methodological move, specifying whenever possible the unmarked case for each essential component of the transaction between real readers and the roles offered them by narratives. The following chapters explore some of these specifications.

Rhetorical narratology also follows speech-act theory in defining the literary speech situation as one that protects the CP; this definition is needed because relevance will always govern. Pratt insists that in such a situation, "the CP is singularly secure and well-protected at the level of author/reader interaction. It is *hyperprotected*" ("Literary Cooperation" 215). For this reason, readers are able to accept flagrant violations of the CP: "[o]ur knowledge that the CP is hyperprotected in works of literature acts as a guarantee that, should the fictional speaker of the work break the rules and thereby jeopardize the CP, the jeopardy is almost certainly only mimetic" (215). In the example with which I began this chapter, the narrator of *The Portrait of a Lady* claims not to know whether Isabel believed everything Mr. Goodwood said. But in a narrative display text, we assume, unless given reasons to the contrary, that the narrator "knows the story . . . [and] evaluates adequately"; that is, we assume that the narrator adheres to the Gricean maxims of quantity and quality. This narrator has just told us that "[t]he world . . . had never seemed so large to Isabel"; how could he know this about her but not be able to assess her belief? And how can we keep reading when confronted by such a contradiction? Yet we do. Speech-act theory explains that we may take the violation as contributing to the work's mimetic effect; we assume that it isn't *James* who is uncertain or self-contradictory but either Isabel or the narrator. As Pratt says, "Ultimately, the CP can be restored by implicature. Given such a guarantee, the Audience is free to confront, explore, and interpret the communicative breakdown and to enjoy the display of the forbidden" (215). Just like elements that are embedded in the text of a lit-

erary work, "the hyperprotection is there to be exploited" (221). However, it is not in the text but in the context, the literary speech situation. If my friend utters these same contradictory statements about
someone he claims to know really well, I'll probably break in with
"But you just said . . ." If he doesn't remove or otherwise clarify the
contradiction, he loses my trust, my willingness to participate in the
speech situation with him. Hyperprotection is present or not depending on what the situational context determines regarding relevance. In
a literary speech situation, the goal of maximum cognitive effect with
minimum processing effort leads directly to the reader's assumption,
when encountering any apparent violation of the cp, that "something
is to be discovered." Although just what that something is may be far
from apparent, the actual processing of the narrative can continue.
The principle of relevance does not stipulate that all questions must
be answered: cognitive effect does not depend on closure.

Summarized, Pratt's key points regarding the speech-act analysis of
literary works are these:

> 1. A literary text exists in a context that determines how it will be received.
> 2. Because readers share this context, they will take the literary work as a
> display text whose purpose is to stimulate an imaginative, affective, and
> evaluative involvement.
> 3. Readers believe that the writer believed that this involvement is worth
> their time.
> 4. The unmarked case of a genre establishes the norm against which readers
> recognize variations or departures.
> 5. Such departures are by definition marked.
> 6. Such departures are also hyperprotected: readers assume that when a text
> violates any of the maxims supporting the cp, this violation is part of the
> text's display rather than a transgression of the cooperation between the (as-
> sumed) author and reader.
> 7. A reader always begins a novel with the assumption that the speech situa-
> tion is identical to that of real-world narrative display texts, especially that
> the speaker (narrator) will observe the cp and that the narrative is tellable.
> This is the unmarked case for the novel genre.

As this summary makes clear, speech-act theory always keeps in view
the recipient of the act. Furthermore, it insists that according to the
principle of relevance, all human communication is governed by a basic drive to establish conditions maximizing cognitive effect and minimizing processing effort. Hence, for instance, both writers and readers
assume that a published text is "worth it," worth the effort to read as it
was to write and to publish. These fundamental points are also basic to
rhetorical narratology. The cognitive and communicative principles of

relevance guarantee that as long as the parties involved assume that the communication is rational, texts will be understood as having the purpose of display and will be processed either automatically or consciously, depending on whether they are unmarked or marked.

Speech-act theory can serve this foundational role for the study of literary narrative because its premises have been scrutinized, challenged, and refined but never shown to be invalid. A few years after completing *Toward a Speech Act Theory*, Pratt reflected on what she termed the theory's "ideology." She determined that the major benefit of the theory, to both linguistics and literary theory, has been to move the focus "out of the realm of language as autonomous, self-contained grammatical system into the realm of language as social practice" ("The Ideology" 6). But there are still some limitations, the first of which is that "speech-act theory implicitly adopts one-to-one speech as the norm or unmarked case for language use" and so tends to discuss *the* reader and *the* text. This model "makes it easy to overlook the fact that, though literary production and reception often take place in private settings, literary works are public speech acts (in the sense that they are institutional, and have no personalized addressee), and people are playing generalized social roles when they participate in them" (Pratt, "The Ideology" 7–8). However, because speech-act theory does draw attention to such roles and to the public nature of the speech acts, it also "has the potential for correcting" this limitation (8). The seven key points I've just summarized are not limited in this way; the elements of display, marking, the CP, and hyperprotection all make most sense in a context of public reception, as do implicature and illocutionary act.

A second limitation is ethnocentric: the present typologies of speech acts, especially as elaborated by John Searle, are based on an assumption that there exists an autonomous, consistent self, but not all cultures share this assumption, and so the theory can't be extended (*Expression and Meaning* 8). However, even though this assumption is culturally shaped, it remains valid for Western-language speech-act situations, as long as the model self is kept free of attributes that typify one gender, ethnic background, belief system, and so on. That is, Western cultures share the notions that one's identity persists over time and that one is one's self rather than anyone else, but we also recognize that each self is constantly evolving, subject to all kinds of shaping forces and able to contain contradictory elements. Third, the role of author has been understood in terms of the same "concept of a unified, personalized speaking subject," a concept that has necessitated the formulation of entities such as "implied author" as well as "the notion of an authentic, essential 'real author' out there somewhere" (10). Pratt recommends rethinking these concepts and taking "authorship" as "a certain, socially constituted position occupied by a speaking subject and endowed with certain characteristics and certain relationships to other dimensions of that subject. Alternatively, we could say that an implied author exists in all speech acts—an author is implied in a text only in the same way subjects are implied in any speech act they perform" ("The Ideology" 10). All of these concepts of authorship, traditional as well as revised, have a place within rhetorical narratology. The traditional concept of a single, live author is necessary for any meaningful discussion of constructive intention, while the concepts of authorship as a socially constituted role and author as implied by any speech act or text are needed for a complete description of a narrating situation. Speech-act theory does privilege the individual voice but is easily extended to the analysis of other types of voices, such as the communal voice that Susan Lanser discusses in *Fictions of Authority*.

Pratt says that the whole notion of *cooperation* as a basis for speech acts may also be incomplete: "affective relations among participants—degrees of hostility, intimacy, mutual concern, and so on— have a radical impact not just on what people do, but also on what rules they operate by in a situation" (13). Marie-Laure Ryan usefully reminds us that cooperation implies total sincerity, a condition difficult to achieve in practice and the definition of which requires the use of imprecise "fuzzy sets" (*Possible Worlds* 62–63). Nevertheless, the principles of relevance suggest that, all other things being equal, cooperation establishes the unmarked case in any speech situation; it defines a context within which interpretation can take place. Other relationships are marked in relation to this context and are recognized as such by participants in the situation. Similarly, rhetorical narratology recognizes that cooperation can carry expectations that are shaped by degrees of power and authority relative to one's gender, social position, race, and so forth; this recognition actually strengthens the theory.

Pratt concludes her retrospective by noting that one key point of speech-act theory remains unshaken: the nonfiction/fiction distinction so important to much traditional literary-critical analysis is irrelevant when we pose the speech-act question of what the language is doing. "We must talk not about assertions that stand in relation to the real world," she writes, "but about utterances which postulate fictional states of affairs that are placed in some complex, but positively specifiable relation to the real world" ("The Ideology" 16). More recently, Petrey, drawing on John Austin's version of speech-act theory rather than on Paul Grice's, has reached these same conclusions, the Austinian orientation facilitating both the kind of correction for which Pratt calls (treating audience as composed of many individuals rather than a single reader) and a clarification of the differences between the speech-act and the deconstructive approaches to language.

Petrey asserts that "speech-act theory's concern for the *social* process of verbal performativity is unique among contemporary critical schools. . . . The principal tenets of speech-act criticism are that language in society invariably enacts collective life and that literature is invariably language in society" (165). The practitioner of speech-act analysis is interested in what words do and in whether those actions are "successful or unsuccessful—in Austin's terminology, they're either felicitous or infelicitous" (12). Derrida's critique of speech-act theory, Petrey notes, "is based on the nature of speech rather than the felicity of the acts it performs" (139). "Derrida concentrates on language as language, Austin on language as collective enactment of reality; one emphasizes locution, the other illocution" (147). An utterance's "illocutionary force" has less to do with the actual locution than with the conventions that are invoked by the locution and the context in which it is uttered (12). This is true even of one of the most often quoted examples of a "constative" locution (an utterance that, supposedly, strictly says rather than does): "The cat is on the mat." Petrey points out that it is nearly impossible to find a "situation in which to *say* 'The cat is on the mat' is not also to *do* something with, to, for, despite, or against someone else at the same time"; this so-called "minimal constative utterance . . . can have a vast range of performative impact" (30–31). Bach and Harnish elaborate on this point, providing a substantial list of the illocutionary acts a constative can perform, such as asserting, describing, disputing, and responding (41).

Petrey also shares Pratt's assessment of the poetic language fallacy and underscores her insistence that the proper object for analysis is *literary* rather than *fictional* discourse, where "literary" is primarily a context that draws attention to and may also be invoked by textual features such as (for fictional narrative) past-tense narration and free indirect discourse. Petrey points out that Austin's strict concentration on spoken utterances caused him to term literature a "parasitic" use of language, unable to have any illocutionary force. But "because the illocutionary act's defining feature is its conventionality," and because literature is "thoroughly conventionalized," Austin was mistaken (51–52). "To adopt a speech-act perspective on literary texts (rather than on fictional discourse) is to see that literature, like any other linguistic performance, is a collective interaction as well as a verbal object. Like any other linguistic performance, therefore, literature is illuminated rather than impoverished when its interpreters consider it in relation to its users" (70). The reference to *users* draws attention to the entire socially constituted context of literature. Petrey criticizes Searle's article "The Logical Status of Fictional Discourse" for restricting illocutionary force to the single individual rather than to the community; Searle's "approach to fiction purposely and purposefully ignores fiction's circulation within a community" (68). But he also finds Searle's treatment of *literature*—as opposed to *fiction*—on the mark: he quotes Searle that "[r]oughly speaking, whether or not a work is literature is for the readers to decide, whether or not it is fiction is for the author to decide" (68–69).

As this review shows, speech-act theory removes certain questions from consideration and focuses on others. Rather than asking how a person recognizes a text as literary, I take "literary" as a context of use and ask how that context influences the relationship between text and audience. The key element in this relationship is display: an audience will accept and expect that the text's purposes include calling attention to the text or the author of the text or both. Elements of the narrative text may be marked or not, with the most important marking having to do with the three ur-conventions of the experience of reading narrative, as I explain in chapter 2.

Narrative and Context: Story, Fictionality, Narrativity

That speech-act theory dovetails with and supports the developing interest in contextualist narratology can be seen in some very recent and important works such as James Phelan's *Narrative as Rhetoric*, Kathy Mezei's "Contextualizing Feminist Narratology," and Monika Fludernik's *Towards a "Natural" Narratology*, as well as in studies a decade or so old that are overdue for serious attention, for example, Thomas Leitch's *What Stories Are*. All of these works, as well as those by Lanser and Rabinowitz to which I've already referred, constitute extensions of either the rhetorical approach pioneered by Booth or the speech-act approach of Pratt. All can be thought of as falling within the realm of what has come to be called *discourse analysis*. Yet that theoretical and methodological "home" has not been recognized. As I pointed out at the beginning of this chapter, the study of narrative continues to be bifurcated: there are strong, ongoing interests in the text-based features present in narratives (such as focalization) and in the narrative *use* of language, but these two approaches have not been scrutinized for their common ground. Speech-act theory, I argue, provides this commonalty. I intend rhetorical narratology to map the shared area and by doing this to demonstrate that those topics having to do with voice and audience, hence directly with the transaction among author, audience, text, and various contexts, belong at the center of the discipline.

This center can be seen in some principles shared by Phelan, Mezei, Fludernik, and Leitch regarding how narrative is defined and how it should be analyzed. Phelan concentrates on a narrative's rhetorical dimensions: who is telling the story, who is the audience, what is the narrating situation, and what is the purpose of the narrative (4). Phelan insists that "narrative is not just story but also action, *the telling of a story by someone to someone on some occasion for some purpose*" (8). A narrative is a locution, but as Phelan repeatedly demonstrates, every verbal narrative is also an instance of *narrating*, with illocutionary force that can be experienced by an audience as emanating from a narrator or an author or both, or even with distinct illocutionary force ascribable to narrator *and* author. Mezei's essay introduces a collection utilizing "the essence of feminist narratology—the *context* of how stories are told, by whom, and for whom," with a particular interest in how gender influences the discourse elements of narratives ("Contextualizing" 1). Mezei notes that narratology in recent years has been characterized by an increasing diversity of approaches as well as by a discomfort with text-centeredness, traits shared by recent feminist theory. Fludernik, in her lengthy and unfortunately not very readable book, includes narratives that narratologists have not much studied, such as oral and medieval. "Natural" denotes the "*cognitive frames* by means of which texts are interpreted"; her model allows for "narratives without plot, but there cannot be any narratives without a human (anthropomorphic) experiencer of some sort at some narrative level" (*Narratology* 12–13). Both written and spontaneously produced oral narratives constitute forms of discourse that are "structurally determined symbolic media which operate within specific generic, cultural and contextual frames" (15).

The unassuming title of Leitch's book belies its scope; in a relatively small space, he deals extensively with the concept of tellability as a function of discourse and then treats such staples as plot, character, and fictionality in a refreshingly jargon-free way. Leitch agrees with Pratt and Petrey: "there is no zero degree of narrative presentation or narrative ontology—no way of presenting a discourse which will guarantee its status, irrespective of its situational context, as narrative" (201). Taking issue with theorists such as Chatman who have argued that stories can be said to exist apart from discourse, Leitch makes a strong case that there is no such thing as *story* ontologically distinct from the occasion of its telling; the same *subject* can be treated in various ways (in a film, in a painting, in a novel), but if the similar ele-

ments are separated out from these various manifestations and presented to an audience, they would not intrinsically be recognized as a
story, because they would lack *tellability* (32–33), that which makes a
text recognizable as a *display text*. Thus, "narratology must begin by
recognizing the fundamentally transactional nature of stories and proceed by defining them in terms of their transactional status" (25).

That the contextualist approach to narratology is now generating
both practical and theoretical studies like these suggests that narratology has begun to mature as a field of inquiry, that now, roughly thirty
years after it was first named, some principles can be taken as given. In
fairness to Chatman, whose critique of speech-act theory I've targeted
several times, I want to mention that his article "Narratological Empowerment" and his textbook/anthology *Reading Narrative Fiction*
take quite seriously the need to bring these principles into class-
rooms—another sure sign of the discipline's maturation. As already
noted, the most important widely accepted principle is the distinction
between *story* and *discourse*, between the "what" of a narrative and its
"how." (Leitch accepts this distinction as a useful tool for the study of
narrative, insisting only that for something to be taken by an audience
as a story, it must be recognized as a display text.) Dorrit Cohn summarizes how the story/discourse distinction is articulated by various theorists: Genette, for instance, separates story from "narrative + narrating," Prince equates story with "narrated" and opposes it to "narrating,"
and Rimmon-Kenan speaks of "text + narration" rather than discourse
("Signposts" 777). Cohn finds this binary distinction problematic and
offers a "tri-level model—reference/story/discourse" ("Signposts"
779), but the "reference" category seems to have more in common
with what Ryan speaks of as the single "reference world" on which
both fiction and nonfiction can draw ("Postmodernism" passim). Nor
does Cohn's model alter the separation between story and discourse,
which is the main point behind Chatman's critical move and the reason it has found such wide agreement among narratologists, even
though they may not agree on the theoretical bases of the distinction
or on its range of applications. Probably the most important disagreement centers on the question of whether "story," as "the signified or
narrative content," can exist independently of the "narrative," as "the
signifier, statement, discourse or narrative text itself" (Genette's definitions, from *Narrative Discourse* 27). As noted, I find Leitch's case
against the difference convincing, and in what follows I will use
"story" and "narrative" interchangeably to refer to the narrative text.
This narrative text will contain both story elements and discourse elements, as described by Chatman (the "what" and "how"); Leitch's argument, and mine, is that no audience will experience the abstracted

"story" elements of a narrative text as a narrative. In order to stress this transactional relationship between narrative text and audience, I will use "narrating" and "narration": rhetorical narratology will always study a narrative text—a story—as part of the dynamic process in which it is experienced by an audience as coming into being word by word within a situational and cultural context. It is the narrating/ narration that an audience experiences, although retrospectively the audience may evaluate both the story and the discourse as part of the process of seeking a theme.

A second principle is that *fictionality*, which is not necessary for narrative but is a component in the most often discussed narratives (novels), is established by context. (By *fictionality* I mean the quality that attaches to an event that is taken as not actually having happened, or to a text narrating such events.) Käte Hamburger and Ann Banfield have both argued that fictional discourse is defined by the presence of certain kinds of sentences; Banfield makes the strong claim that "[n]arrative fiction is structured linguistically by the conjunction of two unspeakable sentences, the sentence of narration and the sentence representing consciousness" (257). Banfield would argue that a string of sentences like the following, from Henry James's *The Bostonians*, marks a narrative as fictional: Verena Tarrant "wanted, in spite of the greater delay and the way Olive would wonder, to walk home, because it gave her time to think and think again, how glad she was (really, positively, now) that Mr Ransom was on the wrong side. If he had been on the right—! She did not finish this proposition" (296–97). This narrator provides a few words that can be taken as Verena's actual thought ("really, positively, now"), a few more that function as transposed inner speech ("If he had been on the right"—quoted thought would use "were" rather than "had been"), and a sentence that narrates an important event in this moment of Verena's mental life: "She did not finish this proposition." Hamburger would make a similar argument, although she would look at slightly different features of the text. The problem with concentrating on strictly textual features, however, is that readers pay very little attention to the "unspeakable" nature of the different types of discourse. This problem leads Suzanne Fleischman to define the "pragmatic structure of fiction" as a communicative context with an embedded fictional speaker and hearer, thus preserving "a Speaker and an Addressee, not necessarily as part of the text but as part of the context" (107–08). What is true of discourse within narrative is also true of the worlds created by narrative fiction: our "intuition" that these worlds "are a culturally marked class" stems from context, because "this markedness is not textually indicated" (Ronen 96).

Dorrit Cohn, summarizing Hamburger's work, reaches the same conclusion I do that fiction is a context; it can be supported by textual details and may even be strongly suggested by them, but such details—"unspeakable" sentences or whatever—are not in themselves sufficient to cause a text to be taken as fictional. Cohn notes that such a sentence as "Now was his last chance to see her; his plane left tomorrow" can only occur in a novel (or, she would probably agree, in a historical work that attempts to involve readers in the personages' lives), but in the novel, the sentence's "literally unheard-of departures from standard grammatical norms" will go unnoticed by readers. "We are in a linguistic domain where the past tense no longer needs to refer to the speaker's own past time" ("Fictional" 8). The convention by which we read fiction does not require that all of the sentences of a fictional text must be of this form, but "it is in the nature of fiction to *enable* this type of un-natural discourse; . . . fiction is recognizable as fiction only if and when it actualizes its focalizing potential" (9). Cohn stresses that the "enabling" takes place in the domain of the interaction between reader and text; "fiction, in short, is not a matter of degree but of kind," a matter of reading a text "in one key or the other" (16). This key determines how "unspeakable" sentences are read, although it could also happen that if a historical study contained a great number of these sentences, readers might experience too much dissonance, because they would be listening for the "history" key. In all of these cases, listeners are following the principles of relevance by searching for a perspective, a "key," that will maximize cognitive effect while minimizing the effort they have to expend.

Cohn concludes by suggesting that the "simultaneous narration" used by some recent first-person fictional works such as Coetzee's *Waiting for the Barbarians* "can have no conceivable analogue in the real world—a world known to be ruled by a law that says: live first, tell later" (19). This new type of discourse situation, "quite as unnatural as the one that traditionally rules third-person fiction," may be creating a new "realm set apart from real-world discourse, safeguarded from confusion with autobiography by the very language it employs" in the same way that the "unspeakable sentences" discussed by Banfield and Hamburger distinguish third-person fiction from history and other reports whose purpose is to tell what actually happened. Cohn's conclusion, however, may be too extreme in the sense of attempting to establish a separation when the fact is, as Genette insists, that "genres can indeed change their norms" ("Signposts" 773). Specifically addressing Cohn's argument, Genette notes that while some borderline cases, because of their formal features, may now have the effect of sharpening the division between fictional and factual, they may not continue to do so: "[n]othing is used up more quickly than the sense of transgression" ("Signposts" 773n25). I would also emphasize that, while it is true that a string of "unnatural" sentences occurring in a work of history or autobiography might cause readers to feel that the author had crossed the boundary of factual knowledge, this single feature is not sufficient to cause an audience to take an entire text as fictional, whereas a contextualizing marker *will* do so, for instance, the word "romance" in the title, an author's disclaimer of resemblance to persons living or dead, or the placement of the physical text on a shelf labeled "Novels." Such a marker establishes the situational context within which the text's *purpose* will be understood. One of the best descriptions of this principle comes from a recent article by Marie-Laure Ryan, "Postmodernism and Panfictionality":

> Fictional communication presupposes a layered situation, in which an author addresses a real or "authorial" audience through a narrator addressing an imaginary or narratorial audience. The author and her audience are located in the real world, while the narrator and his audience are members of the so-called fictional world. The phenomenology of the mediation between these two distinct acts of communication has been described in terms of such concepts as make-believe, role-playing, and recentering into the fictional world. The author invites the authorial audience to imagine a world on the basis of the narrator's discourse, and to regard this world as real in make-believe. By accepting the invitation, the reader becomes immersed in the fictional world, and identifies with the narrative audience. (167)

By accepting this invitation, the reader is acting in accord with the principles of relevance; the reader becomes "immersed in the fictional world" but never forgets that an authorial voice is also potentially present, and this situation is as easy for readers to process as is the situation of holding a three-way conversation. By "immersed in," however, Ryan does not, I think, want to suggest that readers feel themselves to be a part of the fictional world, a feeling that depends on the type of world this is, the nature of the beings inhabiting it, and so forth. The principle of alternativity will always operate. I become painfully immersed in the world of Beckett's Unnamable or of Kafka's Joseph K.; with no surprise or sense of alienation I can pretend to be a member of the audience that is receiving each of these narrations; yet, simultaneously, I never forget that my actual-world experience does not include disembodied, talking mouths or law courts in attics. (The painter, Titorelli, tells Joseph K., "There are Law Court offices in almost every attic, why should this be an exception?" [Kafka 164].)

A third principle is that *narrativity*, like fictionality, is a function of context. In *A Dictionary of Narratology*, Gerald Prince offers this definition:

[t]he set of properties characterizing narrative and distinguishing it from non-narrative; the formal and contextual features making a narrative more or less narrative, as it were. The degree of narrativity of a given narrative depends partly on the extent to which that narrative fulfills a receiver's desire by representing oriented temporal wholes (prospectively from BEGINNING to END and retrospectively from end to beginning), involving a CONFLICT, consisting of discrete, specific, and positive situations and events, and meaningful in terms of a human(ized) project and world. (64)

Prince's diction reveals that precision is impossible: "more or less," "as it were," "depends partly." Prince notes that narrative is distinguished not only by formal but also by contextual features that are implied by the subsequent sentence: the audience will determine whether a text is coherent, has a plot, and is significant. In a very recent survey of approaches to narrativity, Prince again reaches this conclusion:

Perhaps narrativity . . . should be conceived not as immanent to a text but as both textually exterior and interior, all at once out of the text (it is a flexible grid that allows us to view it in certain ways, to give it a certain kind of orientation or force) and in the text (its application is encouraged or called for by various textual features). . . . if A is thought to have a certain kind (or degree) of narrativity, it is because it is taken to involve [features] x, y, and/or z (and because the latter are assigned a certain weight). ("Remarks" 104)

Similarly, Fleischman's definition of "the pragmatic structure of fiction," quoted earlier, places fiction within "the domain of 'communicative language,' though there is ample linguistic evidence . . . to support the view of narrative as a grammatically and pragmatically marked category of utterance" (109). The key words here are "grammatically *and* pragmatically marked," exactly as Prince says, although Fleischman reaches her conclusion from very different evidence:

[I]t appears that as part of their linguistic competence adult speakers possess a typology of narrative forms. The most basic divisions of this typology might be along the lines *realis* vs. *irrealis* (real vs. hypothetical, fiction vs. nonfictional), and *time bound* vs. *timeless*, or *accessible* vs. *ephemeral* (whether or not a story is still available—through writing, audio or video recording, or a society's collective memory), though these oppositions are not always clear-cut. Second, there appear to be grammatical features, including tense-aspect categories, that correlate predictably with these narrative primes. Relying on our (unconscious) knowledge of these correlations, which are culture-bound, skillful narrators can use them for particular purposes—for example, the joketeller . . . who adopts the PAST tense so that listeners will be inclined to interpret his tale as a true story. Narration in the PRET [preterit], the unmarked tense of the narrative mode, correlates with stories that are or purport to be *realis* (including conventional fiction, which purports to be someone's experience) and *time-*

bound. Genres that choose a basic reporting tense other than the PRET tend to be *irrealis, accessible,* and/or *timeless*. (123–24)

One of the ways fictional narrative is distinguished from "chronicles or other reports of past experience is its ability to recreate the experience of the events, in other words, to replicate *post hoc* the contingent prospection of the current report form—whose data source is not memory but direct perception, whose aspect is the [imperfective], and whose tense par excellence is the [preterit]" (131). "[E]ffective storytelling," Fleischman argues, works to "mask the inherent retrospectivity of narration" by manipulating tense and aspect (131). Fleischman's use of the phrase "purport to be" underlines her emphasis on the *pragmatic* marking or, as I would put it, on the contextual and relativistic nature of narrativity. Verb tense and aspect can suggest to an audience that they are experiencing a fictional narrative; according to Fleischman, "narrative constitutes a special category of linguistic performance whose grammar differs in certain significant respects from the grammar of nonnarrative language" (313).

I insist, however, that grammar alone cannot convince an audience that the purpose of the *text* is display, which it must be in order for the text to be taken as a narrative. Grammar can only function this way if the context is one that accommodates a fictional narrative. When I use an "unspeakable" verb form in a letter the point of which *is not* to narrate but *is* to display, and if I believe that I've communicated that point, then I don't worry that my addressee is going to attach the wrong purpose to my verbal act. I would not quite say that context can force my utterance to be construed as narrative or can block such construal, but in this arena the pragmatic component is far stronger than the formal or grammatical.

Still, theorists have invested a great deal of effort attempting to specify the formal features of narrativity, from Vladimir Propp's early structuralist approach in *Morphology of the Folktale* (1928, translated into English in 1968) to Marie-Laure Ryan's *Possible Worlds, Artificial Intelligence and Narrative Theory* (1991). Ryan's book intends to provide formal, objective answers to questions that most narratologists treat intuitively or in an ad hoc fashion, such as how a protagonist's motivation to act influences the outcome of a plot. Ryan's intention is admirable, although her method only works well with simple, brief stories. Like every other such model, it also contains a set of starting propositions that rely on the theorist's world-knowledge and story-knowledge, such as that humans sometimes seek and enjoy revenge but that revenge plans sometimes backfire. Without these propositions, the model doesn't work. *Possible Worlds* is most useful in that it brings such details to attention, especially the aspects that influence tellability. But the models and maps of even such a simple narrative as "The Fox and the Crow" are already complex, as Ryan points out: "[a] semantically complete representation of a plot is a structure of such complexity that it can only be held and manipulated by the neural network of the brain—or by an artificial simulation of this network" (*Possible Worlds* 232).

In spite of the seventy years, or more, of attempts to define narrativity, there is still no rigorous, complete answer for the rhetorical question: How do the formal features influence readers' experience of narratives? Nor have even the poststructuralist formalists been able to account for how and why, given the appropriate context cues, readers can accept almost any aberrant form as a narrative, or at least as an attempt at a narrative that implies a story (the story of the attempt to generate a narrative). In two recent articles, Ryan admits that the reception of a text crucially determines its type. Discussing "the modes of narrativity," Ryan writes that her criterion is "the focus of the reader's attention" ("Modes of Narrativity 383). The same point emerges in this useful distinction between summary and narration: "summary represents a text while narration represents a world. . . . Actual narration is verbal performance; summary is not. Actual narration invites reader participation in the fictional world; summary maintains a distanced contemplation" (Ryan, "Allegories" 269–70). Similarly, Robert de Beaugrande demonstrates that while "story grammars" can be somewhat useful, they should always be applied with sensitivity to the context: "[i]f we try to abstract the grammar away from considerations of interest, suspense, surprise, creativity, culture, and society, our results, no matter how well formulated, will remain inconclusive at best, and irrelevant at worst" ("The Story" 416).

A more detailed, contextualist description of narrativity is provided by Leitch, who defines the term as what the audience does in order to construct a narrative from the data presented in a discourse. "At its simplest level," he writes, "narrativity entails three skills: the ability to defer one's desire for gratification (so that even if the opening five minutes of a film do not make obvious sense or provide pleasure, we still assume that the film will ultimately justify our attention); the ability to supply connections among the material a story presents; and the ability to perceive discursive events as significantly related to the point of a given story or sequence" (34). He also notes that successful narratives avoid over- and underspecification, the former because it does not provide enough room for the audience's narrativity to operate, and the latter because it calls for the audience to put too much

work into constructing the story: "[n]arratives cultivate an appropriate degree of narrativity, which may vary widely from one story to the
next" (35, 37). By specifying these skills of narrativity, Leitch provides
one measure of tellability and helps explain why a sequence of events
abstracted from a story is not going to be regarded by an audience as a
story, although it will almost certainly be recognized as providing material for a story.

Fleischman discusses the skills from a more technical angle. She asserts that "adult linguistic competence includes as one of its components a narrative norm—a set of shared conventions and assumptions
about what constitutes a well-formed story" (263). She describes this
norm in "the Western narrative tradition" as including the following
tenets:

(a) that narratives refer to specific experiences that occurred in some past world
(real or imagined) and are accordingly reported in a tense of the PAST; (b) that
while narratives contain both sequentially ordered events and non-sequential
collateral material, it is the events that define narration; (c) that the default
order of the *sjuzhet* in narratives is iconic to the chronology of events in the
fabula they model; and (d) that narratives are informed by a point of view that
assigns meaning to their contents in conformity with a governing ideology,
normally that of the narrator. Though these tenets of normative narration are
commonly infringed, the rhetorical or stylistic effects produced by infringe-
ments are possible only because the norm is in place. (262–63)

Fleischman bases her concept of the "narrative norm" on research into
the macrostructure of natural narratives done by William Labov and
others. She summarizes the following components found by Labov in
this macrostructure:

> Abstract: what was this about?
> Orientation: who, what, when, where?
> Complicating Action: *then* what happened?
> Peak: what was the high point?
> Evaluation: so what?
> Resolution: what finally happened?
> [Coda: what is the relation to the present context?]

The complicating action is the only essential component; the coda is
bracketed because it occurs less frequently than any other; the other
components tend to be found in *"effective* narration" (135–36). A narrative that only answers the question "Then what happened?" will be
perceived by the audience as having a fairly low degree of narrativity;
the more of the other questions the narrative answers, the greater will
be its perceived degree of narrativity.

Fleischman's "narrative norm" and the skills of narrativity identified by Leitch also apply to the traditionally discussed elements of plot, characters, and theme. The first two skills help explain why not every sequence of actions constitutes a *plot*, which must display *telos*, a "necessitous end" (Leitch 130). To be recognized as a plot, a sequence must "ultimately justify our attention," and the events in the sequence must display some kind of connection. The importance of the appropriate degree of specificity can be seen in characterization: "[w]hat makes most characters tellable . . . is subtraction rather than addition, the presentation of a character in terms of a type which is ultimately inadequate, or in terms of a role which is obscurely or incompletely defined" (159). On the topic of "point," which includes but is broader than theme, Leitch writes that "fictional works convey serious speech acts in the same way nonfictional works do: through the implicata required by the particular generic conventions they invoke. Although fictional works are committed to the serious speech acts they convey, however, it is not a defining commitment of fiction to convey a serious speech act; no work of fiction is committed as such to anything more than the minimal criterion of tellability" (182). Leitch is speaking of fiction, but the same holds true for narrative, with the additional criterion of *display* as the point of the speech act.

Essentials of the Narrative "Script"

Because narrativity is located in the transaction between audience and text, it is always present as an aspect of the audience's *potential* experience and thus of the "script" with which the audience approaches a story. The term *script* is similar to *frame* as used by Ian Reid, Inge Wimmers, and Monika Fludernik, among others, but is preferable because it reminds us that reading is a dynamic process whose movement itself is structured. Reid stresses framing as a process by quoting Derrida's aphorism "Framing occurs, but there is no frame" (45), yet his promising concentration on this process is replaced by a relatively traditional close reading of texts in order to demonstrate the functioning of "exchanges" within the texts. He does provide, however, interesting case studies of the material and historical circumstances surrounding some of these texts in his chapters 5, 8, and 9. I suspect that Reid would agree with me that *framing* is *scripted*; this distinction allows his discussion to be more finely tuned. Wimmers, too, recognizes that "[r]eading is a complex process that gradually involves us, as we read, in multiple, interlocking 'frames of reference,'" the most important of which is "prior knowledge of genre conventions" (3); *script* stresses that these "frames" are going to be accessed in a somewhat predictable order.

In chapter 5 I propose a general *script* to describe an audience's experience, through time, of a narrative; my present purpose is to sketch the set of preconscious but learned behaviors that enables an individual to have a structured experience of a narrative. Fludernik implies this set in noting that when reading a text as narrative, a reader applies "a *holistic* understanding of the frame of storytelling" and thus seeks such "anthropomorphized props" as narrator, narratee, and characters (*Narratology* 341, emphasis added). I agree with Fludernik that the elements of narrativity are not to be found within a text but result from the context within which an audience approaches narrative, a context that includes a script (*Narratology* 47). As I've shown earlier, Ryan points out that because narrativity is not a textual but a contextual element, it can be treated by novelists as an "optional ingredient," an example being the multiple sequences of events that can be derived from Robbe-Grillet's *The Voyeur* (*Possible Worlds* 267). Ryan here is using "narrativity" in a different sense from that used by Leitch, but her point is similar to his—an actual reader still wants to be able to find connections among the events, although these connections can be many. Leitch reads *The Voyeur* as "pure narrative" without teleology or theme; he sees it as "engaging and rewarding the reader's narrativity without providing as a bonus any teleological wisdom whose manifestation would make it more than minimally narrative" (128–29). What I would say is that in general the "new novel" adopts the illocutionary stance of calling narrativity into question, but it can only do so because narrativity exists as an element in the audience's script.

This script includes the expectation of *progression, point,* and *authorial reading,* all of which are crucial in rhetorical narratology and all of which are suggested or implied by Prince's definition and Leitch's discussion of narrativity and by Fleischman's treatment of the "narrative norm" component of "adult linguistic competence." The fact that these three quite disparate theorists have some important commonalties stands as evidence, again, for the maturation of this field of study. To Prince's "oriented temporal wholes" and "conflict" and Leitch's "ability to supply connections" and "to perceive discursive events as significantly related to the point," I link *progression,* a function of both the plot of the story and the tensions (if any) in the discourse. To Prince's "meaningful in terms of a human(ized) project and world" and Leitch's *telos,* I link *point,* which traditional studies of narrative would explain as theme or as rhetorical effects such as the exciting of pity or terror, and which the more rhetorically oriented studies consider as *tellability.* Practically speaking, *point* and *tellability* are identical; I'll generally use *point,* as the more economical term, to denote a narrative's meaningfulness as experienced by the audience of the narrative. To Prince's "project" as well as "prospective" and "retro-spective" orientations (both of which can be incorporated under the heading "teleology," in contrast to the "ending" that resolves conflict) and Leitch's "ultimately justifying our attention" and "point of a given story or sequence," I link *authorial reading*, which denotes the expectation of an audience that a narrative has been designed with some end in mind. This term *should not* be taken to mean the search for an interpretation sanctioned or consciously designed by the actual person who authored the narrative. Authorial reading involves a split perspective—attending both to the author's *display text* and to the discourse of fictional speakers within that text (Lanser, *Narrative Act* 292).

As implied by the connections I've drawn with Prince and Leitch, almost every narratologist's tool kit contains the same basic set of concepts, although the shapes and names of these "tools" vary. I've selected *progression, point,* and *authorial reading* because of their generality and because they are commonly used by the most persuasive rhetorically oriented theorists of narrative, for example, Phelan and Rabinowitz. Three dramatically different examples will further demonstrate the commonalty of the concepts. Marie-Laure Ryan proposes as the "basic conditions of narrativity" that "a narrative text must create a world and populate it with characters and objects," that "the narrative world must undergo changes of state that are caused by physical events," hence must display a "temporal dimension," and that the physical events must display a "coherence and intelligibility" that we can term "plot" ("Modes of Narrativity" 371). Ralph Rader, whose many articles over the years comprise a fascinating body of rhetorically grounded criticism, defines the novel as "a work which offers the reader a focal illusion of characters acting autonomously as if in the world of real experience within a subsidiary awareness of an underlying constructive authorial purpose which gives their story an implicit significance and affective force which real world experience does not have" ("Emergence" 72). Rader refers to "the universally registered bi-planar quality of the novel as generating an illusion of an apparently autonomous life-world experienced as is our own . . . within a clear sense that the whole is the deepest kind of 'let's pretend' construction imposing a coherence and consummation which each of us seeks in our life worlds but never achieves," or, more concisely, to the "experiential" and "phenomenological reality" of "the common reader's response to novels as, on the one hand, 'just like life' but, on the other, as having something to say that life does not'" (76–77). Leitch names two general rules for narrative: tellability and coherence. Each entails a set of "subsidiary rules": tellability entails the rules of display, economy, and suspense; coherence, the rules of closure and significance

(116–17). Leitch, Rader, and Ryan all are talking about what I term *progression, point,* and *authorial reading,* as well as *naturalization* (to be discussed in the following chapter). Point, for instance, is related to intentionality: while I may ask someone, "What's the point of this story you're telling me?" I mean, "What's *your* point? What design do *you* have on my feelings, thoughts, or actions?" It's also related to progression: a narrative's pattern of conflicts, tensions, and resolutions contributes both to my sense of the suitability of the ending and to my sense of the narrative's teleology, its designedness.

With a speech-act theoretical base, the elements I've been discussing (story/discourse, fictionality, narrativity, progression, point, authorial reading, and naturalization) comprise a contextualist, *rhetorical* narratology that can describe and at least partially explain how actual readers interact with narratives. These elements shape the narrative-reading script within which what Chatman terms the "structure of narrative transmission" will be apprehended by an audience (*Story and Discourse* 22). This structure includes the narrating situation (how the story is ostensibly being told) and, potentially, a number of "voices" that are either audible in the text itself or inferred by a reader: extrafictional voice, implied author, narrator(s), and focalizer(s). It also includes the following "audience positions" that are likewise either demonstrably in the text itself or recoverable by a reader: narratee, narrating audience, and authorial audience. The rhetorical-narratological analysis of a given work will determine which of these "voices" and "audience positions" are most important, how they interact, what functions they perform in addition to narrating, to what extent they are marked and protect the CP, and how all of these components may influence the way an actual reader relates to the work. Such an approach is essential, because how we readers "receive" a narrative influences the narrative we feel ourselves actually to be receiving. As a very simple example, whenever a narrator directly addresses a narratee within a work, the actual reader can choose to stand outside this "conversation" or to identify with the narratee. Such choices, on the part of an actual reader, will at least in part be based on the reader's determination of the work's "constructive intention"—the actual reader will in a sense be asking, "In order to be the best possible reader of this work, where should I place myself with respect to this narrator and this narratee?"

Prospect of Chapters

In the following chapters, voice and audience positions and other elements of narrative discourse will be interpreted within the narrative script, according to which these elements are intended to be recognized as carrying the features of display and tellability and are intended to invoke the audience's narrativity. The script causes readers to search for an authorial intention to move them rhetorically, in the direction of action, thought, or feeling—the point of the narrative. This approach to narrative discourse is consistent with the forward-looking suggestion offered by Shlomith Rimmon-Kenan that the perceived "crisis of narratology" can be addressed by correlating "language as medium and language as act" with the theoretical entities of "the narration, the text, and even the story" ("How the Model" 164). To explain the "structure of the narrative transmission" from "author" through "text" to "reader," in chapter 2 I identify the two basic positions that an actual reader may be invited, by a text, to occupy: authorial audience and narrating audience. (From now on I'll generally use the term *reader* rather than *audience* when I'm referring to the actual recipient of a narrative. This use will help avoid confusion with the terms *authorial* and *narrating audience*.) I then describe how these two positions interact, rhetorically, with three ur-conventions to which all narratives must adhere.

In chapter 3 I extend the discussion of audience positions to include "narratee," and I identify the several kinds of "voices" that can be involved in the "transmission" of a narrative: actual author, extrafictional author, implied author, narrator, and focalizer. These "voices" (I use the term metaphorically), together with the various audience positions that are offered to an actual reader, constitute the most important portion of the structure of narrative transmission. They influence how a reader experiences the narrative as it develops through time as well as how a reader assesses the narrative upon completion. Figure 1 shows the voice and audience positions as they will be developed over the next two chapters. This figure is best read from the inside out, as it were: the innermost positions are the most clearly located within the world of the narrative, and the outermost, at both sides of the figure, are the most clearly constructed by the reader, extraneous to the world of the narrative but essential for any interpretation of that world.

Chapter 4 takes up several more specific issues, including the gendering of narrating voices and the representation of speech, that have been of great interest to narratologists during the past two decades. Finally, in chapter 5 I provide an extended illustration of the methods and concepts of rhetorical narratology, using two contemporary novels, *Written on the Body* by Jeanette Winterson and *Waiting for the Barbarians* by J. M. Coetzee. I demonstrate that analyzing the structure of narrative transmission, while it cannot predict specific rhetorical effects, can identify some important illocutionary acts, hence can

Fig. 1. Structure of Narrative Transmission

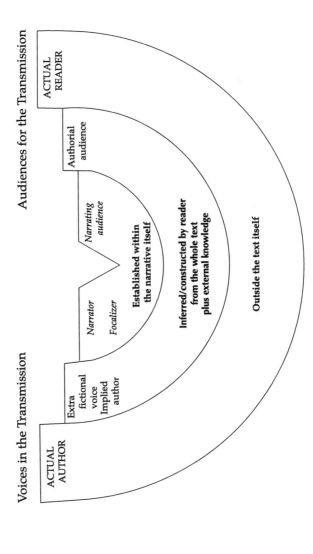

Voices in the Transmission

Audiences for the Transmission

ACTUAL AUTHOR

Extra fictional voice Implied author

Narrator
Focalizer

Narrating audience

Authorial audience

ACTUAL READER

Established within the narrative itself

Inferred/constructed by reader from the whole text plus external knowledge

Outside the text itself

identify at least some aspects about which an actual audience is likely to construct implicatures and, from them, to infer "points." That is, I show that a fairly straight line can be drawn between discourse features and interpretation.

All of my examples are *fictional* narratives, primarily novels. I draw on several well-known novels for most of my examples, especially *Bleak House* and *In the Labyrinth*, in order better to illustrate the various vantage points offered by rhetorical narratology. This is the technique used by Genette in *Narrative Discourse*, although my example texts have the advantage of being better known than his; like Genette, I use these examples both to generate theoretical insights and to provide my readers with a greater sense of continuity from chapter to chapter.

In concentrating on fictional narratives I realize that I may be casting my net in a pond rather than a sea. But these are the texts of most interest to me as a teacher; it was in trying to help students articulate their own responses to and difficulties with such classics as *Moby-Dick* and *Great Expectations* that I first realized the need for a comprehensive pragmatics of narrative. I believe that the principles and practices I describe in the following chapters apply, mutatis mutandis, to any narrative and to many other products of human language, but, aware of what happens to someone who seeks the key to all mythologies, I have kept my scope modest.

And a second caveat, which I will repeat in the following chapters: although rhetorical narratology aims to be relatively comprehensive, it does not aspire to the status of even a protoscience. Chatman offers his system as "well-formed," by which he means logical, self-consistent, and including the following: a clear method (e.g., inductive or deductive), a model of demonstrable adequacy, taxonomies whose distinctions are both interesting and adequate to the range of phenomena, and timeliness (*Story and Discourse* 264–65). However, it is important to note that Chatman refers to his system as a model rather than as a scientific theory. He recognizes that the state of knowledge about narrative is not yet and may never be to the point where a theory can be offered that contains or implies tests of its own validity. My model does meet Chatman's criteria. In particular, it is more adequate to both the range of narratives, as texts, and to the human experience of narrative than are Chatman's, Genette's, Phelan's, and Lanser's, to name only those I've found most useful. But it is still only a step or two, not a leap.

2

Audience

Audience and the Ur-Conventions of Narrative

Every narrative implies a rhetorical situation that is fundamental to all analysis: an audience listening to someone telling a story. From the people to whom the *Beowulf* poet addressed his "Hwaet!" (which roughly translates as "Listen! I have a story to tell you") to the strange "you" present in the opening of Alain Robbe-Grillet's *In the Labyrinth*, audience is essential. Without an audience there could be no narrative, and both authors and readers know this, the former often emphasizing that necessity by incorporating one or several auditors into a story (Robbe-Grillet's "you"). As Pratt has demonstrated, a reader begins a novel by assuming that its speech situation is like that of "real-world display texts": there is a speaker who is observing the cooperative principle (cp). In a situational context in which narrative is taken to be the purpose of the transaction between text and audience, this is the assumption that follows from the cognitive and communicative principles of relevance. Roland Barthes asserts that recent literary theory has removed "the Author" from the text "by showing that the whole of the enunciation is an empty process, functioning perfectly without there being any need for it to be filled with the person of the interlocutors" ("Death" 145). In fact, he refers, albeit obliquely, to speech-act theory by terming writing a performative, "in which the enunciation has no other content . . . than the act by which it is uttered—something like the *I declare* of kings or the *I sing* of very ancient poets" (145–46). Petrey responds that this assertion is too limited: "[t]he multiplicity of conventions in Austin's concept of speech acts is thus reduced to the single convention allowing words to name themselves as words" (148). I side with Petrey; as I explain in chapter 3, several voice or "interlocutor" positions are available in any narrative text, although none can be simplistically equated with the actual author.

The question Barthes raises, whether or not a narrative text can be said to perform itself, is interesting although peripheral to rhetorical narratology; as I've argued in chapter 1, the *concept* of author is essential, but I realize that this is at best barely a majority position. There is almost no disagreement, however, that *reader* is essential; even Barthes keeps the reader in the text. Not to do so would be to ignore one of the defining features of the novel genre, that "reader involvement coin cides with meaning production," as Wolfgang Iser says (*Implied Reader* xi). In fact, one of the more dynamic areas of change in the history of the novel has been the development of the role of the reader embedded in or invited by the text. Iser has documented this development: from the embedded fictitious reader who first became prominent in the eighteenth century (such as Tristram Shandy's famous "dear Madam"), to the reader invited to judge unreliable narrators in the nineteenth, to the twentieth-century reader whose participation in the work is on the level of coproduction because there is no clear narrating voice that can be taken as the source of the novel (*Act of Reading* 203–07).

According to Iser, this later development follows from the nature of fictional language, which has "the basic properties of the illocutionary act," including "the quality of 'performance,' in that it makes the reader produce the code" that governs the selections the text has actually made among all of the possible characters, events, and so forth (61). A text "owes its presence in our minds to our own reactions, and it is these that make us animate the meaning of the text as a reality" (128–29). An extreme formulation of this point comes from Barthes: "writing is not the communication of a message which starts from the author and proceeds to the reader; it is specifically the voice of reading itself: *in the text, only the reader speaks*" (*S/Z* 151, emphasis in the original).

Setting aside for now the thorny issue of that word *only*, the concept of "reader" does play an essential role and is my main interest in this chapter. In fact, Jonathan Culler regards the study of the reader as one of the three important recent developments in the theory of fiction: "[t]he fiction of a reader is absolutely central to the reading of fiction. What we discover when we try to explain fiction by reference to the reader is this central role of fictions of reading," a "circularity" that strikes Culler as essential for the theory of fiction ("Problems" 3–4). Glossing Culler, Inge Wimmers writes that "[t]he extent to which the construct of a reader reading shapes our reading of fiction and, in turn, our discourse about fiction, is a frame of reference we cannot ignore" (163). The construct necessarily arises from the rhetorical situation

that surrounds any fiction: our experience of human language is inseparable from the notion of speakers and listeners. Marie-Laure Ryan
distinguishes between two competing theories of fiction: the referential, which is based in ontology and holds that "to be fictional is a
mode of being," and the intensional, which is based in illocution and
holds that "to be fictional is a mode of speaking" (*Possible Worlds* 13).
Rhetorical narratology comes down on the side of the latter, with the
additions that fictionality is located in how one takes an utterance as
well as in how one utters and that any "mode of speaking" operates according to the principles of relevance.

Many narratologists have developed sophisticated versions of the
communication triangle linking sender, receiver, and message in an
interactive relationship and have then cataloged the types of receivers.
Another type of approach studies the process of reading. With rhetorical narratology I combine these approaches, studying the roles a reader
may adopt in responding, through time, to the narrating situation. Because all verbal structures must be linear, and because readers come
close to doing everything at once, I can't capture what actually happens in reading. However, I do believe that much is to be gained by
specifying the main expectations that authors and audiences bring to
the experiencing of narrative. I begin with a brief consideration of how
readers probably process narrative texts at the level of the sentence. I
then describe what I term (borrowing from Lanser) the three ur-conventions governing the experience of reading a novel; I add a fourth in
the following chapter. In 1981 Lanser noted only one such convention,
naturalization, and said that speech-act theory had not yet adequately
dealt with "the conventions that govern the sending and receiving of
display texts" (*Narrative Act* 287). The picture becomes more complete with the three others I discuss: authorial reading, progression,
and (in chapter 3) heteroglossia. I use these ur-conventions to develop
my critique of the "code" approach to narrative. I conclude the chapter
by illustrating how the ur-conventions may influence a reading of
Bleak House.

    George Dillon has identified three levels in the processing of a text:
perception (the goal of which is to identify the propositional structures
of individual sentences), comprehension (to identify a contextual
frame for the text), and interpretation (to identify an author's constructive intention) (*Language Processing* xvii–xxii). To a certain extent,
perception must happen first; however, Dillon notes that readers often, and automatically, leap directly to *interpretation* if confronted by
a passage whose propositional structure and context they can't iden-

tify. In fact, once readers have gained a sense of the constructive intention, according to Dillon, that sense often—I would say *always*—"governs comprehension and perception in that we tend to see what we have inferred the writer wants us to see" (xx). That inference is the "constructive intention." We assume that the text exists for a reason, and we speak as if that intention originated with the actual author, but we also know that we can't be certain about the individual's purpose; in this sense we are "constructing" an intention and attributing it to an individual we ourselves have imagined. The interplay between interpretation on the one hand and perception/comprehension on the other takes place on many "processing" levels at once, as researchers in the field of artificial intelligence have recently been demonstrating, but Dillon correctly emphasizes that seeking and establishing a "constructive intention" is the most powerful strategy employed by readers. This emphasis fits exactly with the principles of relevance as they influence the reading of any display text: readers assume that the text is worth their time and that apparent violations of the CP (for instance, fractured syntax) are part of the text's display. The principles direct readers to *perceive* and *comprehend* a text with the least possible effort, and as for *interpretation*, some expenditure of effort in this activity is expected by readers as one of the purposes of the exchange. No one can be said to read a text without actually encountering, seriatim, the words that constitute its physical form, but this encounter will be nothing more than what teachers of reading term *word calling* unless it takes place within a context that allows for sense to be made. The ur-conventions constitute this context, once the purpose has been determined to be not just display but narrative.

Authorial Audience

As Dillon says, without making some assumptions readers could only deal with texts on the simplest level of processing clauses and propositions. To say anything more about reading is to enter the realm of fictions (about reading and about readers), which is populated by roles both offered by texts to readers and adopted by readers in the transaction with texts. The best guides through this realm are Peter Rabinowitz's 1977 essay "Truth in Fiction" (termed by Culler "the most useful scheme" for analyzing the roles a novel can offer to readers ["Problems" 3]) and his 1987 book *Before Reading*. Like Iser, Barthes, and others, Rabinowitz starts from the notion that "to read—in the sense of to understand—a text is to imitate it in some way, to produce something 'around' (para) it that is new but that bears some clear relationship to the original text" (*Before Reading* 17–18). He specifies three main types of imitation, three different roles that an audience can play: the actual audience (people who actually read the book); the hypothetical or *authorial* audience (those for whom the author implicitly wrote, to whom the constructive intention is assumed to be addressed); and the *narrative* audience (the imaginary audience for which the *narrator* is writing, "a role the text forces the [actual] reader to take on") (20, 21, 95). James Phelan, discussing Robert Browning's dramatic monologue "My Last Duchess," offers a helpful way of thinking about the distinction between authorial and narrative audiences: the former has a "double consciousness" of the poem's speaker as both real (mimetic) and created (synthetic), while the latter "has a single consciousness of the Duke as real" (*Reading People* 5). Elsewhere, Phelan points out that readers of lyric poetry "intuitively assign" the technical aspects such as rhyme to the author, not to the speaker (*Narrative* 34); to notice these aspects is to participate in the authorial audience. (If speakers within the world of the poem recognized that they were speaking in verse, that recognition could invite actual readers to place themselves within that world.) Rabinowitz says that the authorial and narrative audiences are "*simultaneous* roles that the audience of a text can play" (*Before Reading* 20); he probably does not mean that an actual reader can play both roles at the same time but that the reader is almost always aware of both and can shift back and forth in an instant.

In Rabinowitz's scheme, to read "authorially" is to *pretend* to be a member of the *narrative audience*, that is, to take the fictional work as real (96); this is the first, and the essential, step in interpretation ("Truth in Fiction" 133). A reader who truly loses himself or herself in the world of the work has for the nonce become part of the narrative audience and is no longer conscious of *authorial* intention. "Pretend," however, connotes an active choice and may be too specific: readers certainly may decide to pretend, but they may also just enter without conscious effort into the work's world. I find Ryan's description more accurate because it is more general: reading in the narrative-audience mode is characterized as "immersion," in contrast to the mode of "detachment" ("Allegories" 30–31). The latter we term *authorial*.

Also in order to establish a suitably general description of authorial reading, I need to spell out another small but important point that Rabinowitz, Phelan, and others imply but leave unstated: it is not necessarily the fictional *world*, described by narrating voices, that the reader takes as real but the fictional *work*, that is, the narrating acts of which the novel consists. The actual reader in the role of narrative audience certainly *may* take the world as real, as fully and accurately described by the narrative voices, but this is not essential, whereas one cannot function as a narrative audience without believing in the reality of the narrating voice. In pretending to be a part of the narrative audience of "My Last Duchess," the reader does not have to believe everything the duke says but does have to believe that the duke is really talking to the envoy. At least since the "rise of the novel" in the eighteenth century, authorial reading as described by Rabinowitz has been the unmarked case: readers expect to be able to infer a constructive intention; they expect that they may be asked to act as if they belong to the narrative audience; authors automatically assume these expectations. A narrative that prevents readers from smoothly constructing a coherent intention, that is, one that implies a morally unacceptable narrative audience without also implying an authorial criticism of that audience, is marked.

The difference between marked and unmarked cases in one sense is highly subjective, because seldom does a narrative carry explicit signals that designate the stance of an authorial audience. In another sense, of course, readers can scarcely discuss a narrative without making statements about what the author intended; reading authorially seems to happen automatically and seems inseparable from any discussion of theme, plot, or any other feature that signals or implies the constructed (synthetic) nature of a narrative. Phelan notes this apparent inescapability of the author's presence, which *"need not be signaled by any direct statements on his or her part but through some device in the narrator's language—or indeed through such nonlinguistic clues as the structure of the action—for conveying a discrepancy in values or judgments between author and narrator"* (*Narrative* 46, emphasis in the original). I follow Rabinowitz in granting special status to authorial reading; it is the way most people read, and it "provides the foundation for many other types of reading" (*Before Reading* 30). As the unmarked case of reading fictional narratives, this is analogous to the unmarked case of a real-world narrative display text with an identifiable narrator whose purpose is to narrate and to involve an audience in contemplation. To read authorially is to seek for authorial intention, not, however, intention as "individual psychology" but as "social convention"; it is to accept "the author's invitation to read a particular socially constituted way that is shared by the author and his or her readers" (22). Rabinowitz excludes individual psychology, I think, because he wants to guard against being taken as advocating the old intentional fallacy or other limited biographical interpretations. I second the exclusion, but I admit—as I'm sure Rabinowitz would too—that many people do read exactly this way. Thus, here, authorial reading is a respected critical practice. The *marked* case of authorial reading is that in which the reader experiences the author, not the narrating voice, as violating the cp: the narrated events might not seem tellable, or the author might seem to lack control over generic or usage conventions. Hence relevance could not be established: the reader would likely assume either that the author had no clear intention (failure of the cognitive principle of relevance) or that the author did not select appropriate means to communicate that intention (failure of the communicative principle). Alternatively, the reader might assume that she or he lacked either the intellectual capacity or the experience necessary to process the text. For someone who is not able to shift frames of reference easily, Robbe-Grillet's *In the Labyrinth* will be a marked case; such a person may "go through" the novel but surely won't be reading it.

As I stressed earlier, authorial reading includes recognizing the world of the fictional narrative as constructed but does not require that the fictional be distinguished *as* fictional on the basis of textual elements. Much critical ink has been shed in the attempt to establish this distinction; speech-act theory solves the problem by only considering texts within speech situations. Lanser places the utterances of fictional narrative within a class of speech acts that "operate as *hypotheticals*," requiring a "context of utterance in order to be distinguished" from other types (*Narrative Act* 289). In the process of reading a fictional narrative, this context is established first, authorizing readers to regard the world within the narrative as hypothetical. In the beginning of *In the Labyrinth*, a narrating situation invites readers into a world: "I am alone here now, under cover. Outside it is raining, outside you walk through the rain with your head down . . . The sun does not get in here, nor the wind, nor the rain, nor the dust" (Robbe-Grillet 141). Soon, however, seemingly contradictory elements are introduced into this world: a soldier actually lives and dies, or else he is only a figure in a painting; it is raining, but it is also snowing; the narrating voice in his room may also be the doctor who treats the wounded soldier. And so forth. Confronting these apparent contradictions, a reader has two choices: to take this world as one in which the rules of logic don't hold, or to take the text as a series of narrating acts that do not cohere into a well-formed story. (I say "two choices," but someone with an imagination more flexible than mine might see others.)

The point is not that a reader is actually forced by the text mentally to construct a self-contradictory world and believe in that world, but that the reader has the option to consider the possibility. While the soldier, the rain, and other elements are being described, they do exist in a reader's mind, at least as products of the narrating voice, if not also as components of a hypothetical world that are being taken, for the moment, as real. The authorial audience of *In the Labyrinth* may actually experience a triple rather than a double consciousness: the elements of the world within the novel are plausible and can be taken mimetically except when the narrating voice introduces doubts or contradictions, and this voice can be taken both mimetically (as an actual voice trying to tell either a fictional or a real story) and synthetically (as created by Robbe-Grillet, with the intention of causing actual readers to experience this triple consciousness). This dynamic illustrates what Ryan refers to as the "parasitic" nature of metafiction. *In the Labyrinth* after all does contain substantial passages of "factual discourse presupposing [the] autonomous existence" of a "reference world" that other passages mark as imaginary ("Postmodernism" 169).

None of these experiences could happen were the actual reader not operating according to the cognitive and communicative principles of relevance. These principles, in this speech situation, lead the reader further to assume that the CP is hyperprotected. Were it not for this assumption, *In the Labyrinth* could not be read, except perhaps as the trace of a very confused consciousness. This novel alternates between what Wimmers terms the "reality effect" and the "fictionality effect," between referentiality and overt destruction of the referential illusion, often from one sentence to the next (17–18). Wimmers would say that a reader must either shift frames of reference in order to keep up with these alternations or else must develop a new, more flexible frame. Because they occur in a narrative display text, this novel's many floutings of the unmarked case (for example, that the narrator "knows the story" and "provides all the relevant information" [Pratt 205]) count as implicatures that there is something for readers to discover—a new concept of identity, perhaps, or a new way of reading involving multiple and overlapping frames of reference. This "something" is intended by the author—or so readers will assume who are able to join the authorial audience.

Summarizing much recent work on how readers actually make their way through texts, Rabinowitz writes that reading "is not a natural activity" but "a separately learned, *conventional* activity" (*Before Reading* 27). In order to read, a reader must belong to what has come to be called an "interpretive community" in which certain "social usages" have been established, including that of "authorial audience"— the hypothetical readers with beliefs, values, and reading practices— that make possible a felicitous uptake of the text (22–23). Rabinowitz emphatically distinguishes between his authorial audience and the ideal reader discussed by some earlier reader-oriented theorists. "To join the authorial audience, then, you should not ask what a *pure* reading of a given text would be. Rather, you need to ask what sort of *cor-*

rupted reader this particular author wrote for: what were that reader's beliefs, engagements, commitments, prejudices, and stampedings of pity and terror?" (26). Identifying that "corrupted reader," however, is not an activity that can be fully described or predicted; it depends on the reader's ability. As Rabinowitz puts it, readers assemble texts from "rudimentary directions" that the texts contain, but readers have to "know what directions *are*" (what, in a text, counts as a direction) and have to bring to the assembly process certain "tools"—for instance, a working knowledge of what to expect about a detective novel or a romance (38). Rabinowitz quotes from an unpublished paper by Gerald Graff that speaks to these conditions: students often have difficulty discussing literary works because they don't know "what kind of thing it is that they are supposed to *say*" about literature, and the works don't tell them (38 n.50).

In sum, Rabinowitz provides a plausible description of reading that specifies two types of fictional reader (narrative and authorial), both of which constitute roles that an actual reader not only *can* play but is certain to play, by virtue of participating in this conventionalized transaction. This description, or "scheme" as Culler terms it, marks a major advance in theories of reading narrative. It has been widely applied—most usefully, I believe, by Phelan—and has stood the test. There are only two small changes I need to make. The first is terminological: for Rabinowitz's "narrative audience" I will use *narrating audience*. I make this substitution to emphasize the dynamic, interactive nature of reading. My usage is consistent with Genette's: "narrating" refers to "the producing narrative action and, by extension, the whole of the real or fictional situation in which that action takes place" (*Narrative Discourse* 27). Actual readers receive the *narrating* in real time, experience a narrating voice; both logically and phenomenologically, the narrating precedes the narrative. This emphasis is in keeping with speech-act theory. The second difference is that I don't include "ideal narrative audience," which is "the audience for which the narrator wishes he were writing" (Phelan, *Narrative* 145, quoting Rabinowitz). According to Phelan, distinguishing between ideal and actual narrating audiences can contribute to our understanding of some types of narrative discourse, such as second-person narrative (135). While recognizing that the ideal/actual difference can exist, I find Phelan's examples confusing, because he indicates that narratee at times can be closely allied with narrating audience, at other times with ideal narrating audience. My system is sufficiently sophisticated to handle Phelan's examples, I believe, if the term *narratee* is limited to those instances when an audience is explicitly addressed or invoked, when an actual addressee is called up by the narrator's discourse and occupies the same diegetic level as the narrator. This distinction will be developed in chapter 3.

Naturalization

Naturalization is the second element crucial in establishing a conventionalized role that an actual reader can play. Lanser terms this the "urconvention of novelistic discourse": that "the text will permit the creation of a coherent and human, if hypothetical, world" (*Narrative Act* 113). "[A]lmost all structures of narrative are subjected by writers and readers alike to this naturalizing process," Lanser writes (113). The reader's role is actually to create the hypothetical world, to endow it with the features that enable the narrative to make sense. Lubomir Dolezel applies from literary semantics the basic concepts of *inference* and *encyclopedia* (fictional and actual-world) to explain how readers recover implicit meaning by constructing a hypothetical world. According to Dolezel, literary semantics insists that "(a) there are markers of implicit meaning in the explicit texture; (b) implicit meaning is recovered by specific procedures" (204). A gap or lacuna in a text invites us to combine our actual-world encyclopedia (our store of "shared communal knowledge" [Dolezel 206]) with the fictional encyclopedia that we construct while reading as a basis for inference. These inferences are the implicit meanings.

The immensely varied fictional encyclopedias guide the recovery of implicit meaning in fictional texts. In order to reconstruct and interpret a fictional world, the reader has to reorient his cognitive stance in agreement with the world's encyclopedia. In other words, a knowledge of the fictional encyclopedia is absolutely necessary for the reader to comprehend a fictional world. The actual-world encyclopedia might be useful to a certain degree, but by no means universally; for most fictional worlds it does not provide comprehension, but misreading. (208)

Dolezel, however, does not explain how this fictional encyclopedia is constructed; it seems rather like a black box. His fundamental insight is sound: "inference from presupposition . . . requires knowledge about the world; a logical procedure [inference] has a cognitive base [knowledge]" (Dolezel 205). I suggest that the cognitive base—the fictional encyclopedia—requires the belief that the fictional world is, as Lanser says, *human*, and that unless otherwise noted it is identical to the actual world: if an unnamed river runs through the fictional city of Frankfurt, Germany, this river will be the Main. That is, while Dolezel believes that using the actual-world encyclopedia leads to misreading of most fictional worlds, I argue that such use constitutes the default case. A second correction is also needed. According to Dolezel, "a special compartment of our encyclopedia" contains our knowledge about human actions (e.g., that we usually have motives for our actions) (205). I regard this as too broad a use of the term *encyclopedia* and prefer to speak in terms of *frames of reference* or *scripts*. Once these two corrections have been made, Dolezel's approach is helpful in understanding how naturalization happens.

Lanser's use of the term *naturalization*, the use I adopt here, is related to but more restricted than that of Culler, for whom it denotes a "recuperating" of "the strange, the formal, the fictional" into something which can "speak to us" (*Structuralist Poetics* 134). For Culler, the process of naturalization takes place within a context that regards the novel as "the primary semiotic agent of intelligibility," as "the model by which society conceives of itself, the discourse in and through which it articulates the world" (189). *Naturalization* as I use the term does not carry this same value, one reason being that the value no longer holds—films and television are probably now more important as semiotic agents. In rhetorical narratology, the term refers to the reader's automatic application to a narrative of the actual-world encyclopedia as well as of the frames that organize the knowledge in this encyclopedia. I also want to distinguish my and Lanser's use of the term from that of Monika Fludernik, who, if I'm understanding her correctly, links naturalization to "the frame conception of storytelling" in which all stories have narrators (*Narratology* 47, 341). However, Fludernik also argues that part of the experience of narrative includes "human immundation" or embodiment (311), which seems identical to what Lanser and I mean by naturalization.

Again we can speak of an unmarked case, defined not by textual elements but by the role the reader plays: if the cultural frames of reference evoked by the narrative are very close to those with which the actual reader lives, and if the appropriate frames are *not* brought to the reader's attention but function on a preconscious level, then the reader will automatically apply this ur-convention. "Marked" cases occur when a frame is brought to the reader's attention, for instance, when a narrating voice compares how something *is* in the narrated world to how it *might be* in a different world, or when something in the narrated world could not happen in the actual world—a character is in two places at once, or it is both raining and not raining at the same time. Of course, these cases are somewhat predictable from the texts themselves, as when some law of logic or physics or psychology seems not to hold. *In the Labyrinth* is a fascinating example of the marked case. In a dream or reverie, a figure in a painting may suddenly move, but not in a work that specifies every trace of dust on a mantle. These details can be made to coalesce into a "human, if hypothetical, world," but even the most sophisticated reader must put some conscious effort into this task; it won't happen automatically. Marking for naturalization is relative to cultural context. The point is that marking occurs whenever a reader becomes conscious of the need to apply the ur-convention—whenever a discourse element calls attention to this convention, or story elements are strange enough (Poe's "Ulalume" for a far-afield example) to cause a reader to respond, "Not in *this* world."

Taking narrative as governed by the ur-convention of naturalization resolves several problems that have bedeviled literary theory, Lanser notes. The theorist need not "speculate about the metaphysical nature of textual personae and of linguistic communication itself"; rather than attempting to settle the question of "the ontological status of the narrative voice," the theorist is "free to look instead to the rules for usage that constitute the encoding/decoding of fictional texts" (*Narrative Act* 112). Lanser's specific topic here is the "textual voice," but she insists that at least in Western fiction, there is both a speaking voice and "another, usually silent consciousness that 'hears.' In fact, it is this voice and the structure of communicating personae which the text builds that give the written text much of its power and authority" (114). The authority is constituted in the experience of the reader, who applies, often in a preconscious way, the usage rules for decoding a novel. Lanser's choice of the word "usage" is apt: usage is convention-bound and comes into play as soon as a text is determined to meet the ur-convention, that is, provides sufficient material for the creation of a coherent, human world.

To say that a novel can be decoded, however, is to imply that there exists a code and a set of application rules that alone suffice for interpretation (Cohan and Shires 114). As I will explain shortly, this is almost certainly not the case, which is why I prefer the term *frame of reference*. One of the chief theorists of "the phenomenology of reading," Wolfgang Iser, has asserted that no common code exists in the transaction between reader and literary work: "at best one could say that a common code may arise in the course of the process" ("Interaction" 107). Iser correctly opposes a simple communications approach to this transaction (regarding the reader as receiving whatever message the text is transmitting); he insists that "the message is transmitted in two ways, in that the reader 'receives' it by composing it" (107). Lanser's discussion of the ur-convention actually takes Iser's point into account, because both readers and writers in effect agree to a certain set of assumptions when they enter into a literary transaction (*Narrative Act* 113); I suspect that her use of the term *decode* was casual, not critical. These assumptions establish the ground rules by which both the naturalizing process and authorial reading take place. When we describe an unmarked case, we are specifying such rules but are not asserting that a code exists. The unmarked case is tested by what readers notice about a text or how they behave with respect to it, and this case is linked to textual elements, although never with the same degree of precision that links an encrypted message to its constituting code. Lennard Davis reminds us that reading novels is one activity into which members of our culture have been "socialized." For this reason we are "unconscious of the many bargains we have already struck and forgotten," bargains that tend to "normalize" us into the dominant ideology (Davis 17). Davis makes this point in the context of a political argument, but it also holds more generally: not only reading novels but acting as the audience for any narrative is a process that tends to conserve effort (as the principles of relevance dictate), requiring us to implement those "forgotten" bargains—our frames of reference—without noticing that we're doing so.

Progression

The third aspect of the reading of narrative with ur status equivalent to the naturalizing function and authorial reading is the experience of narrative progression. In one way or another, all narratologists attend to progression. In chapter 1 I discussed *point* as including what Leitch and others term *telos*, the "necessitous end" of a string of actions (Leitch 130). Michael Toolan provides a "minimalist definition" of narrative as "a perceived sequence of non-randomly connected events" and states that readers expect a "narrative trajectory," including a recognizable beginning, middle, and end as well as motivations and resolutions (5–8). The term *progression*, from the subtitle of Phelan's *Reading People, Reading Plots*, best incorporates the additional expectations named by Toolan as part of the trajectory: not just the *point* of the narrative but how the real-time experiencing of the narrative leads to that point. Basic to what Phelan calls the "rhetorical interpretation of narrative" is the presence of *instabilities* within a narrative. Phelan differentiates between "two main kinds of instabilities: the first are those occurring within the story, instabilities between characters, created by situations, and complicated and resolved through actions. The second are those created by the discourse, instabilities—of value, belief, opinion, knowledge, expectation—between authors and/or narrators, on the one hand, and the authorial audience on the other" (*Reading People* 15). For the first type Phelan reserves the term *instabilities*; the second he labels *tensions*. Both types contribute to narrative progression, which is a rhetorical, not a logical, necessity in a narrative, at least one that we call successful. Progression involves readers in the activity of prediction when the text is a novel but probably not when it is a biography or history, although progression will still be created by instabilities that involve readers in the "what next?" game: the main events are known, but the detailed path from one to another is not.

Progression can be usefully related to the basic requirement of tellability. Ryan discriminates between external and internal points that justify the telling of a story. The former include the truthfulness of the fictional to the actual world and arousal of a definite emotion or state. The latter involve evoking or violating, and then resolving, a character's or reader's expectations (*Possible Worlds* 152–53): if a character's expectations, then instability is created, and if a reader's expectations, then tension is created. Ryan identifies a principle by which tellability can be maximized: "*Seek the diversification of possible worlds in the narrative universe,*" by which she means that the more possible outcomes are evoked, the greater the tellability (156). (In Ryan's theory, each possible outcome defines a "possible world.") However, Ryan places an unnecessary limitation on the theory by treating tellability strictly as a function of plot: "[t]he theory of tellability is concerned with potential narrative appeal" and can be connected to "paraphrases and summaries," that is, it can be separated from "the letter of the text," or what she terms the "performance" or "realization" of a narrative (149). In chapter 1 I argued against such a separation.

Even formula fiction allows infinite variations. My older daughter consumed Nancy Drew mysteries at the rate of one a day during part of a summer vacation. These books probably offered her an experience with a recognizable family resemblance to what I get from reading Gabriel García Márquez or Manuel Puig. Nancy Drew and her friends George and Beth, in spite of having solved what seems to be every imaginable crime, still discover one new crime or mystery after another. The key here is that adjective "new." Could anyone ever get away with republishing a Nancy Drew mystery, or for that matter a best seller, entirely unchanged except for a different title? This is logically possible but has probably never happened and never will: to experience progression, readers must encounter something they haven't seen before. (For a more detailed discussion of this point, see Kearns, "Reading Novels" 19, 28.) Robert de Beaugrande cites studies of natural narratives demonstrating the same general point: "story-telling depends vitally on variety as a means to maintain *interest*." Hence, there is no single, "ideal" version of a story; such a version "would not be interesting, or not for long" ("The Story" 395).

The unmarked case of progression is the presence of instabilities and the absence of tensions. That is, to adapt Pratt's remark about dialects in the voices of the mayor of Casterbridge and Jane Eyre, we experience a tension when a narrator expresses values that go against those we can attribute to the authorial audience; we do not notice when the two sets of values are consistent with each other. Or we experience a tension when the CP is flouted in a way that can be attributed to a narrating voice and seems intended to be taken by the narrating audience, but not by the authorial audience, as a violation of the CP; we do not notice when the narrating voice adheres to the CP. Likewise, instabilities *must be present*; we would notice if they were not. If we were reading something that we expected to be a narrative but that simply presented characters going their daily rounds, with no conflicts of any sort, we would probably cease to read. Or, if we were well versed in and sympathetic to contemporary fiction's many formal experiments, we might decide that we were experiencing a sophisticated example of flouting, designed to implicate a tension between an insipid narrating audience (willing to plod through a sequence of predictable events) and an authorial audience that is aware of life's complications and unpredictabilities. By Prince's definition of narrative, quoted in chapter 1, there must be two or more sequential events, "neither of which *presupposes* or *entails* the other" (emphasis added); this lack of presupposition or entailment is a necessary precondition for instabilities.

Exactly how progression will manifest itself in a reader's experience, however, can never be specified; rhetorical narratology is not an exact science. In fact, Leitch asserts that a story's interest can depend on patterns of organization having nothing to do with its narrativity, including the "histrionic, ironic, and digressive patterns," all of which are "antinarrative" (73). Leitch aptly describes narrative as "an area of experience rather than an object of knowledge"; these other patterns "provide an experience whose hermeneutical dimension is antithetical," meaning that they help move readers *away from* the "misleading or incomplete knowledge" that a strongly progressing narrative might move them *toward* (77). Nevertheless, although recognizing that a story's display aspect might be reinforced by irony, digressions, and so forth, I still hold with progression as an ur-convention: a narrative can lack these other patterns and still be taken by readers as a narrative, but it cannot lack progression.

Phelan's method of dealing with progression is strong because flexible, emphasizing the experiential aspect while providing a fairly complete formal structure for analyzing elements that can be demonstrated to lie within a given text. "There are no hard-and-fast rules about the way that progressions may develop," Phelan writes (*Reading People* 105). The method has the additional virtue of being *relatively* free of ideology, especially in comparison to the most widely known discussion of the experience, Iser's articulation of the phenomenology of reading, *The Act of Reading*. Iser treats a novel as "a system of perspectives designed to transmit the individuality of the author's vision. As a rule, there are four main perspectives: those of the narrator, the characters, the plot, and the fictitious reader" (*Act of Reading* 35). These all converge into what Iser terms "the meaning of the text"; the role of the reader is "to occupy the shifting vantage points that are geared to a prestructured activity and to fit the diverse perspectives into a gradually evolving pattern" (35). Iser describes one "essential quality of the aesthetic experience" as follows: "the discrepancies produced by the reader during the gestalt-forming process . . . have the effect of enabling the reader actually to become aware of the inadequacy of the gestalten he has produced, so that he may detach himself from his own participation in the text and see himself being guided from without" (133–34). These discrepancies, Iser says, are patterned by "blanks"—lacks of signs—within the text: "the asymmetry between text and reader stimulates a constitutive activity on the part of the reader; this is given a specific structure by the blanks and the negations arising out of the text, and this structure controls the process of interaction" (169–70). The blanks impede the reader's attempt to make the text cohere but do so in a patterned way that "induces and guides the reader's constitutive activity" (194, 202).

Needless to say, Iser's reader is an idealization, able to be pushed one way and pulled another by a text's "structure of blanks," bringing to the reading experience no limiting predispositions, no deficiencies in understanding literary language, and almost no habits of interpretation. I say "almost no"; there are two. First is the gendering of this ideal reader, a point I'll return to. Second is the reader's willingness to "become aware of the inadequacy of the gestalten he has produced." Indeed, for Iser, the act of reading might better be called "the act of being guided by a text" or, more precisely, "being guided by the text's 'wandering viewpoint'" (the "shifting vantage points"). Iser's description of the novel-reading activity privileges multiplicity and pluralism and makes of this activity a linear rather than a holistic process, but neither multiplicity nor pluralism is logically necessary; both result from the way Iser sees the world and interprets human experience.

Rabinowitz comments on this limitation: Iser "stresses what the text offers, rather than what the reader is presumed to bring . . . And by suggesting that all worthwhile texts develop their own codes . . . he smudges the line between the text's directions and the readerly presuppositions that allow those directions to work" (*Before Reading* 38 n.50). This line, this distinction, is essential. Phelan describes progression in terms of developments that a reader may recognize; the trajectory of plot, character development, thematic development, or whatever will only carry readers along if readers allow themselves to be carried. Iser's description gives much more power to the text; he suggests that a novel not only offers readers a wandering viewpoint but prescribes what they will see at each step along the path. Phelan and Rabinowitz do not treat reading as a coded activity, although some codes are involved: it is an activity whose general shape only, not the details, is established by the ur-conventions and other aspects of the literary speech situation.

Rabinowitz makes the same kind of point about coherence, which is, he writes, "more usefully discussed as an activity by readers rather than as a property of texts. . . . The gaps found in texts . . . may well be intended as opportunities for us to apply rules of coherence in some guided fashion" in order to arrive at a meaning the author desires to convey. "We can find those intended meanings, though, only if we assume that they are there. Indeed, the fundamental rule of coherence is [that] . . . [w]e assume, to begin with, that the work *is* coherent and that apparent flaws in its construction are intentional and meaning bearing" (*Before Reading* 147). Rabinowitz's language exactly illustrates the "hyperprotection" of the CP within a context of display text. Iser's notion of a reader following a wandering viewpoint among a novel's four perspectives stands as a wonderful metaphor, but it is ultimately too limiting, implying one best path connecting a novel's gaps and indeterminacies. No two readers will ever agree on such a path, although if they are familiar with the conventions present in a narrative display text, they will take as part of the display whatever gaps they do encounter.

While Phelan's work avoids the prescriptive certainty of Iser's as well as the latter's tendency to substitute metaphor for analysis, it does have one drawback: its rhetoric tends to place texts rather than readers at the center. Adjusting for this focus, however, is relatively straightforward and worthwhile, because Phelan addresses not only the fact that a narrative is experienced through time but also the ways a narrative may invite and limit thematic interpretation. Phelan says that "[a]lthough thematizing is a fundamental part of interpretation, it is only a part." As a "generalizing move" on the part of the reader, it takes place within and is constrained by the narrative's progression; there are no rules for determining in advance how a character's attributes may contribute to a narrative (*Reading People* 104–05).

In general, Phelan distinguishes between characters' *dimensions* and *functions*, the former being attributes possessed in isolation from the containing text, and the latter being applications of attributes: "dimensions are converted into functions by the *progression* of the work" (9). Dimensions may serve a mimetic, a synthetic, or a thematic function or a combination. I've already used these terms, but a more detailed discussion will be helpful here. Phelan explains that by "synthetic" he means "the 'artificial' component of character" (2); I'm using the term more generally to refer to any element of a narrative that strikes readers, or can strike readers, as constructed, just as "part of knowing a character is knowing that he/she/(it?) is a construct" (2). Similarly, "mimetic" connotes "the way characters are images of possible people" (2); more broadly, I use the term to refer to any element that would fit in a *plausible* (naturalizable) possible world. Such elements include the acts of narrating and of simply uttering: the world *described by* Beckett's Unnamable is nearly impossible to naturalize, but it isn't difficult to imagine a plausible world in which this voice's utterances take place. I have students who connect what The Unnamable says (thinks?) to what may pass through the mind of an aged relative in a nursing home, for instance.

Phelan's "thematic" refers to "some proposition or assertion" that can be attached to the constructive intention that readers infer about a text (3). Phelan goes on to distinguish between the structuralist view of a text, which "foregrounds the text as construct," and the mimetic, which he equates with the rhetorical: foregrounding "the text as communication between author and reader" (8). This distinction is somewhat misleading, however, because Phelan describes attributes as able to participate simultaneously in "the mimetic, thematic, and synthetic spheres of meaning"; the "rhetorical theorist" is not committed to privileging the mimetic function (9). Phelan points out that in fact "[s]ynthetic dimensions will always be synthetic functions because they will always have some role in the construction of the work," and further, that "although every mimetic and thematic function implies a synthetic function, not every synthetic function implies a mimetic or thematic one" (14). Phelan's key methodological move is to consider how all such functions contribute to a narrative's progression—its movement through time—as that progression would be experienced by the authorial audience: "such movement is given shape and direction by the way in which an author introduces, complicates, and resolves (or fails to resolve) certain instabilities which are the developing focus of the authorial audience's interest in the narrative" (15).

Roderick Usher, for instance, in Poe's famous tale "The Fall of the House of Usher," has the attribute of melancholia. An actual reader could interpret the tale as a warning against an excessive indulgence in this mood: you may accidentally put a loved one, still living, in a tomb, and destroy your mansion as well. Because Usher believes that his house and his family are *literally* interconnected in an organic way, a reader might also take the tale as an exploration of the theme of mind-body relations. Neither interpretation is adequate to the tale, because both ignore essential attributes of the narrator, such as his relative rationality, that are developed into a mimetic function by means of the instability between the narrator and his old friend Roderick Usher, as well as Usher's sister. This instability is demonstrably *in* the text as much as any element can be; it's there for the authorial audience to notice. The instability may also serve a thematic function, suggesting that a rational person is relatively powerless when faced with apparent irrationality like Usher's and may even become seduced by the latter, as when the narrator inadvertently contributes to both his and Usher's nervous excitement by reading aloud from the (apparently apocryphal) "Mad Trist" of Sir Launcelot Canning. Phelan's discussion of progression reminds us that when we move from perception and comprehension of a narrative to interpretation, we can't select just any attribute as having thematic significance, unless we want to ignore the narrative's rhetoric. For an attribute to serve a thematic function, it must participate in the progression: it must be linked to instabilities or tensions or both.

Is Reading Narrative a Coded Activity?

Approaching narrative by asking what fundamental assumptions—ur-conventions—readers bring to the experience should be sharply distinguished from the recent privileging of *codes*. A number of different terms have been used that evoke approximately the same meaning as code: *schema, script, Gestalt, frame*—all refer to the patterns by which people make sense of and organize their experiences, patterns that are usually applied without conscious thought but that can be brought to one's attention by something unexpected. *Schema,* for instance, is usually used to describe how a reader organizes world knowledge; schemata are based on cultural norms and, among other functions, define what will be regarded as verisimilar (Goodrich 33). *Script* relates more specifically to well-known, repeated actions; *Gestalt* and *frame* are applied to perceptions. We may not usually think about the ways in which ordering a meal in a sit-down restaurant differs from ordering at Burger King, but we certainly would if we heard a Burger King customer ask to see a menu: "individual menu" is not part of the fast-food script. Another frequently mentioned example: a home buyer and a burglar use different scripts when walking through a house. This second example also reveals that not all scripts are equally available to all members of a society. The burglar can probably act like a home buyer, but the average home buyer probably doesn't know the steps by which a practiced burglar cases a house.

Perhaps because of the influence of Roland Barthes, especially in his *S/Z*, *code* is the term most often used by narratologists; Barthes goes so far as to define reading as "a traversal of codes" (71). The problem of such use is that typically, narratologists have tended to deal with codes as they are present in texts and have regarded as outside their purview how readers might use or be influenced by codes. In the words of one narratologist, "the more far-reaching 'revisionism' of some reader-oriented studies . . . is often at odds with the very project of narrative poetics" (Rimmon-Kenan, *Narrative Fiction* 118). But the growing interest in placing literary works within a cultural and especially an ideological context has led theorists of narrative to turn to the concept of codes and coding as one way to explain the transaction between real readers and texts.

One of the most vigorous proponents of the use of codes in understanding the process of reading is Robert Scholes, whose *Textual Power* (1985) has been reinforced, unlike many critical studies, with a pedagogical work, *Text Book* (coauthored with Nancy Comley and Gregory Ulmer, second edition 1995). Scholes's governing purpose is clear and admirable; as a teacher addressing teachers, he writes, "We must open the way between the literary or verbal text and the social text in which we live" (*Textual Power* 24). The best way to do this is by helping students become aware of "cultural coding"—how they infer a world from the words on a page (26–27). Cultural coding, according to Scholes, is organized around oppositions. Sacred and profane love is one such opposition, which Scholes links to Mars and Venus and exemplifies using interchapter 7 of Hemingway's *In Our Time* (*Textual Power* 34). He provides a wonderfully clear and apt description of the relationship among language, text, and the actual world: "we neither capture nor create the world with our texts, but interact with it. Human language intervenes in a world that has already intervened in language" (112). Scholes correctly insists that no discussion of writer, reader, or text is complete without a consideration of "the cultural system in which all of these individualities . . . take shape and have their being" (47). He continues: "[t]he writer, the reader, and the text—all are coded: by language, the most comprehensive code, and by other social and institutional systems that can be described and understood in terms of the notion of code" (47). Scholes gives the following example of how coding and the expectation that a code is present influence readers' assessment of intention: "[w]e settle our notion of Hemingway's meaning and Hemingway's intention to mean *at the same mo-*

ment, and we can do this only by assuming that a unified Hemingway intended a unified meaning in the first place" (49).

One limitation of Scholes's method is his reliance on binary opposi-tions. In the theory of Barthes, only the symbolic code is structured around antitheses (Cohan and Shires 124–25), but Scholes seems to be-lieve that all cultural coding follows this pattern. A more troubling limitation is his certainty about exactly which cultural codes are pres-ent in a given text and the necessity of enabling students to see exactly these codes, a certainty that may grow out of his belief that codes are much more important than situational context in constructing a meaning for any text. For instance, students "must see naturalism and aestheticism not simply as styles or modes of production in an isolated realm of 'art,' but as world views with social consequences" (*Textual Power* 38). The implication here is that students first must *see* the code of naturalism, just as they must see the sacred/profane opposition in interchapter 7.

Phelan provides a telling criticism of this tendency and implication in Scholes's work: "readings that follow Scholes's principles typically lose precision and comprehensiveness as they gain generality" (*Read-ing People* 75). Methodologically, "the dynamics resulting from the temporal process of reading do not figure in interpretation" as Scholes defines it, yet these dynamics "are as much a part of [a text] as the bi-nary oppositions Scholes makes central" (*Reading People* 75). In fact, as already suggested with the "House of Usher" example, the dynam-ics of progression are more important; they enable readers to discrimi-nate among the many oppositions that even a simple narrative can contain. Phelan also points out that "[b]ecause Scholes wants to get to those cultural codes and because he assumes that interpretation proper is thematizing, the model privileges the propositional elements of the narrative and subordinates or ignores the emotional, affective el-ements" (77). According to Phelan, always to read characters as the-matic instantiations of codes is to ignore their status as mimetic ob-jects. Codes can certainly illuminate our understanding of how a reader will react to a fictional character, "but such illumination should not blind us to their status as analogies rather than identities" (79). Ian Reid appropriately expands the scope of this criticism of the power theorists attach to codes: the codes tend to be "divorced from the contingencies of any situation where one takes a book in one's hand" and tend not to recognize "the problematic nature of heuristic distinctions between what is inside textuality, or inside interpreta-tion, and what is outside them" (58).

With rhetorical narratology, I'm providing a more flexible, less pre-

scriptive approach to codes. Readers approach narrative texts expecting to be able to read authorially, to infer a possible, human world in
the text, and to experience progression. These ur-conventions are rhetorical in nature; they can be served by any code, whether activated by
a text or applied by a reader. Codes are not forced on a reader by a text,
aside from the linguistic code that enables a reader to "perceive" a
text's sentences (to process their propositional content, in Dillon's
model). Iser is wrong that fictional language "makes the reader produce the code" that has shaped the text (*Act of Reading* 61). As Prince
says, there is no way to predict which codes a reader will apply (*Narratology* 108–09).

I can illustrate these strong limitations on the code approach to narrative by means of Barthes's five codes: the proairetic (having to do
with actions), the hermeneutic (having to do with the formal means by
which enigmas can be understood), the referential (having to do with
accepted bodies of knowledge such as science or morals), the semic (relating to characters and characterization), and the symbolic (*S/Z* 17–
20). For at least two of these, Cohan and Shires provide a more accessible description: the hermeneutic is "the code of narrative suspense
. . . [raising] the basic question: what happens next in the story and
why?" (123). And the referential code "marks out an intertextual zone
in which culture mediates subjective knowledge of reality through its
many codes"; they quote Eagleton on *Bleak House* for an example that
the London of this novel "signifies, not 'Victorian England' as such,
but certain of Victorian England's ways of signifying itself" (129, quoting from Eagleton's *Criticism and Ideology* 77). Barthes argues that every "lexia" of a text draws on one or more of these codes and that a
reader understands a narrative by applying them unconsciously on a
sentence-by-sentence basis. (A lexia is "a textual unit or unit of reading
of variable dimension constituting the best space in which meaning
can be observed" [Prince, *Dictionary* 48].) Barthes admits that this
"cutting up" of the text into lexias is "arbitrary in the extreme; it will
imply no methodological responsibility, since it will bear on the signifier, whereas the proposed analysis bears solely on the signified"
(*S/Z* 13).

For example, a reader encounters the following sentence (from Bal-
zac's *Sarrassine*): "[a]t this moment, the light footsteps of a woman in a
rustling dress broke the silence." According to Barthes, we understand, without being explicitly told, that this woman is entering the
room; we are able to understand the detail in this way because it is a
manifestation of the proairetism *to enter*, which includes the action
"to announce oneself by a sound" (*S/Z* 78). However, Barthes says, a
code is not to be thought of as "a list, a paradigm that must be recon-

stituted" (20). Rather, each code functions as a voice, and the text, constituted by the reader in the process of reading, becomes "a stereographic space where the five codes, the five voices, intersect: the Voice of Empiricism (the proairetisms), the Voice of the Person (the semes), the Voice of Science (the cultural codes), the Voice of Truth (the hermeneutisms), the Voice of Symbol" (21).

The problem here should be obvious: this sentence from *Sarrassine* does not explicitly state that someone is about to enter. The sound of footsteps can suggest many different actions, and it is only in the following clause, "Young Marianina came in," that this particular action is selected from the other possibilities (e.g., passing by, eavesdropping, hurrying away). Barthes does not explain how a reader is able to select the "correct" proairetism or what difference it might make to a reading if the correct one is not selected. In fact, this example suggests that coded elements may only be understood retrospectively, which would mean that these are codes of *re*reading. Barthes's method can be successfully applied, but only because the ur-conventions establish a context that tells a reader to naturalize these details in one way into a coherent human world. The context, that is, activates the application of codes, determines how the signifier (the text) will be divided into lexias, and thus establishes very definite limits on what the signified (the interpretation) can contain.

Scholes himself at one time seemed to be sensitive to the danger of attaching too much power to codes and seemed more in favor of a balance between structuralist and rhetorical approaches. Contrasting Barthes's practice, especially in *S/Z*, with Genette's, Scholes wrote that the former "finds meanings that are cultural, collective, almost involuntary as far as the reader is concerned. While Genette . . . locates meanings that are closer to the reader's experience of the text . . . [f]or Genette, the systems relating to the process of reading are more important than the cultural codes alluded to by the text" (*Structuralism* 162–63). Not only for Genette, but for Phelan, Rabinowitz, Lanser, and Booth. With all due respect to Humpty Dumpty, it does matter what names we attach to phenomena. Is there a "diegetic code," as Cohan and Shires, following Barthes, assert, that is, a way to specify how a (prose) narrative "means as a telling" (130–31)? Cohan and Shires actually undercut their claim by noting that the "knowledge of how one medium means as opposed to any other" is socially and historically determined (131); if a code depends this much on context, how can it even be termed a code? Cohan and Shires also write that Barthes's codes, specifically, "succeed when they *appear to trace* a course of meanings originating in the text" (132, emphasis added). A bona fide code should *actually* identify meanings, not just appear to do so.

While reading may not be a coded activity, it can be usefully discussed as rule governed. This is Rabinowitz's purpose with his "rules
for reading." Rabinowitz remains very close to "the reader's experience of the text," using "rule" in the sense of "conventional procedure." Whereas "code" as Barthes and Scholes use the term conveys
the impression of a cultural substrate, something that operates on a
preconscious or unconscious level, Rabinowitz's rules "serve as a kind
of assumed contract between author and reader—they specify the
grounds on which the intended reading should take place" (*Before
Reading* 43). The rules are "socially constructed" and "can vary with
genre, culture, history, and text." A further difference between codes
and rules is that the latter can be misapplied even by well-intentioned
readers; such misapplication is a major cause of misreading (43).
Codes, in contrast, are usually described in a way that suggests they
control readings.

Rabinowitz's rules are divided into four types, all of which connect
very smoothly with the skills of narrativity described by Leitch: defer-
ring gratification, perceiving connections among events, perceiving
connections between events and the narrative's point (34). Rules of *notice* tell us what counts as important in a text; rules of *signification*
tell us how to attach meaning to what we notice; rules of *configuration* tell us how to pattern what we notice; rules of *coherence* instruct
us in the ways of combining a text's details into a pattern that makes
sense (Rabinowitz, *Before Reading* 43–45). These rules are not fixed or
exhaustive; Rabinowitz regards them as complementing other typologies. Nor can they be applied in any predetermined order: "[r]eading is
a more complex holistic process in which various rules interact with
one another in ways that we may never understand, even though we
seem to have little difficulty putting them into practice intuitively"
(46). A particular convention, such as the use of literary parallels, may
involve all four types: we conventionally *notice* parallels; we attach
significance to them; we expect *configurations* of parallels; we bring
them together into a *coherent* structure (46).

A brief survey of some of these rules indicates how flexible (but also
imprecise) they are. Rules of notice include explicit statements by a
narrating voice, special positioning (titles, beginnings and endings of
textual units), and ruptures of continuity. Whatever a text emphasizes
will "serve as a basic structure on which to build an interpretation. As
authorial audience, we read with the prior understanding that we are
more expected to account for a detail that is stressed by a rule of notice
than for a detail that is not" (*Before Reading* 53). Rules of configuration
are somewhat like implicatures; they are the means by which readers
understand what certain details actually signify. This category in-

cludes the convention that authorial statements tend to carry more weight than those emanating from characters within a narrative, the "snap moral judgments" that we conventionally attach to certain actions and appearances, the "rule of realism" (a novel is assumed to be realistic unless it signals otherwise [102]), and assumptions that chain together causes and effects in a temporal sequence. Configuration rules also include causality as well as expectations regarding genre (goodness and virtue will triumph in a traditional melodrama but will be ground into the dirt in the naturalistic novel). Most of the rules in this category derive from what Rabinowitz terms the two "metarules of configuration": that "*some*thing will happen" (the narrative is tellable) and that "not *any*thing can happen" (*telos* must be present) (117).

The configuration rules guide a reader's "experience of an unfolding text during the act of reading"; the rules of coherence, on the other hand, come into play once a reader has finished the text (110). In this category, the fundamental rule is that "the work *is* coherent and that apparent flaws in its construction are intentional and meaning bearing" (147). Rabinowitz distinguishes among three general coherence-building rules that a reader can apply in response to three types of coherence-damaging situations: insufficiencies or gaps in a text (invoking "license to fill"); overabundance of information, including apparent contradictions (invoking "rules of surplus"), and disparate information (invoking "rules of naming, bundling, and thematizing") (148–58). The situations named by Rabinowitz all constitute apparent violations of the Gricean maxims, but the CP is hyperprotected in the literary speech situation, hence the reader not only can but will apply these rules. As always, the principles of relevance underlie the dynamics of interpretation: all of these rules allow a reader to maximize cognitive effect while minimizing processing effort.

Even though reading is a holistic process, some rules probably take precedence, such as the rules of notice and the most general coherence rule named by Rabinowitz: "we should read a text in such a way that it becomes the best text possible" (45). "Metanarrative signs," which "constitute the answer of a text to the question 'How should we interpret you?'" (Prince, *Narratology* 126), also have at least a logical priority and contribute to the immediate context of reading within which other rules will be selected by a reader, often without conscious thought. These signs include elements outside of the narrative (such as titles) as well as moments when a narrating voice expresses an awareness of itself as a narrating voice. They can help readers determine which code to apply and what a particular element of the text might mean within that code (*Narratology* 118). But even if the illocutionary force of a metanarrative sign can be predicted (readers will notice the sign), its effect on interpretation cannot be. As Prince explains, metanarrativity is a relational, not an absolute, property, dependent on the most local context (the text) as well as on the conditions under which text and reader interact (120). This is true even for those signs that fall into two of the types of "rules of notice" Rabinowitz identifies: rules of "position" and of "extratextual deviation." The former have to do with the fact that readers and authors participate in a "speech situation" privileging titles, epigraphs, generic subtitles, divisions within texts, and so forth (*Before Reading* 58); the latter, more specifically with the use of and deviation from subgenres (e.g., detective story). Rabinowitz comments: "the border line between reference and formula—like the border lines between deviations and norms more generally—can be pinpointed only in the context of a particular intertextual grid" (74).

My basic point is that reading narrative is a coded behavior only in a loose sense; at best, rhetorical narratology can classify the available codes, identify readers' typical cognitive structures and moves, and suggest how the elements of these two categories may connect. Just how tentative any such suggestions must remain, pending a great deal of research, can be seen in the links George Dillon offers between three styles of reading and three of Barthes's codes. The first of these, Character-Action-Moral, is practiced by readers who "treat the world of the text as an extension or portion of the real world" ("Styles of Reading" 80–81). The "Digger for Secrets" reads through the lenses of depth and abnormal psychology and is interested in excavating a work's hidden realities (83–84). The "Anthropologist" focuses on "the cultural norms and values that explain what characters indisputably do and say" (84). According to Dillon, these correlate, respectively, with the proairetic, the hermeneutic, and the referential or cultural codes (87). While Dillon's correlations are somewhat idiosyncratic (the hermeneutic code, especially, incorporates much more than psychology), the point remains that some such connection between codes and cognitive structures probably exists. Dillon notes that Barthes's other two codes, the semic and the symbolic, probably do not correlate with specific styles of reading but are incorporated by all. Similarly, there is no "structuralist style as such: the basic moves of structural analysis (finding contrasting groups and repetition of patterns)" are present in each reading style (87).

If Dillon turns out to be correct that these three styles of reading stand as "general patterns of thinking rather than a learned decorum of literary criticism" (87–88), then he will have provided a useful cognitivist base. Even if he is not right about the details, he still offers a possibility worth pursuing. On the other hand, these styles are extremely broad and loose, and it is likely that many readers can implement all three styles, depending on their immediate reasons for reading. It is also likely that different kinds of texts invite different styles of reading. The recent best-seller *Jurassic Park*, for example, probably elicits the Character-Action-Moral style, whereas *In the Labyrinth* gives most readers the impression that there must be some secret, some key, to its labyrinthine contortions. As a college teacher, I try to help my students see that to read this "new novel" solely for plot, character, or theme would be to miss all the fun. Similarly, were I to tell them I was doing a deconstructive analysis of *Jurassic Park*, their (probably politely unvoiced) response would be *"You're* missing all the fun."

In the gray area between what Dillon terms "learned decorum" and cognitive structures that may be "hard-wired" into human beings lie the recently demonstrated differences in how women and men read. These differences provide an additional argument against privileging codes, which, at least in the versions articulated by Barthes and Scholes, ignore gender. But further research in gender differences may require some changes in the relative power I've attributed to each ur-convention. Early narratology had no interest in the question of how a reader's gender influences the transaction with a text (or, for that matter, how a text might be read as gendered in nonobvious ways). Iser's phenomenology of reading demonstrates the same limitation, failing to ask whether all readers are conditioned by their culture to process a text's gaps in the same way or are equally ready to formulate and then discard Gestalten at the behest of a text.

David Bleich's fascinating although limited study of how gender is reflected in reading practices showed that both men and women read poetry similarly, seeking a sense of the author as creator of the work (239, 249). However, in reading narrative fiction, men respond to the narrating voice and regard that voice as the product of an authorial intention, whereas women enter more immediately into the world of the novel (239). Another notable difference is that men are more likely to summarize a story, whereas women infer and dwell on the affective aspects (256). Bleich speculates that these tendencies may be traced to developmental differences in the way men and women experience and relate to language: females, from infancy, identify with their "mother's tongue" and thus experience the most important language user— the mother—as "less other" than males experience her (264–65). A second plausible explanation of Bleich's findings is that males are in general more concerned with authority and ownership (in a sense both the [inferred] author and the narrator possess the narrative), whereas females tend to be more empathetic in social and linguistic situations. This explanation is supported by one of Elizabeth Flynn's research projects, which revealed that male readers are more inclined to domi-nate a text and less inclined to be empathetic—they tend to render a text "voiceless" (272–73). Women are "closer to the interactive center" (276).

Both Flynn and Bleich derive their results from intensive, months-long interaction with small groups of readers. Their studies have the virtues and the limitations of the case approach; both also have the ring of truth. Much more research in this area must be done, but these results do show strong differences in the ways men and women tend to approach texts. These differences add to the argument against the as-sumption on which theories of coding are based—that codes structure reading. As the research base in this area becomes more developed, rhetorical narratology may also need more precisely to discriminate between how various types of readers experience the three ur-conven-tions of authorial reading, naturalization, and progression. It could turn out that for male readers, authorial reading carries more force, whereas naturalizing tends to be the primary move for female readers. This in turn could require changes in the marked cases. For example, I've stated that if a reader doubts that a text really embodies an author-ial intention, the reader will probably balk. But this may be less likely to happen for female readers if they're able to naturalize the text.

Such refinements of the ur-conventions along gender lines are im-plied by Patrocinio Schweickart's seminal theoretical essay "Reading Ourselves: Toward a Feminist Theory of Reading." Schweickart orga-nizes her discussion around a figurative "story of reading" with two "chapters" that apply to how the woman reader relates to male-authored and female-authored texts. In the first "chapter," the woman must become an antagonistic reader of male-authored texts in order to "disrupt the process of immasculation"; in the second, she enters into a dialogic relationship with the female author through the author's text (27, 32, 37). Schweickart's tendency to slip from description to prescription leads her to some overstatements such as that "*how* [fe-males] read is inextricably linked with the question of *what* we read" (25); clearly, this applies to all readers, not just to women. But the dis-tribution of antagonistic and dialogic responses surely differs along the lines she suggests, a difference that may also manifest itself in how the ur-conventions are experienced. Progression, for instance, can result from instabilities, tensions, or both; tensions are created within a nov-el's discourse by conflicts between, typically, the authorial audience and the narrating audience. Yet Schweickart describes the dialogic re-lationship between "feminist reader and female author/text" as cen-tered on "managing the contradictory implications of the desire for relationship (one must maintain a minimal distance [from] the other) and the desire for intimacy, up to and including a symbiotic merger with the other" (38). This dynamic interaction implies that a woman may be less inclined than a man to distance herself from a narrating audience, at least when reading a female-authored text; because, as Phelan explains, tension results from the reader's experience of a difference between narrating and authorial audiences, the female reader might experience either less tension or a different type of tension. If less, then the reader's experience of progression would not be as strong. It could even be the case that women novelists tend to incorporate less tension of this sort; the contract they assume their actual readers to enter into might reflect their own practice as readers of female-authored texts. This would mean that they construct their narratives to privilege separate, individual voices, enabling the greatest possible dialogue both within the text (among its voices) and between text and reader.

Bleich and Flynn would probably say that such a dialogic relationship is not just present when feminist readers encounter female texts but can operate to some degree in the reading experience of any woman, who therefore may feel less discourse tension and consequently experience less progression in a narrative. This is also the thrust of Scholes's delightful essay "Reading Like a Man." Scholes poses the question, "[I]s there any difference between reading *as* a woman and reading *like* a woman?" and answers in the affirmative: neither a man nor a woman can read *as* the other, that is, with a lifetime of experience living within that gender ("Reading" 217–18). This fundamental fact justifies feminists' practice of "reading on behalf of all the members" of "the class *woman*" (207). Pending additional research into these gender differences, however, we can say that naturalization, progression, and authorial reading all remain essential to the experience of reading narrative, even though their relative importance probably differs not only between genders but along other axes as well. We can also say that the phenomenon of gendered reading makes the code approach even more dependent on contextual analysis of the sort provided by rhetorical narratology.

Ur-Conventions, Codes, and Rules in *Bleak House*

In the following chapter I look more closely at narrating voices, always within the framework of these ur-conventions and their unmarked cases, which I summarize in figure 2. As I've said, rhetorical narratology does not aspire to scientific exactitude. This chart does not gener-

Fig. 2. Essential Elements of Reading Narrative

UR-CONVENTION	UNMARKED CASE
Authorial Reading	Reader automatically assumes that author has intended reader to have the experiences reader is having.
Naturalization	Reader is able automatically to create a coherent, human world.
Progression	Reader experiences instabilities in the story but no tensions in the discourse.

ate every possible interaction between a text and a reader. However, it serves as a guide to analysis by setting forth the conditions that govern the structure of narrative transmission.

My rhetorical-narratological synthesis is also useful in that it foregrounds some causal interactions among the elements of several systems I've been referring to in discussing the ur-conventions: those of Rabinowitz, Phelan, and Barthes. First, there is a strong connection, although not an identity, between *instabilities*, the *proairetic, semic*, and *hermeneutic codes*, and *rules of notice and configuration*. An instability will exist between characters (semic code) within the world created by the narrating. It will involve actions (proairetic code), which may be either physical or psychological and which suggest a range of possible actions to follow. It may also elicit from the reader a sense of an enigma (hermeneutic code), and it will certainly be signaled in some way by a rule of notice, for instance, by occurring at a place of emphasis (such as the end of a chapter) or by being repeated.

Chapter 16 of *Bleak House* (published serially in 1852–53) can be used to illustrate these interactions. The chapter begins with the statement "My Lady Dedlock is restless, very restless" (218). Several paragraphs later, we read that Lady Dedlock "has flitted away to town," and the narrating voice then asks,

What connexion can there be, between the place in Lincolnshire, the house in town, the Mercury in powder, and the whereabout [sic] of the outlaw with the broom, who had that distant ray of light upon him when he swept the churchyard step? What connexion can there have been between many people in the innumerable histories of this world, who, from opposite sides of great gulfs, have, nevertheless, been very curiously brought together! (219)

Up to this point, the existence of such a connection has been hinted at, but this is the first time the authorial audience has its awareness of these hints validated by this extradiegetic narrating voice. The *enigma* is quite clear: why is Lady Dedlock, a woman who appears to be the epitome of success, so restless? This enigma is reinforced by the *semic* code: people are restless for particular reasons, including guilt and dis-satisfaction. These details build on the *functional* nature of Lady Ded-lock's inner turmoil, an attribute that was hinted at as early as the sec-ond chapter and has become the source of one of the novel's most prominent instabilities. By placing the reference to her restlessness at the beginning of the chapter, Dickens signals an expectation that readers *notice* this detail. The placement itself functions as an illocu-tionary act: readers familiar with novels divided into chapters know they're to take it thus. In addition to this rule of position, Dickens ap-plies the rule of explicit statement with the rhetorical questions about connections and with the chapter title, "Tom-all-Alone's."

I'm referring here of course to "Dickens" as the source of the inten-tion I infer while reading authorially; "he" has crafted the chapter with such obvious rhetorical flourishes and is easily identified with the nar-rating voice and the voice of the novel's prefatory statement about spontaneous combustion. The chapter's codes and rules only make sense in such a context: a human using language to work on an audi-ence in just these ways I feel myself worked on. For me, while I'm read-ing, this voice exists in the present—one reason, by the way, for the convention of referring to the voice as doing things now: "Dickens ap-plies the rule." This present-tense existence is another reminder that the unmarked case of the novel-reading situation is the narrative dis-play text; I describe my encounter with this text using forms that are grammatically identical to those my younger daughter uses in relating someone else's conversation: "Then she goes, '*I* wouldn't wear shoes like that,' and I'm like, 'Just because *your* grandmother won't buy *you* Doc Martens.'" But at least with writers like Dickens, whose effects tend toward the oratorical, I simultaneously think about the actual Dickens who create*d* this novel using more or less the same rules I ap-ply in reading it; the dead author and the living reader do seem to coop-erate in this endeavor, our cooperation made possible by the rules we share and by the principles of relevance that enable us to decide which of those rules pertain to this specific transaction.

The chapter's enigmatic nature is developed by the shift to a descrip-tion of Jo the crossing sweeper, resident of Tom's, and then to Lawyer Tulkinghorn in his chambers:

From the ceiling, foreshortened Allegory, in the person of one impossible Ro-man upside down, points with the arm of Samson (out of joint, and an odd one) obtrusively toward the window. Why should Mr. Tulkinghorn, for such no-reason, look out of window! Is the hand not always pointing there? So he does not look out of window.

And if he did, what would it be to see a woman going by? There are women enough in the world, Mr. Tulkinghorn thinks—too many; they are at the bot-

tom of all that goes wrong in it, though, for the matter of that, they create busi-
ness for lawyers. What would it be to see a woman going by, even though she
were going secretly? They are all secret. Mr. Tulkinghorn knows that, very
well.

But they are not all like the woman who now leaves him and his house behind; between whose plain dress, and her refined manner, there is something
exceedingly inconsistent. She should be an upper servant by her attire, yet, in
her air and step, though both are hurried and assumed—as far as she can assume in the muddy streets, which she treads, with an unaccustomed foot—she
is a lady. (222–23)

The fact that this most observant of persons does not see something
that the reader is permitted to see rings the chimes of notice even
louder. We follow the enigmatic figure as she locates Jo and has him
lead her to the pauper's cemetery where "Nemo" was buried; Jo notices, just as does the narrating voice, that this woman may be dressed
as a servant but that her hands and rings contradict the disguise. The
rule of position is evoked again, to create notice, by the way the chapter concludes: " 'Sir Leicester would have done better to try the other
side of the house, my dear,' says Mrs. Rouncewell to Rosa. 'His dress-
ing-room is on my Lady's side. And in all these years I never heard the
step upon the Ghost's Walk, more distinct than it is to-night!' " (226).
The Ghost's Walk has been called to the reader's attention in chapter 7,
titled "The Ghost's Walk"; the tread is heard whenever calamity or
disgrace is coming to Chesney Wold, and Lady Dedlock can hear it over
any other noise.

A second set of interactions can be seen among the *semic code,* the
rule of signification, and the *thematic function.* By this point in the
novel, Dickens probably expected his readers to have inferred that
the mysterious woman is Lady Dedlock, that Nemo had been her
lover, and that Esther is their child. That is to say, although the narrating audience, by definition, is taking the enigmas at their surface
value, the authorial audience is already ahead of the game; this difference creates a discourse *tension* that can further how an actual reader
determines the work's themes. The death-bed curse of Lady Morbury
included the statement, "I will walk here, until the pride of this house
is humbled" (90). Both Sir Leicester and his lady have repeatedly been
described as prideful, an attribute that becomes thematic by means of
the described activity of the ghost, by the contrast of My Lady in that
"scene of horror" (as she terms it), the graveyard, and by the detail of
her repugnance toward Jo: "She drops a piece of money in his hand,
without touching it, and shuddering as their hands approach" (225).
Up to this point, although we know her to be prideful, we have not
seen My Lady actually display such a strong reaction to someone who

has been set up as a sympathetic figure. Readers easily apply here the significance rule of snap moral judgments: certain actions are readily interpreted as damning. But it is the semic code that allows readers automatically to read Lady Dedlock's shudder as connected to her pride and probably also to her restlessness; the passage does not use either of those words, but the former, especially, is firmly fixed in our awareness of how people conventionally behave, so much so that it seems explicit. Relevant too is the psychological component of the cultural code. No specific reference is made to psychology, but it is common knowledge that restlessness must have a cause, that pride creates shudders of revulsion, and so forth.

Finally, readers who are in the authorial mode are probably applying the *configuration rule of balance* to predict that Esther and My Lady are on converging paths ("readers can usually start with the presumption that diverse strands of action will in some way be linked" [Rabinowitz, *Before Reading* 132]) and that because Esther is so empty of pride, their convergence will have thematic significance as well as resolving an instability that the text has offered for notice by frequent repetitions: "motherless" girl and "childless" woman. This level of interpretation is more abstract than most of what Barthes models in *S/Z*, but it can be related at least to the *proairetic code*. The mysterious woman is obviously engaged in the action-series we would call "searching"; Lady Dedlock's restlessness manifests itself in what seems to be a search for something—anything!—to relieve her "boredom." Esther too is on a quest, as she has explained very early in her portion of the narrative: "I would try, as hard as ever I could . . . to be industrious, contented, and kind-hearted, and to do some good to some one, and *win some love to myself if I could*" (Dickens, *Bleak House* 18, emphasis added). When actual readers move from Mrs. Rouncewell's remark about where Sir Leicester should sleep to the next chapter, headed "Esther's Narrative," they may feel only slightly less directed than in passing from chapter 6, the close of a portion of that narrative, to the first sentence of chapter 7: "[w]hile Esther sleeps, and while Esther wakes, it is still wet weather down at the place in Lincolnshire" (81).

As this brief analysis of some of the rhetorical features of *Bleak House* shows, neither Barthes's system nor Phelan's nor Rabinowitz's works in any way like an analytical machine; all are flexible, even improvisatory, although some followers of Barthes have tried to make his system prescriptive. When combined they enable readers to connect the details of individual lexies (of greatest interest to Barthes) to the larger but still local structures (rules of notice, signification, and configuration; attributes becoming functional as instabilities) and finally to interpretation (rules of coherence, thematic function). They don't predict any definite responses of actual readers but do suggest what actual authors may have had in mind when constructing their narratives and what readers who read authorially may determine about constructive intention. They could not serve any of these purposes unless authors and readers shared the preconscious awareness (one could also call it a linguistic intuition) that both story and discourse are always present in a narrative and that discourse elements carry illocutionary force that contributes to the implicatures derivable from these elements. Readers do what they do, in response to an author's actions embodied in the text, in order to preserve the principles of relevance, which dictate that within this particular situational context, cognitive effect is supposed to involve interpretation based on codes, rules, and the ur-conventions of narrative.

3

Narrating Voices and Their Audiences

The Rhetorical Significance of Narrative Transmission

The study of point of view, including analysis of narrators, has been of major interest to theorists of narrative during the past four decades; Wallace Martin states that for American and German theorists it is "the defining feature of narration" (9). Yet as narratologists frequently point out, the traditional terminology at best provides a place to begin and can fail to get at the most interesting effects. This limitation can be illustrated by considering the following beginnings, from Melville's story "Bartleby the Scrivener" (first published in 1853) and Dickens's novel *Bleak House*:

I am a rather elderly man. The nature of my avocations, for the last thirty years, has brought me into more than ordinary contact with what would seem an interesting and somewhat singular set of men, of whom, as yet, nothing, that I know of, has ever been written—I mean, the law-copyists, or scriveners. I have known very many of them, professionally and privately, and, if I pleased, could relate divers histories, at which good-natured gentlemen might smile, and sentimental souls might weep. But I waive the biographies of all other scriveners, for a few passages in the life of Bartleby, who was a scrivener, the strangest I ever saw, or heard of. While, of other law-copyists, I might write the complete life, of Bartleby nothing of that sort can be done. I believe that no materials exist, for a full and satisfactory biography of this man. It is an irreparable loss to literature. Bartleby was one of those beings of whom nothing is ascertainable, except from the original sources, and, in his case, those are very small. What my own astonished eyes saw of Bartleby, *that* is all I know of him, except, indeed, one vague report, which will appear in the sequel. (13)

I have a great deal of difficulty in beginning to write my portion of these pages, for I know I am not clever. I always knew that. I can remember, when I was a very little girl indeed, I used to say to my doll, when we were alone together, "Now, Dolly, I am not clever, you know very well, and you must be patient with me, like a dear!" And so she used to sit propped up in a great arm-chair, with her beautiful complexion and rosy lips, staring at me—or not so much at

me, I think, as at nothing—while I busily stitched away, and told her every one
of my secrets. (15)

Conventional textbook terminology would describe both passages as
first-person, retrospective narratives, in which the narrators seem to
be personally involved. Such a description, however, says nothing
about their vastly different rhetorical effects, the first inviting readers
to share the narrator's sense of himself as an author and his wonder-
ment at this character named Bartleby whom he has selected as his
subject, the second involving us with a person who expresses a difficulty with her role as narrator yet is able to go on at great length. These
openings display two different attitudes toward the narrating act in
which each is engaged, the lawyer of "Bartleby" very much in control
and with a sense of himself as a public person, while Esther Summerson presents herself as retiring and diffident: although the novel places
her in the central role, she repeatedly refers to herself as peripheral,
fearful lest her "vanity" give her a more important place than she feels
she deserves. The effect is even more complicated because Esther enters the novel in the third chapter, the other "portion" of the narrating
coming from a distinctive and powerful voice that seems to relish its
task. Here are that voice's first sentences:

London. Michaelmas Term lately over, and the Lord Chancellor sitting in Lincoln's Inn Hall. Implacable November weather. As much mud in the streets, as
if the waters had but newly retired from the face of the earth, and it would not
be wonderful to meet a Megalosaurus, forty feet long or so, waddling like an el-
ephantine lizard up Holborn Hill. Smoke lowering down from chimney-pots,
making a soft black drizzle, with flakes of soot in it as big as full-grown snow-
flakes—gone into mourning, one might imagine, for the death of the sun.
Dogs, undistinguishable in mire. Horses, scarcely better; splashed to their very
blinkers. Foot passengers, jostling one another's umbrellas, in a general infec-
tion of ill temper, and losing their foot-hold at street-corners, where tens of
thousands of other foot passengers have been slipping and sliding since the day
broke (if the day ever broke), adding new deposits to the crust upon crust of
mud, sticking at those points tenaciously to the pavement, and accumulating
at compound interest. (1)

This narrating voice has a personality every bit as definite as Esther's.
To characterize this voice, with its flair for metaphor and a willingness
to dive into the muddy, sooty details of the scene, as "omniscient" is to
beg the question of the way it invites readers into the scene, as if we
should be at home in this world (no need to define "Michaelmas Term"
or to specify which lord chancellor) even though our familiar distinctions between human, animal, and mineral may not hold.
   While this voice seems to share with Esther the world of the novel

and the task of writing, its family resemblance is closer to that of the lawyer-narrator of "Bartleby": it is comfortable with the speaking role, conveys a sense of public awareness, and is easy to characterize as male. The lawyer implies a narrating ability that extends beyond his present purpose—if he wanted to, he could bring his readers to tears and laughter. He asserts that his story is tellable; the *Bleak House* voice implies the same when he goes on to focus this powerful descriptive language on the main object of interest: "[t]he raw afternoon is rawest, and the dense fog is densest, and the muddy streets are muddiest, near that leaden-headed old obstruction, appropriate ornament for the threshold of a leaden-headed old corporation: Temple Bar. And hard by Temple Bar, in Lincoln's Inn Hall, at the very heart of the fog, sits the Lord High Chancellor in his High Court of Chancery" (2). On the other hand, the effect of this voice's present-tense narration is quite different from that of both the lawyer and Esther. Because of the differences in assertiveness, gender, and verb tense, *Bleak House* might even be described as having two different narrating audiences, even though both narrators are ostensibly telling portions of the same story and describing the same world. Esther would almost fit better in the lawyer's somewhat humane realm than in the implacable setting of *Bleak House*. Furthermore, her narrating audience—the one located within the world of the novel—knows that she knows how the story ends, whereas the omniscient voice can see everything that is happening but doesn't necessarily have foreknowledge, leading to a different effect for a narrating audience, hence to a potentially fascinating tension for the authorial audience.

These examples demonstrate how important it is to assess what Chatman terms the "structure of narrative transmission" (*Story and Discourse* 22), rather than the much simpler point of view, by asking such questions as the following. How many narrating voices are present? Where do these voices stand with respect to the audience? To the story? What storytelling conventions do they evoke? How are the narrating voices characterized? Is a listener, a "narratee," specified? What standpoint is being offered to the authorial audience? What assumptions, especially concerning values and experience with other texts, do the narrating voices make about their audiences? What discourse elements are important in transmitting the story to the actual reader? All of these questions have to do with the effect that F. K. Stanzel terms *mediacy*, which he considers to be the distinguishing characteristic of narration as a type of literary art (*Theory of Narrative* 4). This general characteristic generates both narrator ("the modality of the narrative") and point of view (the narrative's "perspectivization") (21). Even in the case Stanzel terms "figural" narration, in which a "reflector" replaces the mediating narrator and thus creates an "illusion of immediacy" (5), the questions of transmission are still fundamental to analysis. They tell us how to look at that display act that is narrative.

As my examples from "Bartleby" and *Bleak House* show, transmission is not just a theoretical issue concerning how narratives in the abstract, as some sort of logical category of language, can be studied; it is also central to the rhetoric of narrative—how audiences and narratives interact. Although mine is not an empirical study, the question of what happens to actual readers of narrative—to me, to my students, to the children with whom I've shared stories—is always on my agenda. Elrud Ibsch points out in her review essay "The Cognitive Turn in Narratology" that while research in this area was just beginning before 1990, the work that had been done confirmed some long-held theoretical assumptions and challenged others. One study in particular, by Ludwig and Faulstich, suggested that discourse factors (including first-/third-person narrating and internal/external perspective) influence how readers initially receive a narrative but that the characteristics of individual readers have more to do with how readers interpret a narrative (416–17). Ludwig and Faulstich themselves, according to Ibsch, warn against generalizing from their results, feeling that the people they used as subjects should have been "highly socialized readers" (418). That qualification is important—not that their student readers reacted inappropriately to narratives but that effects are going to differ. I would also mention that they used a short narrative, Hemingway's "Old Man at the Bridge"; the effects of narrative transmission, as well as of other rhetorical elements such as progression, may be different in the reception of longer texts. It would not be surprising if in longer narratives these elements played a greater role in shaping interpretation.

Because I'm taking the strong-contextualist position, I approach the questions of transmission by concentrating on the narrative as a set of multilayered speech acts governed by ur-conventions and conforming to the cognitive and communicative principles of relevance. The ur-convention of most interest in this chapter is the first, the reader's practice of authorial reading. Phelan makes a crucial point, however, in insisting that the concept of authorial reading (and by extension the entire structure of voice and audience positions) is most helpful as a "heuristic for reading" that recognizes differences among actual readers. The model "invites a sharing of experiences, especially sharing that involves discussion of the textual grounds for those experiences, so that different readers can continue to learn from each other" (*Narrative* 147). Some of the most interesting and powerful of these experiences are stimulated by narrating voices—their different types, their relationships to the story and the audience, the specified or implied addressees, and their variations within a narrative.

Concentrating on narrating voices rather than on point of view or narrator marks a departure both from traditional studies of narrative and from taxonomies devised more recently by narratologists with a structuralist orientation. The concentration also addresses Andrew Gibson's recent criticism of narratology for privileging notions of vision and voice (86–87, 144). Gibson is wrong that narratologists have avoided problematizing these notions, although he aptly reminds us that something like "discourse *space*" is a metaphor and must be questioned as to its suitability as a basis for framing theory (16, 20, 26). For years narratologists have agreed that the term *point of view* and its various family members (such as *first-person* and *omniscient*) do not adequately describe the many dimensions involved in how a story is actually told. Complex narrative situations can't be analyzed with the relatively primitive tool point of view, as Genette says; the attempt to do so has led to such methodological lapses as "christening 'narrator' a focal character who never opens his mouth" (*Narrative Discourse* 64–65). A textbook example of this particular lapse is Donald Hall's attribution of "unreliable narrator" status to John Marcher, of James's story "The Beast in the Jungle" (120). Marcher is the focalizer; to equate him with the narrator is to miss the opportunity for irony that exists when narrator and focalizer are distinct. In trying to develop better tools for analyzing such situations, however, narratologists have created forbiddingly elaborate diagrams (such as Stanzel's "typological circle" [*Theory of Narrative* xvi] or Chatman's "Diagram of Narrative Structure" [*Story and Discourse* 267]) and equally forbidding sets of terms. Commenting on this barrier to clarity, Lanser criticizes Genette's "neologistic" and "counterproductive" terms based on the root word *diegesis* (*Narrative Act* 133). Genette's Gallic fecundity is all the more regrettable because *diegesis* itself and several of the derivatives are useful, but they get lost in the crowd.

Furthermore, some of structuralist narratology's best-known analytical tools are not sensitive to rhetorical effects. For example, Genette describes his system as built on "categories borrowed from the grammar of verbs" (*Narrative Discourse* 30). This grammar leads him to organize "temporal relations between narrative and story" under *tense*, "modalities (forms and degrees) of narrative 'representation'" under *mood*, and "the way in which the narrating itself is implicated in the narrative" under *voice* (31). The categories are helpful, but in developing the details of his system Genette gives relatively equal weight to aspects of narrative that do not have equal rhetorical impact. Of the three, *voice* has the greatest influence on a reader's page-by-page experience of a narrative, as the research of Ludwig and Faulstich suggests (Ibsch 416); this is the case, I believe, because voice has the most to do with the ur-convention of authorial reading. *Tense* has the least influence, in general, because it is not essential to, although it may influence, a reader's application of any of the ur-conventions. This difference in rhetorical importance is not reflected in Genette's terms. Like verbs, narratives display voice and tense, but unlike verbs, narratives have shades or degrees of each, degrees that the "grammar of verbs" can say nothing about.

A third problem is that the category of *mood* is less intuitive for native speakers of English than for speakers of more highly inflected languages. According to Genette, "'[d]istance' and 'perspective' . . . are the two chief modalities of that *regulation of narrative information that is mood*" (*Narrative Discourse* 162), but most readers experience "distance" at least partially as a function of "temporal relations between narrative and story," or *tense*. Esther and the omniscient narrator are located at different *temporal* distances from the events in *Bleak House*, a fact perhaps as important to readers' experience of the novel as the difference in narrating persons (mood). Likewise, perspective would strike most readers as having something to do with how "the narrating itself is implicated in the narrative," that is, with *voice*.

In spite of these problems, Genette's discussion of narration is still the most thorough and will be important in this chapter. A different organization than his, however, is needed in order best to explore the rhetorical effects that can be created within a narrating situation. I've sketched the basics of this organization in chapter 1. They derive from Chatman's diagram of the persons—I call them positions—that can be involved in the transmission and reception of a narrative:

Fig. 3. Chatman's Structure of Narrative Transmission

	VOICE				AUDIENCE	
Real author	Implied author	(Narrator)		(Narratee)	Implied reader	Reel reader

(*Story and Discourse* 151)

In this diagram, narrator and narratee are optional; Chatman hedges somewhat in noting that some stories are more accurately described as "minimally narrated" than as totally lacking a narrator (*Story and Discourse* 196), one classic example being Hemingway's "The Killers." Although Chatman and a few others have floated the possibility of narratorless narrative, most narratologists hold that a narrator must be present. According to Ryan, the "no-narrator" theory is not consistent with the principle of intentionality on which "contemporary philosophy of language" is based; the theory can't "explain how the sentences of impersonal fiction can convey meaning without projecting an intent" (*Possible Worlds* 69). Monika Fludernik represents the opposing view, harshly criticizing the position that both a narrator and an implied author belong in the structure of narrative transmission. She says (correctly, I think) that this position results from the "frame conception of storytelling rather than from any necessary textual evidence" ("if there is a story, somebody must needs tell it"), but she doesn't convince me that this is an "absurd" position (*Fictions* 448). She does usefully note that another script is also prominent, that of "reflectoral narration," which "structures narration around the script of *experiencing* or *viewing*" rather than telling (449).

I come down between Fludernik and Ryan. Fludernik doesn't seem to be addressing the fundamentally intensional nature of narration: part of my reading *frame* most certainly includes the concept of *agent*, and this actor or agent is the source of the narrative that I'm being offered for experiencing or viewing. I agree with Ryan that the principle of intentionality requires such an agent (as do the cognitive and communicative principles of relevance), but the agent need not be located within the narrative, which is where *narrator* must be placed. Instead, I use the term *implied author* to denote the source to which a reader will attribute a narrative. If this really is, as Fludernik says, a *frame conception*, that means it has a cognitivist basis and is not simply a cultural predisposition. Her use of the term *schema* to name the same tendency suggests that she may not have been sufficiently critical of her own language; *frame* is the better term, because the expectation of agency is an innate part of human linguistic equipment.

In Chatman's diagram, implied author and implied reader are "immanent to a narrative"; real author and reader are "outside the narrative transaction as such, though, of course, indispensable to it in an ultimate practical sense" (*Story and Discourse* 151). The positions on the "voice" side of the diagram can be discussed by means of "the notions of illocutionary action . . . and implicature," as Susan Lanser says; the notions "facilitate an approach to the questions of attitude, distance, 'affect,' and tone" that are crucial for an understanding of the relationship between a text and its reader (*Narrative Act* 79–80). She points out that "[w]e can explain a narrator, then, by looking at the speech acts s/he performs in the context of their performance" (80), and the same approach allows us to describe how "narrative perspective and voice . . . are retrieved in the conventional reading of literary discourse" (226). In fact, almost everything that's truly interesting about any voice in a narrative has to be inferred or constructed, on the basis of what a textual element implicates and what the rules for reading and other conventions allow us to understand about the illocutionary acts to which it likely contributes. What a narrator means may be more important than what a narrator says, and any voice that we hear "behind" a narrator—a voice of an implied author, for instance—is wholly derived from implicatures and illocutions. The same holds for an actual reader's relationship to the narrating and authorial audiences.

In chapter 2 I refined this diagram on the audience side by replacing "implied reader" with "authorial" and "narrating" audiences. In this chapter I add some complexity to the voice side and further explain the audience side, adding the position of "narratee." (See fig. 1 for the complete diagram.) Each side allows for options, but of different types. The audience side offers actual readers various roles to play: for each position, a reader can move anywhere along an axis of response, from total acceptance to total rejection. On the voice side, the positions of narrator and focalizer can be occupied by any number of characters or voices during a single reader's experience of a single narrative, while the implied author and extrafictional voice will remain fixed once they're established for an actual reader. Moreover, the two sides are not symmetrical in function. "Narrator," for instance, does define "narratee" but only partly shapes "narrating audience," which is also influenced by "focalizer." "Extrafictional voice" has no analogous component on the audience side but contributes to a reader's sense of the "authorial audience."

This multiplicity and fluidity has only recently begun to be explored by narratologists applying Mikhail Bakhtin's concept of *heteroglossia*: the "internal stratification present in every language at any given moment of its historical existence" (262–63). Incorporated into a novel, heteroglossia functions as *"another's speech in another's language,* serving to express authorial intentions but in a refracted way. Such speech constitutes a special type of *double-voiced discourse"* (324). In fact, the novel genre itself, according to Bakhtin, is defined by its embodiment of heteroglossia. From now on, I'll be treating the reader's expectation of and experience with heteroglossia as a fourth ur-convention, applicable, however, only in *fictional* narratives, hence not universal in the way that authorial reading, naturalization, and progression are. (I think Bakhtin is correct that the experience of heteroglossia is potentially present in every instance of human language use, but not all types realize this potential. The novel does so because its heritage is linked with class struggles and the rise of mass culture, among other reasons.) Heteroglossia is closely connected to the ur-convention of authorial reading: any utterance of any textual voice can in principle be regarded as synthetic and as furthering a constructive intention. (The intention is refracted through a voice that may be serving a mimetic or plot function within the world of the narrative.) Like the other three ur-conventions, this one exists symbiotically with the cooperative principle (CP) and with the assumption that a fictional narrative, offered as such within the appropriate situational context, is tellable.

Because of the ur-convention of heteroglossia as well as the asymmetry between the two sides of the narrative-transmission diagram, the relationships among reader, text-as-utterance, and message are neither predictable nor stable. To be sure, as Lanser says, point of view is a "structure of discourse"; it is "the medium *par excellence* for regulating interpersonal relationships and communicating values and attitudes" (*Narrative Act* 85). The success of such communication depends on how the speaker relates to the "listener, the message, and the verbal act," but each of these relationships involves "social realities which in some sense 'precede' the production of discourse" (86). Further complicating the picture, these relationships "are dialectically intertwined," even though some structure results from the condition that if the communication is to be successful, the relationships must all lie "within the conventions of acceptability for a particular audience and a particular speech event" (94–95). Thus, even though "[a]ll discourse manifests a structure" of relationships among listener, message, and verbal act (97), the intertwining allows only the most general predictions about how individual acts of communication will be influenced by this structure. Every narrative situation will involve these elements, but their relative prominence will depend on how a reader processes them and will probably change during the course of the narrative.

For instance, Lanser attributes to the skill with which the communicator performs the speech act a certain "*mimetic authority*, as opposed to the *diegetic authority* that comes directly from the person of the author or from a narrating voice" (89–90). But a narrator who tells her own story in an unskillful or awkward manner may still carry mimetic authority; she may even be more credible as a mimetic figure than a skillful narrator would be, while still conveying the same authority with respect to the narrating itself (the diegesis). Esther Summerson, with her many coy pauses and self-deprecations, may strike some readers as unskillful compared to the omniscient voice. Certainly her voice is less assured—less oratorical, less insistently didactic and metaphorical. On the other hand, she carefully preserves a linear chronology while also employing foreshadowing. Readers may even decide that her allusions to a certain dark young man comprise a sophisticated implementation of notice and signification: she is trying to dramatize, retrospectively, her inner conflict regarding her suitability for Alan Woodcourt while also implicating that this element of the plot is less important than her repeated finding and losing of her mother.

The omniscient narrator, however, violates linear narration at least once, at the beginning of chapter 55, which jumps back in time to pick up the narrative of Mr. George after chronicling Mr. Inspector Bucket's discovery of Mademoiselle Hortense as the murderer of Lawyer Tulkinghorn. This analepsis is necessary because the narrator, reaching a fork in the narrative road, chose to follow Mr. Bucket, leaving Mr. George in the narrative lurch. As the omniscient narrator's *only* analepsis, this choice suggests that the narrator has a fascination with Mr. Bucket's power; the reader may not share the fascination but must go along with the narrative line. Mr. Bucket says to Grandfather Smallweed, "I am damned if I am a going to have my case spoilt, or interfered with, or anticipated by so much as half a second of time, by any human being in creation. . . . Do you see this hand, and do you think that *I* don't know the right time to stretch it out, and put it on the arm that fired that shot?" (731). This little display on Mr. Bucket's part can yield a great deal of pleasure to the actual reader who likes to see unsavory characters get their just desserts, but a different actual reader who is concerned about Mr. George's well-being may not be able easily to follow the lead of the omniscient narrator here and may resent the temporal juggling, preferring to get on with the line of the story concerning Mr. George, who is languishing in prison under the charge of murder. That is, some actual readers may prefer Esther's values, as implicated by her narrating acts, over the values of the omniscient voice: her combined mimetic and diegetic authority may yield a greater moral authority.

What these complexities and difficulties add up to is, first, that analysis of narrating voices must take into account the many potential relationships among the speaker, the listener, the point, the story, and the verbal acts that bring into existence the story and the speaker. Second, the analysis can never predict actual perlocutionary effects but can only sketch some possibilities. Lanser terms the relationships dialectical, but a more accurate description might be "complex system" in the mathematical sense: the variables are so intricately interwoven that no precise description is possible. The system is saved from chaos—people are able to make sense of narratives at all—only if the context permits reading the texts as narratives; the principles of relevance then direct the reader to apply the ur-conventions of authorial reading, naturalization, progression, and (for fictional narratives) the *expectation* of complexity that results from language's inherent heteroglossia. Apparent violations of the CP will be interpreted as implicatures, since this principle is hyperprotected for literary texts. We expect the two voices of *Bleak House* to complement each other some-how, even though our first encounter with Esther's voice seems to be changing the rules established by the novel's opening chapters. We take Esther's mannerisms as significant, even though we may find them irritating. When the mystery of her parentage is revealed only halfway through the novel, we keep reading, assuming that the re-maining 470-odd pages (in the Oxford Illustrated Dickens) contain ma-terial just as tellable and just as worth displaying as did the first 410.

Voice Positions: Extrafictional Voice and Implied Author

Although *implied author* is not precisely a voice, the ur-convention of authorial reading dictates that developing a constructive intention is one of the most important moves a reader makes. The "person" to whom this intention is attributed, I term, following Booth, the *im-plied author*. This "author's second self" is constructed by the reader on the basis of a text's "extractable meanings" as well as "the moral and emotional content of each bit of action and suffering of all of the characters" (73). Actually, the more accurate term might be *inferred author*, because each reader will infer from a work the attributes of its creator, whereas "implied" suggests that a text somehow projects this quality (Genette, *Narrative Discourse Revisited* 150). But because "implied author" is so well established, it's worth keeping.

This position involves what Lanser calls the "extrafictional voice," which is the source of the first textual elements a reader encounters: the text's "historical information" such as title, introduction, and or-ganization (*Narrative Act* 122). The extrafictional voice is "the most direct textual counterpart for the historical author, carries all the di-egetic authority of its (publicly authorized) creator and has the on-tological status of historical truth" (122). Lanser continues: "[w]hat-ever information is provided, whatever expectations are called forth, the reader's mimetic participation in the text includes the building of an author-image from this historical material" (124).

However, an important qualification is needed. Authorial reading, as an ur-convention, is an essential component of the context within which *any* narrative will be understood by an audience. But only when the narrative is fictional do I need to separate extrafictional voice, im-plied author, and actual author; the governing convention or un-marked case of factual narrative is that of identity between the actual author's voice and the voice embodied within the narrative. Mediacy distinguishes fictional narrative, not narrative in general. According to Ruth Ronen, "[t]he fact that fictional texts have authors affects truth determinations regarding fictional propositions: only some fictional propositions come from an authorial source, whereas others come from a source to whom the power of narration has been delegated (as demonstrated by the difference between an omniscient narrator, a person narrating about his younger self in the first person, and an unreliable narrator)" (92). By contrast, the authorship of a factual narrative reflects a different type of intention, even among postmodern readers who "know" that factual narratives are no less constructed than are fictional narratives. In this book I'm focusing on the latter type. Much of rhetorical narratology applies to both fictional and factual narratives, but some important components do not. In developing the structure-of-narrative-transmission model, I will explain all components as they apply to fictional narrative, because I believe this to be the more complex type.

In a fictional narrative, the "author-image" or extrafictional voice contributes to the reader's construction of an implied author, although more is involved, as I will explain shortly. The elements that the reader uses to construct this voice belong to the world the reader occupies; not only do they have "the *ontological* status of historical truth," but they are experienced that way as well—we would never doubt that the author named on a title page was the actual author. (The obvious exception, but one that does not contradict this point, is the general category consisting of hoax, plagiarism, ghost writing, etc.) The extrafictional voice provides the reader provisionally with at least two pieces of information that influence the sense of the implied author: the actual author's gender and distance, historically and geographically, from the world of the novel. A third piece of information may also be provided: the subgenre to which the work belongs. According to Lanser, readers will assume the narrating voice to be male unless the *author* or the narrator is noted as female; that is, the male voice is the unmarked case (*Narrative Act* 166). The actual author's distance from the work's world, combined with subgenre signals, implies a level of involvement with or detachment from the story itself on the part of the author. The historical and geographical distance of the world of the novel, established early in the text, will also set certain expectations about style, subject matter, and ideology. Reading the title *The Blithedale Romance*, I expect to have my emotions engaged and do not expect to encounter a slice of life, whereas the label "historical novel" will cause me to infer an author who pays attention to facts; I also expect a fairly objective tone from the narrating voice (unless of course that voice is a character in the story).

From this "historical material," encountered only briefly and superficially, a reader constructs, usually without much conscious thought, a very sketchy portrait of the implied author. Lanser asserts that "[a]ll other voices that the text creates are subordinate to [the extrafictional voice], less directly related to the historical transaction between author and audience, and weaker in diegetic status" (*Narrative Act* 128). This subordinating, however, will usually only happen at the beginning of the reader's encounter with the text; the extrafictional portrait is so thin that it can easily be altered as the reader enters the story. Any ordinary "conventional reading of fiction" assumes an "authorial presence" who is "ultimately responsible for the text" (132). This "authorial presence" may be distinct, in the reader's experience, from the voices that tell the story, but it is not necessarily more powerful as a diegetic presence than these voices. For instance, a personalized narrator will be experienced as having strong diegetic status, at least for the duration of the reading. And the reader's sense of the implied author will be much more strongly shaped by interacting with the contents of the text itself. Lanser says that like the implied author, the extrafictional voice "may not be a narrating presence within the fictional tale itself" (123), but she also says that "[t]races of the unmasked fictional *narrator* may be found in the organization of discourse, sometimes in the titling of chapters, always in the deep structure of the verbal act, from its most general framework to choices of syntax and lexis for each voice represented in the created world" (132, emphasis added). Conventional critical usage, however, has attached the term *implied author* to these traces, a usage more in keeping than *unmasked fictional narrator* with how readers experience this aspect of the narrative. Who is responsible for the chapter titles in *Bleak House*? We automatically answer "Dickens himself," even if we don't know this for a fact (which it is). Esther is explicitly writing a narrative, but we certainly don't view her as coming up with the title "A Progress" for chapter 3 or "Esther's Narrative" for chapter 17 (among others). Nor are we likely to take the omniscient voice as having generated the titles for "his" chapters, although to do so would not seem as counterintuitive as attributing to Esther the authority of "her" chapter titles.

Returning to Phelan's point that to distinguish among a text's voices is a helpful heuristic and leads us to discuss the "textual grounds" for our experiences with texts (*Narrative* 147), I note that the extrafictional voice is important in that it consists of *textual* elements that contribute to the reader's construction of the implied author, which otherwise is not a textual entity in the same way a narrator is. Booth writes that "though the author can to some extent choose his disguises, he can never choose to disappear" (20). This does not mean that the real author, or his or her disguised "second self" the implied author, is located within the text; instead, the implied author is derived by the reader from the narrative speech act, with a bit of guidance from the details of the extrafictional voice. As Booth says, no fact is ever given us in a " 'natural,' unadorned form," neither in books nor in life; "[t]he author cannot choose whether to use rhetorical heightening. His only choice is of the kind of rhetoric he will use" (112, 116). Because of the ur-convention of authorial reading, readers will always infer an authorial presence who is responsible for creating the text, who is the source of the work's *narrative* discourse (Lanser, *Narrative Act* 132). Patrick O'Neill puts the point somewhat differently in distinguishing between narrator and implied author: the latter "always deals in the signal information that tells us how the semantic information [provided by the narrator] should be understood" (69).

There are two unmarked cases that govern the reader's construction of the implied author. I've already mentioned the first: the extrafictional voice and the implied author are taken as identical because they share crucial identifying features such as gender, historical era, and social class, as well as the ideologies that attach to these features. Although the implied author has no speaking part in a narrative, the "voice" will always be conceived by readers as single, self-consistent, and "public," in Lanser's terminology. Lanser distinguishes between public and private narrating voices—between "fictional narrative acts designed for an apparently public readership and those narratives designed for reception only by other characters or textual figures" (137 n.35). One way to tell these voices apart is that "the public narrator generally defines for the reader the story world in which s/he will function as creator and authority," while the private narrator is "bound to the fictional world"; the latter is "not capable of addressing personae outside the fictional context" (138), whereas the former is. Whenever a reader has the feeling that an authorial voice located within the text is occasionally rising above the story level and commenting directly to an authorial audience, the reader will attach these comments to the extrafictional voice in the unmarked case. As long as the addressed public is not too far removed from the actual readers encountering the extrafictional voice, they are unlikely to pay the voice of this implied author any unusual attention: reading authorially, we expect to encounter an authorial voice. We quite comfortably, and unthinkingly, attach the label "Dickens" to the omniscient voice in *Bleak House*, not least because the voice of the preface to the first book edition (published in 1853) is so similar to the omniscient voice both in tone and in values.

My argument that readers automatically identify the extrafictional voice with the implied author hinges on the assumption that readers tend to construct both of these voice positions as monologic. Nevertheless, I recognize that individual readers with critical antennae different from mine may reach different conclusions. Robyn Warhol, for one, sees *Bleak House* as "a genuinely polyvocal novel that explodes the idea of an omniscient narrator-as-person. The narrative voice that alternates with Esther's is never a 'who,' but is rather a conglomeration of disparate languages and perspectives" (*Gendered Interventions* 149). Outside of Esther's narrative, according to Warhol, the narration "continually shifts in style and perspective" (151). These shifts give Warhol the impression that no narratee is being addressed, an impression that "renders the moment of direct address at Jo's deathbed so memorable" by inviting "a unique moment of discursive contact between narrators and readers" (153). Yet Warhol's reference to "the chameleon narrator" hints that she too may sense behind these many masks one extrafictional voice, a "Dickens" who, like Charlie Hexam in *Our Mutual Friend*, can "do the Police in different voices" (153, 246). My approach actually supports Warhol's larger argument, that the deathbed scene is powerful not only because the discourse suddenly shifts from distancing to engaging but because the extrafictional voice weighs in here with "his" own voice. If the non-Esther sections were narrated with voices that readers truly recognized as distinct rather than as masks of "Charles Dickens," the deathbed scene might carry less power.

The case of *Bleak House* also raises another theoretical issue: how far does the extrafictional voice extend into Esther's narrative? To ask this question is to recognize that the extrafictional voice and the implied author are not *functionally* identical. Genette has argued persuasively that, *logically*, the concept of implied author is unnecessary in analyzing narrative discourse, that it can always be replaced by either actual author or narrator (*Narrative Discourse Revisited* 142–44). Perlocutionary effect, however, is not determined by the rules of logic but by marking within the larger context surrounding the discourse (e.g., narrative, fictional, naturalizable). Marking can be established by two different relational vectors in one novel: the extrafictional voice smoothly connects to the omniscient narrator but not to Esther. A reader who actually believes in Esther, who is able to enter her life-world and become the narrating audience for her chapters, will probably have a stronger sense of authorial double-voicing than is created by the omniscient portions alone. The extrafictional voice I hear in the preface (I'll speak personally here), connect to the actual author's name, gender, and era, blend with the omniscient narrator, and credit with all chapter titles, including those of Esther's portion—this voice does not seem large enough, emotionally, to contain Esther Summerson, in whom I do believe and whose world I do enter.

To put the point somewhat differently: reading authorially, I know that Charles Dickens created Esther and intended that she serve definite rhetorical purposes, but I also sense that "Charles Dickens" the implied author, as Dickens's second self, is another fiction rather than *extra*fictional. (I suspect that this response of mine is similar to what causes Elizabeth Preston to introduce the helpful but not well-defined concept of "dialogic implied author, multiple and fluid in his or her own identities" [153].) He is not contained within the fictional world of the novel, but he is part of the fiction-making context in which I collaborate as a reader. In short, *Bleak House* begins as an excellent example of the unmarked case (identity between extrafictional voice and implied author), but, depending on how an individual reader reacts to Esther's narrative, it may become marked. Should this happen, the reader may justifiably question whether Dickens was wholly aware of the power of his novel to generate a critical look at Dickens's own authoritarian tendency: his fictional second self may be conceived of as a better person than the self projected through the extrafictional voice.

But as I've pointed out earlier, we still are not likely to regard that voice as authoring everything in the novel, including chapter titles. We probably have the sense that Dickens is "speaking through" this voice more than through Esther's, but we also know that Dickens extends beyond the voice's boundaries. Ulf Olsson is discussing something like this phenomenon when he raises the possibility of a voice that is "heard" but is not the voice of either narrator or author. Olsson is criticizing narratology's apparent "longing to authorize fiction," a longing that manifests itself in the metaphor of voice (85). He asks, quite reasonably, "who is the person" of the narratological voice, and answers, not so clearly, that it may be located in tradition or history (85, 91). An answer more in keeping with speech-act theory is that the person is the extrafictional voice in the unmarked case, and even in the marked cases this voice evokes a "person" by negation.

A less theoretically complex example of the marked case is *The Scarlet Letter*: the implied author violates readers' expectation of consistency. A clear extrafictional voice is established by the prefatory "sketch," ostensibly about Hawthorne's stint as a customshouse officer. In this sketch the narrating voice explains how he located the manuscript and the "affair of red cloth" forming the basis of the story to follow. This sketch is lengthy; within its many pages it clearly locates the narrating voice in the town of Salem shortly before 1850, and it establishes the qualities of wry humor, geniality, and empathy. The same temporal location and qualities are carried directly into the narrative (set in Boston, "not less than two centuries ago"); they support a reader in identifying the extrafictional voice of the sketch with the narrating voice of the novel and in labeling both as "Hawthorne." This strong link, however, is violated several times when the narrating voice expresses beliefs that belong to a Puritan contemporary of Hester Prynne's rather than to someone writing around 1850. For instance, Roger Chillingworth's eyes are variously referred to as burning with a red light and with a blue. The Puritans were able to believe in such phenomena because they were convinced that Satan's emissaries were walking the earth of the New World, whereas the phenomena are anachronistic for a narrator positioned, as Hawthorne positions his, around 1850. Another discrepancy is that the narrating voice is not always sympathetic: several times he simplistically links moral and physical deformity. (For a discussion of these discrepancies and their rhetorical effects, see Kearns, "Narrative Voices in *The Scarlet Letter*.") These discrepancies complicate our experience of the implied author, of the novel's norms and perspectives, because we expect "the" implied author to be singular.

This difficulty can be resolved—the undeniable readability of *The Scarlet Letter* can be explained—by invoking the fourth ur-convention, the expectation of heteroglossia. Readers expect novels to embody various voices. Usually these voices belong to characters; occasionally a narrator's voice will differ from that of the implied author. It is also possible for the narrating to be shared by several voices, with the transitions from voice to voice coming abruptly rather than being signaled either verbally or textually (for example, by different typefaces or by blank spaces on the page). Hawthorne may have been aiming for such an effect, either consciously or not, in order further to dramatize both the historical distance of the Puritans and their continuing influence on his own society. He thus creates a tension that contributes to the novel's progression. Because these disruptions, although vivid, are brief and infrequent, they don't seriously challenge the CP. The reader who notices the shifts but doesn't see a purpose for them can still read on, treating them as authorial lapses; the reader who does grasp them will have a richer reading experience.

The second unmarked case is that of a clear separation between the narrating voice(s) and the implied author: the speaker(s) cannot be confused with the name on the title page. Lanser would term these "private" narrating voices, because they can't reach outside the world of the narrative. They are intradiegetic, hence by definition distinct from the voice of the implied author. Esther's entrance into *Bleak House* in chapter 3 will surprise first-time readers, but only for a moment; once we recognize that this is a new "I," not the omniscient voice, our association of the implied author with that voice will return, although it will expand or otherwise alter because of this new type of material that contributes to our sense of the constructive intention behind the novel. Nineteenth-century American literature offers an example of the marked version of this case: *Adventures of Huckleberry Finn.* If for no other reason than because Twain offers a prefatory "notice" in what every reader will take to be his own voice (Mark Twain, the public self of Samuel Clemens), readers will not confuse Huck's voice with that of his creator, who intones that "[p]ersons attempting to find a motive in this narrative will be prosecuted; persons attempting to find a moral in it will be banished; persons attempting to find a plot in it will be shot." But Huck, too, addresses "his" readers at the very beginning, taking on a public status that conflicts with his identity as a character in another book: "[y]ou don't know about me without you have read a book by the name of *The Adventures of Tom Sawyer;* but that ain't no matter. That book was made by Mr. Mark Twain, and he told the truth, mainly."

We might attempt to resolve this conflict by distinguishing between Huck as narrator and Huck as character, except that these two roles are not distinguished in the novel; Huck is a single entity, and one of the ways we know him is as the teller of his story. Alternatively, we might say that in the fictional world to which Huck belongs, *Tom Sawyer* is to be taken as biography ("the truth") rather than as fiction, taken thus by Huck's fictional readers, his narratees. This second resolution, however, is not rhetorically plausible; having taught this novel often, I know that actual student readers feel themselves to be addressed by Huck's opening "you," but these readers also know that *Tom Sawyer* is fiction. Not that Huck is less fictional than Tom, but by overtly staking a claim to readers' attention, he seems to lift himself momentarily out of the fictional realm and onto the same diegetic level as the extrafictional voice. (I'll shortly discuss this phenomenon of crossing narrative levels, which Genette terms *metalepsis.*) *If* readers are somewhat unsettled by this opening, then *Huckleberry Finn* becomes a marked case: we can't place Huck strictly in the world of the story, because he is speaking *out of* the story, to "us," about his existence in the realm of *Tom Sawyer.* There is also the question of the intradiegetic transmission of the narrative: what is this boy doing writing a book and signing it "The end. Yours truly, Huck Finn"? Twain brings this question to the forefront in the final paragraph by having Huck observe, "if I'd a knowed what a trouble it was to make a book I wouldn't a tackled it and ain't a-going to no more" (Clemens 265). Even though most of the novel's details point to a clear separation between implied author and narrator, the boundaries are not quite as well defined as in *Bleak House.* Hence the identity of the implied author may become an issue—may become marked—for actual readers.

The implied author functions rhetorically to evoke the ideology, the "general cultural codes" that establish "the norms of the narrative," as

Chatman says (*Story and Discourse* 149). "Norms"—this element of the description should be noted. Questions about the implied author's relationship to the listener, to the story, and to the verbal acts of the text will come up only in marked cases; ordinarily, the implied author's *distance* from the story, a distance that includes but is not limited to diegetic level, will remain stable once it is established. Because of the ur-convention of authorial reading, readers expect consistency in the distance and in the text's norms. We expect a stable perspective, including a self-consistent implied author, from which to experience the novel's events and hear its voices. Because, as Chatman (among many others) says, the implied author is the vehicle for the narrative's ideology, marked cases probably are more likely to bring ideology into a thematic role. This may happen with *Bleak House*: a reader on whom the omniscient narrator's self-assuredness grates in comparison to Esther's humility and who senses Dickens's *best* second self behind these two voices may become more attuned to and critical of the tendency of the *Bleak House* world to grind down human beings, for instance, or more sensitive to the apparently absolute power of men over women in this realm. But such rhetorical effects can only be generalized about, never predicted, because each reader individually constructs and responds to the implied author.

Marking, I repeat, is determined pragmatically rather than according to any transcendent standard. For this reason it depends on a given reader's familiarity with the type of work being read. According to Genette, the classical unmarked case with respect to the narrating is that there will be no shifts in status or in level: the narrator's "relationship to the story is in principle invariable" (*Narrative Discourse* 245). For the contemporary novel, however, at least when experienced by knowledgeable readers, there is nothing remarkable about a "variable or floating relationship" between the narrator and the characters (246). This is not to say that these days a novel can do nothing to cause readers to sit up and take notice. For readers familiar with contemporary fiction, the unmarked case is one in which the narrating *level* is preserved (either within or outside of the narrated world); the narrator can without notice change *status*, can move between being present in and being absent from the story.

Narrating Voices and Their Levels, Relationships, and Acts

My emphasis on the reader's role in creating an implied author establishes the single most important difference between that voice position and narrators, those voices located within the narrative. The reader constructs an implied-author persona on the basis of inferences, with occasionally a few tangible details added (such as Twain's "Notice"); the reader locates narrators in the text and knows them as we know someone we can't see but who is addressing us directly or whose conversation we're overhearing. An actual reader will also expect implied author and narrator to have different rhetorical purposes. The narrator's purpose implicitly includes proving that his or her version of the story is true, whereas the implied author's purpose is "to make the whole package, story and discourse, *including the narrator's performance*, interesting, acceptable, self-consistent, and artful" (Chatman, *Story and Discourse* 227, emphasis added).

As with implied author, a narrator is almost always going to be assumed by the reader as part of the literary speech situation. (The bulk of *The Kiss of the Spider Woman* consists of untagged quoted speech and thus may seem to be free of a narrator. On the other hand, some intradiegetic source may be assumed for the footnotes that become more and more obtrusive, and near the end an intradiegetic narrator does appear.) Culler points out that "making narrators is not an analytical operation that lies outside the domain of fiction but [is] very much a continuation of fiction-making: dealing with details by imagining a narrator; telling a story about a narrator and his/her response so as to make sense of them" ("Problems" 6)—in short, assessing the structure of narrative transmission. Culler says that this readerly urge to humanize or reify narrators stems from a "powerful humanistic ideology" that needs to be scrutinized (11), but clearly it also follows from the fact that most human language use serves the purpose of communication. Speech-act theory treats this urge as an element of the CP: because a reader must cooperate with someone, she or he constructs that someone to account for the existence of the communication, the text.

Narratologists agree that the terminology of even recently updated introduction-to-literature textbooks—for example, Laurie Kirszner and Stephen Mandell, *Literature: Reading, Reacting, Writing*, Michael Meyer, *The Compact Bedford Introduction to Literature*, and Carl E. Bain et al., *The Norton Introduction to Literature*—does not adequately discriminate among important aspects of the narrating. (All of these, however, do foreground point of view, and the Norton at least mentions the difference between narration and focus. Textbooks are always a generation or more behind mainstream critical theory.) Genette points out that the term *first-person* is flawed because its formal signal, the presence of first-person verbs, can actually "refer to two different situations . . . the narrator's own designation of himself as such . . . or else the identity of person between the narrator and one of the characters in the story" (*Narrative Discourse* 244). I can overtly involve myself in the *telling* of a story; I can also tell a story in which I am involved as a character. Both are instances of first-person narration, according to textbook definitions, although most readers probably would use the second as their main example, feeling that telling a story about myself is "more" first-person.

To discriminate between these and other situations that are muddled by traditional terminology, Genette develops a scheme that is based on two questions. First, can the narrator "use the first person to designate *one of his characters*"? If so, the narrator is "present as a character," and we term the narrating act *homodiegetic*. If the narrator is "absent from the story he tells," we term the narrating act *heterodiegetic* (*Narrative Discourse* 244–45). Second, does the narrating act take place within the world it is about or within the narrated time frame, or does it take place outside that world or frame? If within, then the act occupies the *intradiegetic* level, which corresponds roughly to Lanser's "private narrator"; if outside, then it occupies the *extradiegetic* level, Lanser's "public narrator." Genette's explanations are difficult to follow, but the following diagram, based on one he provides in *Narrative Discourse* (248), is helpful:

Fig. 4. Narrating Situations

	LEVEL (Where does the narrating occur?)	
	Extradiegetic (Act is outside the world of the story or the narrated time frame.)	*Intradiegetic* (Act is within the world of the story and the time frame.)
RELATIONSHIP (Where is the narrator located with respect to the story?)		
Homodiegetic (Narrator present as a character in the story.)	*Homo/Extradiegetic* Ex: The narrating lawyer of "Bartleby"	*Homo/Intradiegetic* Ex: Esther Summerson of *Bleak House*
Heterodiegetic (Narrator not present as a character in the story.)	*Hetero/Extra* Ex: The "omniscient" narrator of *Bleak House*	*Hetero/Intra* Ex: Scheherazade

The basic structure of this diagram is Genette's, but the parenthetical explanations and the examples are mine, excepting Scheherazade of *The Thousand and One Nights*. Like everything else in rhetorical narratology, I intend this diagram as a heuristic, not as a key to all narratives. Its purpose is to distinguish *some* textual features that seem to relate to how readers experience narratives, rather than to force narrating voices into definite boxes. Suppose I have a friend with a strong background in modernist fiction who wants to take the lawyer-narrator of "Bartleby" as intradiegetic. She argues that even though the narrating is in past tense, the most interesting story is that of the lawyer's attempt to understand what his experience with the pallid scrivener really means, an experience that continues to the present moment of narrating. I would disagree; I take the lawyer as extradiegetic and overtly public. The diagram would help us, as Phelan says, share our experiences and focus on "the textual grounds for those experiences," so that we "continue to learn from each other" (*Narrative* 147).

As Genette points out, stories with several narrators require a more complex description of the narrating situation. For instance, Chekhov's story "Gooseberries" (first published in 1898) opens thus:

The sky had been overcast since early morning; it was a still day, not hot, but tedious, as it usually is when the weather is gray and dull, when clouds have been hanging over the fields for a long time, and you wait for the rain that does not come. Ivan Ivanych, a veterinary, and Burkin, a high school teacher, were already tired with walking, and the plain seemed endless to them. . . . Now, when it was still and when nature seemed mild and pensive, Ivan Ivanych and Burkin were filled with love for this plain, and both of them thought what a beautiful land it was. (136)

The *level* of this opening narrating situation is extradiegetic: applying Lanser's test, the narrating voice is able to address someone who is "outside the fictional context," this "you" who is, however, familiar with the world evoked by the opening, who knows that rain is impending. The *relationship* is conventionally heterodiegetic: a narrator who looks into other characters' thoughts is usually not present in the story as a character. Then Ivan Ivanych tells a story about his brother's progress from minor bureaucrat to gentleman farmer and about his own reaction to the offensively superior attitude the newly made gentleman began to display. The *level* of this second narrating situation is intradiegetic, and the *relationship* is homodiegetic: Ivan is a character in the story, although he is not the protagonist. The story concludes as it began, with the same extra/heterodiegetic narrating situation.

Genette does not give his diagram a title, but on the same page he refers to "narrator's status." My title, "Narrating Situations," shifts the focus of analysis from the person to the act in order better to accommodate a fact Genette himself states repeatedly: novels and short stories, among other narratives, frequently contain several of these situations. The use of embedded narratives like Ivan Ivanych's in "Gooseberries" is probably the most common type of departure from single-situation narration. We also find novels with several voices occupying the same situation (such as Faulkner's *As I Lay Dying*) and occupying different situations (*Bleak House*). For a given narrating situation, the unmarked case would seem to be that the *level* is consistent, although the *relationship* can alter. I intend to be tentative about this designation for two reasons, both resulting from my strong-contextualist position. First, even more than with implied author, a given reader's reaction to narrating situation depends on that reader's experiences with and tolerance for other narrative types as well as the ability to internalize (cease to notice) features in the discourse. Second, the phenomenon of the marking of narrating situation probably also depends on the number and type of the situations within a narrative. The opening of *Huckleberry Finn* can be considered a marked case, in that Huck seems to be both inside and outside the world of which he tells: inside, because he explicitly places himself within that world, yet outside, because he explicitly states that he belongs to another book's world. (By contrast, most of Faulkner's characters live in and around Yoknapatawpha County, but each novel and story treats that county as a real world, not a book world.)

A more vividly marked case would be a character who referred to his role in another *novel* as such; this character would seem to be stepping outside of that world, would seem at least for the moment to be shifting to a different diegetic level. When Proust does this sort of thing, according to Genette, he is attacking "the best-established convention of novelistic narrating by cracking . . . the very logic of its discourse" (*Narrative Discourse* 252). Genette's comments hold for other writers as well: the "logic" challenged by Twain momentarily, and by writers like Robbe-Grillet or Italo Calvino exhaustively, is the contract into which readers believe they're entering; each narrating level and relationship will remain discrete. This contract or logic defines the unmarked case, which, in spite of the caveats I've noted, is probably fairly firm. My own experience is a case in point: although I've been reading and teaching the "new novel," "magical realism," "minimalist fiction," and other relatively experimental forms for two decades, I still am able to experience the breaking of the contract when I begin a new piece by Robbe-Grillet, or even when I reread *The Voyeur*. I adjust fairly quickly, of course, by activating the reading frame within which I contextualize these works, but this activation is a conscious process, hence an instance of *marking*.

Narrating voices do not just exist on levels and in relationships; they also perform acts. Speech-act analysis reveals that at any moment in the narration, several different kinds of acts can be performed simultaneously. Understanding this principle, and identifying the acts, is just as important for analyzing narrating situations as is the specifying of level and relationship. According to Chatman, the "narrator's central speech act" is *narrating*, but other speech acts are involved too; for instance, overt narrative commentary can include the acts of interpreting, judging, and generalizing, all of which are illocutions—actions that are performed or intended by the commentary (*Story and Discourse* 161, 165, 237–48). As Genette says, "Narrative always says less than it knows, but it often makes known more than it says" (*Narrative Discourse* 198).

For Genette's "often" I would substitute "always." Narrative does this, makes known so much more than it says, in the same way that any other speech act does, by means of invitations to the reader to infer, to construe, to interpret—that is, by means of *implicatures*. Logically, of course, what I *know* by means of an implicature is less certain than what I know by means of direct statement. But rhetorically, this is not the case. As I showed earlier, it's nearly if not wholly impossible for any utterance to be strictly constative, because humans are always *doing* with language as well as *saying*. And I think Genette would agree. Narrative's function, Genette says, is to tell a story; for this reason its "characteristic mood" is the indicative. However, this mood involves various "degrees of affirmation," a fact that accounts for the presence of "perspective" (on the events) and "distance" (from the events) in a narrative (*Narrative Discourse* 161–62); perspective and distance "make known" without stating. They also contribute to the ur-convention of heteroglossia by which readers not only accept but expect complexity in narrating voices.

To analyze how the acts of narrating voices relate to the narratee and implied reader and to the message the voice is conveying, Lanser offers a paradigm of *status, contact,* and *stance*. Her description of these terms is unclear, but the many criteria she describes are helpful, as long as they are applied more broadly, not limited to a single element. I've already mentioned that the narrator's skill influences how the reader assesses the narrator's "authority, competence, and credibility" (*Narrative Act* 86). The reader's sense of a psychological "contact" with the narrator is also directly influenced by "discourse register, tone, and other equivalents of visual/auditory contact" and by "direct comments that call attention to the speaker's relationship to the audience" (91–92). Especially important is the " 'culture text'—the particular set of expectations, values, emotional conventions, norms, and assumptions dominant or at least acceptable within a given community"; it will involve "both ideological and psychological attitudes toward a given 'content'" (93).

More helpful than Lanser's criteria, because more easily related to the rhetorical effects that can be stimulated by the various acts of narration, is Genette's list of five essential "functions" of the narrator: (1) the narrative function, (2) the directing function (directing attention to the narrative text), (3) the function of communication (concerning the narrator's orientation toward and contact with a narratee), (4) the testimonial function (the affective, moral, and intellectual relationship the narrator has with the story), and (5) the ideological function (commenting on the action in a way that seems to carry authorial authority) (*Narrative Discourse* 255–56). To illustrate, the previously quoted beginning of "Gooseberries" contains the passages "as it usually is when the weather is gray and dull" and "you wait for the rain that does not come." These passages perform the function of communicating with a narratee and also perform a blend of the testimonial and ideological functions: the statements about the weather are expressed, at least in this translation, as a bit of world knowledge, carrying a sense of ontological irony that transcends individual experience and becomes ideological. Compared to Chatman's list of the nonnarrative illocutionary acts and to Lanser's paradigm, Genette's list has the added strength of correlating with Searle's taxonomy of illocutionary acts as presented in *Expression and Meaning* (although not on a one-to-one basis), hence of having a more solid basis in speech-act theory. (I'm combining Searle's informal description of these acts with the formal terms I listed in chapter 1.)

> *Assertives*: "we tell people how things are"—Genette's *narrating*, which includes describing, as well as *ideological*
> *Directives*: "we try to get [people] to do things"—Genette's *directing*
> *Commissives*: "we commit ourselves to doing things"—*testimonial*
> *Expressives*: "we express our feelings and attitudes"—*testimonial*
> *Declarations*: "we bring about changes through our utterances"—*directing*, *communication*, and *testimonial* (*Narrative Discourse* 12–19, 29)

My only revision to Genette's list is to broaden it: hereafter I will treat the functions he names as able to be performed by the *narrating*, rather than attaching them strictly to a narrator. Such a broadening is consistent with Genette's description of the ideological function (a narrator gives the impression of serving as the mouthpiece of the implied author) and facilitates the description of discourse elements that may not attach to a narrator (e.g., chapter epigraphs).

These functions also interact with Rabinowitz's "rules of reading" and Phelan's dynamics of progression as I described them in chapter 2. The interactions can't be spelled out in any precise way; they exist as differences of emphasis and are always subject to the immediate narrating situation. Nevertheless, because they relate to elements that are demonstrably *in* texts, they make possible a certain amount of objective formal analysis and some predictions regarding likely rhetorical effects. Generally, the testimonial and directing functions are important for instabilities and for the rules of notice and signification: a narrating voice establishes its credibility by means of testimonial assertions, tells readers what's important, and calls attention to those attributes that are being developed into dimensions stretching throughout the text and contributing to mimesis or theme. The communicating function relates to tensions by specifying a position with which an actual reader may identify and that probably differs from that of the narrating or authorial audiences. The ideological function is especially important for tensions (in those cases when narrating and authorial audiences differ) and for rules of signification, configuration, and coherence. Conveying the impression that it carries the stamp of authorial approval, this function will stand out in any reader's attempt to establish a constructive intention.

In chapter 16 of *Bleak House*, the omniscient voice's rhetorical questions concerning the connection between Tom-all-Alone's and Chesney Wold perform at least two of these functions. Because a reader easily can identify this voice as authorial, the testimonial and ideological functions are prominent. Although the voice is not testifying to the truth of the story itself, he is demonstrating a sense of outrage about the way the fictional world is organized, and his illocutionary act asserts a powerful connection among Jo, the mysterious lady, the dead law-copyist, and Lady Dedlock. We do not doubt that Dickens held these views, so similar are they to everything else we have heard from this voice and from the extrafictional voice of the preface. The function of communication is less important here, mainly because although the passage's overdetermination implies a narratee for whom everything needs to be made explicit, this narratee at this point would react no differently to the assertions than would the narrating or the authorial audience. Least significant, in context, is the directing function; the voice's attention is directed less at the narrative itself than at the world in which the narrating takes place.

These functions contribute to a reader's experience of the novel's mimetic and thematic dimensions. One of the fascinating aspects of *Bleak House* is that the novel's world itself has attributes that operate very like a character's attributes in furthering plot and theme. For example, although the London of the novel is physically large and densely populated, experientially it is tiny; to the inhabitants of this realm, there's nothing unusual about how often their paths cross. A reader may have suspected this before, but when the voice asks, "What connexion can there be . . ." he is validating the suspicion, asserting that indeed the world is organized this way, so that readers should continue to seek out connections between not just these locations but the two narratives. Thematically, the fact of these connections translates into an obligation characters have to attend to and care for even those individuals who are most distant in the social or economic scale, individuals like Jo and Guster and Nemo, as well as like Sir Leicester and Lady Dedlock.

To summarize thus far: in analyzing the structure of narrative transmission, rhetorical narratology begins by identifying a work's narrating voices. I then ask Genette's two questions: what are the *levels* of the various *narrating acts*, and what are the *relationships* of the *narrating voices* to the stories they are narrating? Third, I ask what other acts—especially illocutionary acts—these voices perform and how those acts may move readers aesthetically, ethically, emotionally, intellectually, and so forth. This procedure has a practical basis in the rhetorical interaction between text and reader, but because of this basis the procedure can't spell out every step. If a complete model could be developed of the processing of a narrative by a reader, it would have to be so complicated that it would be useless as an analytical or pedagogical tool. Rhetorical narratology does not aspire to scientific precision but operates with a set of assumptions—ur-conventions—and questions that do a reasonable job of concentrating critical attention on a narrative's important features.

The two passages from "Gooseberries" discussed earlier help to illustrate this lack of precision: "as it usually is when the weather is gray and dull" and "you wait for the rain that does not come." These passages perform several functions. But how did I select the passages in the first place? The presence of "you" and "usually" is a clue that testimonial and ideological functions may be operating here, but in another context these words might carry no weight at all or would function differently. As Genette says, the "five functions are certainly not to be put into watertight compartments . . . It is rather a question of emphasis and relative weight" (*Narrative Discourse* 257), and, he might add, of the habits, beliefs, and experience of individual readers who assign the emphasis and weight.

Concentrating on the narrating act addresses the problem of the "humanistic ideology" that Culler says underlies readers' and critics' tendency to create the fiction of a personalized narrator. The problem is not the tendency itself but two almost universal assumptions in

Western cultures: that an identity either remains constant or changes over time in psychologically plausible ways, and that narrating is usually done by single individuals. This assumption has led critics to conceive of "the" narrator of *The Scarlet Letter*, for instance, as exhibiting a split personality (both Puritan and modern). By first identifying some of the novel's important narrating acts, however, and then asking what each of these acts implies about the voice that performs it, we are better positioned to understand the novel as having several narrating voices. When we read that Chillingworth's eyes sometimes burned "blue and ominous" (109), we should take this assertion as an illocutionary act of judgment, an act that we might have difficulty attributing to the same narrating voice who repeatedly stresses suffering and forgiveness. We are more likely to "hear" two voices rather than one, once we decide not to force on the utterance a single identity; we are more likely to be sensitive to the cultural work that Bakhtin rightly attributes to novels.

Voice Positions: Focalizer

The final position on the *voice* side of my diagram for the structure of narrative transmission is *focalizer;* this position is not present in Chatman's diagram but is closely tied to the narrator. Genette makes one of his most important contributions to our understanding of the narrating situation in distinguishing between *"who is the character whose point of view orients the narrative perspective?* and the very different question *who is the narrator?*—or, more simply, the question *who sees?* and the question *who speaks?"* (*Narrative Discourse* 186). Like many elements of narratology, this distinction seems ancient but actually dates only from the 1966 publication of Emile Benveniste's *Problèmes de linguistique générale* (Culler, *Structuralist Poetics* 197). The orienting perspective Genette terms the *focalizer,* although he correctly dwells less on the focalizer as an identity within the narrative than on the focalization itself. When he does speak of a person who fills the role, he says that the narrative is "focalized through" that character or perspective, a locution in keeping with my emphasis on the act of narrating. Focalization is best understood as "a *relation* between the narrator's report and the characters' thoughts, to which the narrator either has no access, or has (and is limited to) access, or has (but is not limited to) access" (Nelles 368). Focalization is so important in the study of narrative because it is "an absolutely crucial, entirely unavoidable, and fundamentally characteristic component of narrative as a discursive system" (O'Neill 106).

In spite of his fondness for tables, Genette does not provide one for the focalizing; his treatment of the topic in *Narrative Discourse Revisited* (72–78) suggests that he might even be opposed to a table or other scheme: "I see no reason for requiring narratology to become a catechism with a yes-or-no answer to check off for each question, when often the proper answer would be that it depends on the day, the context, and the way the wind is blowing" (74). However, different types of focalization do yield different rhetorical effects, hence I offer the following sketch, drawn from Genette's language (*Narrative Discourse* 189–90), based on the narrator's possible *relationships* to the story:

Fig. 5. Types of Focalization

TYPE	CHARACTERISTIC	EXAMPLE
Nonfocalized, or Narrative with Free Focalization	Narrator > Character (Narrator says more than character knows.)	"Omniscient" half of *Bleak House*
Narrative with Internal Focalization (Fixed or Variable)	Narrator = Character (Narrator says what character perceives and knows.)	Fixed: *What Maisie Knew* Variable: *Mrs. Dalloway*
Narrative with External Focalization	Narrator > Character (Narrator says less than character knows.)	"The Killers"

The first type, nonfocalized narration, roughly corresponds to what is usually termed omniscient narration. To *focalize* a narrative is to *limit* in some way the perspective available to a reader, but the nonfocalized narrative conveys the impression that there are no limits on what the narrator *is able* to say. Nelles reasonably suggests replacing the term *nonfocalized* with the term *free focalization* as carrying "the more appropriate connotations of an extended range of narratorial options, of a narrator not tied to or limited by the knowledge of characters" (369); "free" better conveys the rhetorical effect of such focalization. However, even though the term *omniscient* is inadequate and misleading, it is so thoroughly embedded in textbooks and critical discourse that I suggest keeping it, with two clarifications: if applied to a narrator, it only stands as shorthand for extra/heterodiegetic, and if applied to focalization, it means that there are no *overt* limitations on perspective. Of course there can be unmarked limitations. Is the heterodiegetic narrator of *Bleak House* in fact *able* to say anything about Esther or the other members of her immediate circle? If so, he never exercises that ability. It is as if he simply doesn't see or know anything about them, except at the beginning of chapter 7: "[w]hile Esther sleeps, and while Esther wakes, it is still wet weather down at the place in Lincolnshire" (81).

The omniscient narrator seems free to look anywhere, into any mind or other dark corner. Internal focalization gives a reader the impression of seeing and hearing what a character sees and hears; external focalization, the impression of being excluded from some of this internal knowledge. As with much else in rhetorical narratology, drawing absolute lines is not possible, but Genette offers a test, borrowed from Barthes, for distinguishing between externally and internally focalized narration. If the narrative (or the section of narrative under consideration) can be translated into first person with no changes other than in the pronouns and verb forms, then the governing mode is internal. Genette quotes Barthes's example: "James Bond saw a man in his fifties" can be translated into "I saw a man in his fifties" and thus would be termed *internal*; "the tinkling of the ice cubes against the glass *seemed* to awaken in Bond a sudden inspiration" cannot be translated in this way, hence we would term this *external focalization* (*Narrative Discourse* 193–94). Internal focalization exists in three different types, according to Genette: fixed (e.g., *What Maisie Knew*), variable (e.g., *Madame Bovary*), and multiple (e.g., in epistolary novels). The distinction between variable and multiple, however, seems unnecessary; rhetorically, they have the same effect. Hence I drop multiple and speak only of two types, fixed and variable. Last but not least, if the narrating act is either homodiegetic or intradiegetic (that is, if the narrator is telling his or her own story or is otherwise located within the world of the story), then I term this an example of internal focalization, in which narrator and focalizer are identical.

An "enriched typology of focalization" is proposed by David Herman, emphasizing not the internal/external distinction but various "ways of encoding epistemic modalities into narrative discourse"; such modes as the counterfactual and the hypothetical "are crucially connected with what we call the meaning of narratives" (244). Herman bases his typology on "intensional" properties of expressions and on the context-dependent nature of expressions: "we cannot expect attitudes of knowing, believing, hoping . . . to remain constant across changes of context . . . or in the face of more or less embedded contexts" (235). Modes of focalization can be taken as encodings of "propositional attitudes," which in a narrative context (or any other, for that matter) will influence "the meaning of the discourse" (235). Herman appropriately offers this typology not as a finished system but as a step toward articulating "narrative semantics with what we know about the semantic component of grammars generally" (246). However, like other studies that draw on possible-world semantics, Herman's is pretty far removed from the concerns of rhetorical narratology. My sense is that not all of the textual features on which Herman bases his analysis make a difference to readers; although the exploration is definitely worth carrying out, it lies beyond my scope here.

The free-focalized narrative was more prominent in the earlier history of the modern novel, while external focalization, the least common form, has been practiced primarily in the twentieth century. Internal focalization, perhaps because of its flexibility, is the type most common in fictional narratives of the past several centuries in the Western tradition. Genette points out that "internal focalization is rarely applied in a totally rigorous way. Indeed, the very principle of this narrative mode implies in all strictness that the focal character never be described or even referred to from the outside, and that his thoughts or perceptions therefore never be analyzed objectively by the narrator" (*Narrative Discourse* 192). Some of the most interesting effects in modern fiction result from the impurity of internal focalization, effects which Mieke Bal puts under the heading of "ambiguous focalization" (*Narratology* 113). I opened chapter 1 with such an example, from James's *The Portrait of a Lady*, in which the narrating voice expresses on one page an inability to look into Isabel's mind and then a page later states not only her thoughts but also the images that her experience stimulated in her mind.

Genette terms such a moment of ambiguity an *alteration*, which, "especially if it is isolated within a coherent context, can also be analyzed as a momentary infraction of the code governing that context without thereby calling into question the existence of the code" (*Narrative Discourse* 195). He distinguishes between two types of alterations: "giving less information than is necessary in principle" and "giving more than is authorized in principle in the code of focalization governing the whole" (195). Genette also offers this caution: "[w]e should not confuse the *information* given by a focalized narrative with the *interpretation* the reader is called on to give of it (or that he gives without being invited to)" (197). Genette is saying that we should not confuse locutions with illocutionary acts; "information" is the locution, and the reader's sense of being "called on" to interpret the information a certain way, such as when encountering an alteration, results from something in the discourse—an illocutionary act. In her fixed, internally focalized narrative, Esther frequently withholds information, for instance, after Mr. Woodcourt has been to dinner and Ada has laughingly invited her to "have a little talk about Richard": "[b]ut, I don't think it matters what my darling [Ada] said. She was always merry" (*Bleak House* 202). Esther's locutionary act is to refuse to report the conversation. Her act also *means* that at this point she doesn't want to say anything more about Woodcourt. For the authorial audience, her reticence, especially because it comes at the end of a chapter, constitutes an illocutionary act, at the discourse level, on the author's part—an act of calling attention to Esther's limitation as a narrator.

Genette does not provide any details on the focalization codes, but specifying the unmarked cases provides a start toward determining what constitutes more or less than the authorized amount of information. The crucial criterion, although not a hard and fast one, is contained in Genette's formulas relating what the narrator says to what characters know and is similar to the way we distinguish marked cases of narrative levels. For any of the three types of focalization, the unmarked case is that in which the narrator either preserves the same level of knowledge about a character or *plausibly* modulates that level in one direction or another. That is, a narrator might come to know more or less about the workings of a character's mind and might allow the narrative to reflect that gradual increase or diminution; readers will not notice as long as the level is preserved or modulated in this way. We may notice, however, if the level of knowledge about a focalizing character shifts as dramatically as it does near the end of *The Portrait of a Lady*. The rhetorical effect of such a marking is not to change the type of focalization but *perhaps* to push the narrator more into the story, more into an intradiegetic position, hence to change how a reader experiences the narrator's mediation. *Perhaps*, because this example also illustrates the inherent subjectivity of such effects: for some readers the narrator's expressed uncertainty—his sudden drawing back from the kind of information he has been providing throughout—works as an "alteration" without breaking the code established within the novel. Other readers may be led to rethink the mimetic validity of this scene and many others in which the narrator has asserted a knowledge of Isabel's mental processes. Lanser notes that focalizing characters carry strong mimetic authority, "the authority of lived (fictional) experience" (*Narrative Act* 142). Readers who experience not an alteration but a violation of the focalization code won't doubt that Isabel had some kind of powerful experience with Caspar Goodwood but will be unsure about its details and meaning, because the narrator's diegetic authority has lapsed.

Because the defining difference between altering and violating focalization is the perlocutionary effect on actual readers, I find it necessary to qualify Genette's claims that readers adopt, revise, and switch focalization codes. The term *code* conveys a much greater sense of precision than any theorist has achieved in describing a code. As I explained in chapter 2, humans use codes *only* to strengthen what Sperber and Wilson term "ostensive-inferential communication" (*Relevance* 63). Communication is "a matter of enlarging mutual cognitive environments, not of duplicating thoughts" (193); if the codes really did structure literary speech acts, there would be no need to discriminate between locutionary and illocutionary acts or between these acts and perlocutionary effects. Barthes's test for internal focalization by itself does not constitute a code, any more than does an omniscient narrator's ability to look into various characters' minds. Thus, when I refer to focalization codes, I mean neither more nor less than loose collections of textual features that help readers establish a perspective on the narrative. My emphasis on marking and on the rhetorical effects of focalization accords with a suggestion recently advanced by Manfred Jahn that a theory of focalization should treat "narrating and focalizing as mutually dependent activities" and should also recognize the reader's role (263). Genette's theory has several problems, as Jahn demonstrates; I don't agree with Jahn that "imaginary perception" offers a solution but do second his resurrection of James's house-of-fiction metaphor, because that metaphor keeps rhetorical effect "in the picture," as it were.

As with focalization, so with all of the voice positions I've been discussing: none of them can be rigidly defined or prescribed. Criticizing Chatman's assertion (in *Coming to Terms*) that the distinction between "story space" and "discourse space" is absolute, Harry Shaw argues that narrators enter story space because one of the functions of novels is to help us "make sense of the world," because narrators can strike readers as lifelike in the same way characters do, and because the roles assigned to narrators are shaped by cultural forces and reflect particular historical moments (96–97). Shaw suggests that *"the force of general narratological concepts undergoes modification when they are placed in subordination to broader cultural presuppositions"* (113). Such modifications are happening whenever one generation's marked case becomes another's unnoticed norm: for instance, if the postmodern narrative ever succeeds in breaking down the solid bond between extrafictional voice and omniscient narrating voice. But I also want to make explicit here a point I've been implying all along: the ur-conventions of narrative, and the CP without which these conventions could not exist, count as "broader cultural presuppositions." Voices and audiences will certainly change in how they interact with each other, but they will not cease to exist, any more than narrativity and fictionality will become absolute rather than relational categories.

Reader/Audience Positions

Genette's distinction between the narrating *perspective* and the narrating *distance* has primarily to do with the relationship between the narrator and the story. However, as Lanser makes clear, equally important in the literary speech-act situation, and equally important for rhetorical narratology, is the relationship between the narrator and the audience, a relationship that also involves both perspective and distance. The pertinent positions in Chatman's diagram are the *narratee* and the *implied reader*, although it is more accurate to describe this realm of the narrative speech act using three terms rather than two: *narratee* and Rabinowitz's *narrative audience* and *authorial audience*. As explained in chapter 2, the narrative audience is the imaginary audience for which the narrator is writing or to which the narrator is speaking. As also explained, I use the term *narrating audience* rather than *narrative audience* in order to emphasize the act of narration.

The seminal work on the narratee is Gerald Prince's "Introduction to the Study of the Narratee," published in 1973 and reprinted in 1980 in the influential collection *Reader-Response Criticism: From Formalism to Post-Structuralism.* (A more condensed version is contained in Prince's *Narratology* [16–26].) Prince says that every narrative "presupposes not only (at least) one narrator but also (at least) one narratee" ("Introduction" 7); the narratee is the addressee of the narrator. However, the better term for the *inevitably* presupposed audience is *narrating audience,* a qualification that is consistent with Prince's other definitions. He distinguishes among the narratee, the "virtual reader" (that reader whom the author "bestows with certain qualities, faculties, and inclinations according to his opinion of men in general"), and the "ideal reader" ("the one who would understand perfectly and would approve entirely the least of [the author's] words") (9). By this distinction, the virtual reader corresponds to the narrating audience, and the ideal reader corresponds to the authorial audience.

I qualify Prince's system in one other way by insisting that the narratee, like the narrator, must have a relatively visible textual presence. Hence the term should be limited to those textual signals that do not require of the reader a great deal of constructive inference in order to say something specific about a narratee. Three of the many signals Prince lists meet this criterion. There are two types of direct addresses to a narratee: references to "the reader" and similar phrases, and passages using the second-person pronoun in a way that clearly intends a specific individual or group. The third signal is *overjustifications* that function on the level of metadiscourse, such as when the narrator "confesses himself incapable of describing a certain feeling" or "asks to be excused for a poorly phrased sentence" ("Introduction" 15). If none of these three signals is present, the text is unmarked with respect to narratee: readers do not notice if no narratee is present. Prince provides a much more substantial list of characteristics that define what he terms the "zero-degree" narratee (meaning the unmarked case). This narratee knows the language in which the story is told, is familiar with the conventions governing the telling of stories, has a perfect memory for the story, lacks any personality or other identifying characteristics, has no previous knowledge about the story or the world in which the story takes place, is not able to interpret or judge the story's events and characters, has no experience with any other texts, has no "common sense" or world knowledge, and "does not organize the narrative as a function of the major codes of reading studied by Roland Barthes in *S/Z*" (10–11). But if these characteristics all define the unmarked case, then they will be marked when a narrating voice uses one of the three textual signals I've noted. Readers will only know that a narratee has a personality trait, has had experience with other texts, and so forth if those characteristics are mentioned within a direct address or overjustification. In the context of such signals, Prince is correct that "deviations from the characteristics of the zero-degree narratee" provide the material from which "the portrait of a specific narratee is gradually constituted" (12). I would not go as far as Chatman, who argues that the concept of zero-degree narratee serves no theoretical or practical purpose. This narratee is by definition deficient in the enabling medium of discourse, aware not of connotations but only of denotations, as Chatman explains (*Story and Discourse* 253–54 n.4). "[W]hat purpose," Chatman asks, "is served in imagining a reader who comes to a narrative without these competencies?" As a strong contextualist, I answer that the concept serves exactly the purpose of reminding us that every narrative does presuppose certain competencies that influence the degree to which actual readers take texts as marked.

Of these appropriate narratee-invoking signals, the use of *you*, as distinct from the non-narratee-invoking *you*, is somewhat fuzzy, but a simple example will help. The opening of "Gooseberries" addresses "you," but there is nothing about this "you" to distinguish it from a general "one," hence I would say that as a signal, it's directed at a more general *narrating audience*. It works like the inclusive "we," which Chatman aptly characterizes as "'[n]ot only we two, but every other like-minded (that is, "reasonable") person in the world'" (*Story and Discourse* 256–57). Prince claims that "all signals of the narration" can be interpreted as "a function of the narratee" ("Introduction" 12). But this claim ignores the difference in rhetorical effect between a specific narratee whom an actual reader can identify with or not and the *narrating audience* whose values and perspective an actual reader would likely accept unthinkingly. In the "Gooseberries" example, "you" characterizes a narrating audience that most readers will not notice, whereas had Chekhov written "those readers who have traveled through this country will know the kind of weather I mean," actual readers would more likely respond with something that, if verbalized, might be "I've not been there, but I can imagine."

Narratee thus represents a tool the writer uses to position actual readers with respect to a particular experience, value, or response, more than with respect to the entire world invoked by a text. In contrast to "Gooseberries," the opening of *Huckleberry Finn* uses the same word, "you," but it functions as a signal of a *narratee* because the experience attributed to "you" is so precise and so clearly fictive: having read *The Adventures of Tom Sawyer* not as a fiction but as biography or history, or at least existing in a textual world in which such reading is possible. This narratee then vanishes, a fairly common occurrence. Likewise, a narrative may have several narratees. An example is *Moby-Dick*, whose early narratees are addressed as "landsmen" and are implied to be generally obtuse; actual readers who are reading authorially can recognize that they should align themselves *against* these narratees and *with* the uncharacterized narrating audience, which by definition is sympathetic to Ishmael's attempt to understand his voyage on the *Pequod*. Later the novel inscribes narratees who have been metaphorically sailing with Ishmael as he has explored the meaning of his participation in Ahab's quest; these narratees constitute authorial invitations to actual readers to feel that they belong in *this* select company.

The other signals Prince lists as belonging to the function of narratee more accurately have to do with the position of narrating audience. These include impersonal expressions and indefinite pronouns ("one," "we"), some questions (actual or rhetorical, e.g., "What had he been? But perhaps he had been employed at the Ministry" [Prince's example, from *Pere Goriot*]), some negations ("No, it was not to his mistress that Vincent Molinier went" [Prince quoting from *The Counterfeiters*]), comparisons drawing on and references to other texts or to world knowledge ("Everyone knows . . .") ("Introduction" 13–15). The narrating audience is more invoked than addressed, invoked by the attribution of knowledge or values. The unmarked case of this audience occurs when the actual audience accepts these attributes without thinking anything about them—a relativistic description, to be sure, but the only one that is consistent with a rhetorical approach. Not every narrative has a narratee, but every narrative by definition has a narrating audience, one who will take the act of narration and the world within which it occurs at face value. *In the Labyrinth*, as I'll explain shortly, can be made sense of if read as a not-very-competent narrator's attempt to tell a story. This novel's narrating audience never balks at the self-contradictions and reversals—that is to say, nothing is inscribed in the text that could be taken as responding to such a balk.

These refinements of Prince's scheme are consistent with the rhetorical functions he attributes to the narratee. "In all narrations," Prince writes, "a dialogue is established between the narrator(s), the narratee(s), and the character(s). This dialogue develops . . . as a function of the distance separating them from each other" ("Introduction" 19). And further, "[t]he most obvious role of the narratee . . . is that of relay between the narrator and the reader(s), or rather between the author and the reader(s). Should certain values have to be defended or certain ambiguities clarified, this can easily be done by means of asides addressed to the narratee. Should the importance of a series of events be emphasized, should one reassure or make uneasy . . . this can always be done by addressing signals to the narratee" (21). Such signals constitute "the most economical and the most effective sort of mediation" between author and reader (21). Like any other character in a novel, the narratee can serve other functions too: thematic, mimetic (to help characterize the narrator or to make the narrating seem more natural), and synthetic (to develop the narrative's structure) (22–23).

These additional points from Prince's "Introduction" need to be qualified in two particulars. First, the narratee can only be taken as a mediator between actual author and actual reader in the special case of a narrator barely removed from both the extrafictional voice and the implied author. Otherwise the narratee embodies a set of values and attitudes that an actual reader may be led, by *other* aspects of the structure of narrative transmission, to identify with, reject, or partially accept. Second, the narrating audience, by definition never the recipient of direct addresses from the narrator, is better thought of as the context within which occurs the dialogue Prince mentions, rather than a participant in the story.

A text in which the narrating audience is subtly but definitely marked is Henry James's *The Bostonians*. The narrator is in an extradiegetic and heterodiegetic relationship to the story, a relationship that implies a narrating audience who is sympathetic to the narrator's low opinion of Verena, the young woman around whom the plot centers. In the narrator's eyes, Verena has no worth in her own right as a character. However, James has crafted this novel to allow the possibility that Verena has much more willpower and a much more independent identity than the narrator recognizes. Readers who are sensi-

tive to this possibility can feel themselves standing in an ironic relationship to the narrator, witnessing his failings and believing that
James intended precisely this effect. Even though this novel's structure of narrative transmission makes it quite easy to draw a direct line
from extrafictional voice to implied author to narrator, there are features in both the plot instabilities and the discourse tensions that constitute a recommendation from the implied author to actual readers
that they decline the narrator's invitation to join him in disparaging
the young woman. (For an extended discussion of the narrative discourse in this novel, see Kearns, "Narrative Discourse and the Imperative of Sympathy in *The Bostonians*.")

Readers who accept this invitation are aligning themselves with the
authorial audience, which is the final position in my version of Chatman's diagram. Authorial audience is the counterpart of implied author and is identical to implied reader in Chatman's diagram. This is
the audience that recognizes the possibility of a rhetorical, extradiegetic intention behind every locution in the story, that sees elements
like setting and characterization as reflecting an authorial purpose in
addition to seeing them the way the narrating audience sees them, as
descriptions of how the (story) world is. Authorial audience may be
identical to or different from the narrating audience; *The Bostonians*
violates the convention that generally the two audiences will be identical if the primary narrating voice is extra/heterodiegetic. Like implied author, the authorial audience is neither named in nor invoked
by the text but is constructed by the actual reader in response to questions like "How did the author want us to react to this event?" or
"How does the author enable me to experience dramatic irony in this
scene?" An authorial audience exists for every narrative, because every element in a narrative can be taken as an illocutionary act on the
part of an implied author. Practically speaking, few readers will construct this voice position until they have finished the book ("Now,
what did Dickens want me to think about all this?"), unless it is
marked in a way that seems to break it free of the text's narrating.

For instance, a narrator performing the ideological function so that
an actual reader feels addressed with authorial authority places the
reader in a position to draw back from the narrative's events and reflect
on its thematic dimension. Dickens employs this technique when he
has his omniscient voice comment on Jo's death: "[d]ead, your Majesty. Dead, my lords and gentlemen. . . . Dead, men and women, born
with Heavenly compassion in your hearts. And dying thus around us
every day" (*Bleak House* 649). This voice first characterizes a set of
narratees (your Majesty, lords, etc.) against which we actual readers
can define ourselves. He then generalizes in a movement that invites

all of us to include ourselves—we would all like to think of ourselves as compassionate. But if we do, we must accept some responsibility for the deaths of unfortunates like Jo. The *author* is telling *us* this; the assertions are no longer confined within the realm of the narrative but are intended to reach across the diegetic gap to touch actual readers directly.

This example from *Bleak House* illustrates one common marking device for inviting a reader self-consciously to adopt the role of authorial audience during the reading rather than afterward: a shift in narrating level that Genette terms *narrative metalepsis.* He explains: "[t]he transition from one level to another can in principle be achieved only by the narrating, the act that consists precisely of introducing into one situation, by means of a discourse, the knowledge of another situation. Any other form of transit is, if not always impossible, at any rate always transgressive" (*Narrative Discourse* 234). When a character in a Robbe-Grillet novel steps out of a painting or when Tristram Shandy asks the reader's help in filling up a blank page, the narrating is transgressing, inviting the reader to notice that a boundary has been crossed. Genette writes that such "games, by the intensity of their effects, demonstrate the importance of the boundary they tax their ingenuity to overstep, in defiance of verisimilitude—a boundary *that is precisely the narrating (or the performance) itself*: a shifting but sacred frontier between two worlds, the world in which one tells, the world of which one tells" (236).

Gibson has taken Genette to task for holding "that there be no seepage or osmosis across the threshold" between levels (215). On the one hand, this critique is accurate; the "frontier" is "sacred" in Genette's theory. On the other hand, the critique is beside the point, because here, as he so frequently does, Genette implies exactly the rhetorical awareness that Gibson is suggesting with his postmodern theory of narrative. The frontier is sacred only in the sense that transgressions are marked. Genette's description shows that narrative metalepses function as illocutionary acts: they intend to *demonstrate* the presence of a boundary. Their perlocutionary effect is to unsettle actual readers, perhaps with the purpose of making us feel that the fictional realm is not quite as separate from our own as we thought. Narrative metalepses work as displays—they call attention to themselves. As displays, and because they operate within the realm of literary discourse, they are hyperprotected. This means that they can have the perlocutionary effect of unsettling readers without necessarily causing these readers to opt out of the speech situation, as might happen with texts that lacked the element of display (news reports, for instance). Narrative metalepses carry a tag, as it were, addressed to the authorial audience and instructing, "Hyperprotect this discourse element, which you are to take as implicating X." A metalepsis is created if an extradiegetic narrator enters the story and speaks to a character. The narrator's words are the locution; they perform the illocutionary act of drawing the authorial audience's attention to the boundary between "the world in which one tells" and "the world of which one tells." The agent of this act, of course, is the implied author.

Voices and Audiences in *In the Labyrinth*

As I have pointed out several times, rhetorical narratology is not a science and cannot predict the perlocutionary effects of textual elements. It does provide the student of narrative with a general procedure: determine which of the positions in my expanded version of Chatman's diagram are important in a particular text, explain how they interact, and place the interactions in the context of typical unmarked cases in order to suggest their perlocutionary effects. Seldom are all of the diagrammed positions relevant to the actual experience. I've been drawing on Robbe-Grillet's *In the Labyrinth* for examples; I'll now formalize the analysis somewhat in order to illustrate in a more methodical manner the steps by which rhetorical narratology assesses this particular narrative's structure of narrative transmission.

The first task is to establish the relationship among extrafictional voice, implied author, and narrating voices in order to determine where and how readers may experience (or construct) authorial authority. This so-called new novel begins with what looks like a conventional preface, signed by "A. R.-G.":

This narrative is not a true account, but fiction. It describes a reality not necessarily the same as the one the reader has experienced: for example, in the French army, infantrymen do not wear their serial numbers on their coat collars. Similarly, the recent history of Western Europe has not recorded an important battle at Reichenfels or in the vicinity. Yet the reality in question is a strictly material one; that is, it is subject to no allegorical interpretation. The reader is therefore requested to see in it only the objects, actions, words, and events which are described, without attempting to give them either more or less meaning than in his own life, or his own death. (140)

Most readers are inclined to take this preface as having authorial sanction, although the concluding injunction is puzzling and although we have no guarantee that "A. R.-G." refers to the author himself. Nevertheless, we may feel justified in granting diegetic authority to the extrafictional voice, in assuming that whatever "material reality" we encounter will be just that—tangible and credible. But then we begin the narrative itself:

I am alone here now, under cover. Outside it is raining. Outside you walk with your head down . . . outside it is cold, the wind blows between the bare black branches . . . Outside the sun is shining, there is no tree, no bush to cast a shadow, and you walk under the sun shielding your eyes with one hand. (141)

The presence of a narrating "I" marks the narrating act as intradiegetic in level (the act seems to be taking place within the world of the story) and possibly homodiegetic in relationship (the narrator may be present as a character). These characteristics will lead readers to separate the narrating voice from the implied author. The latter is always a construct, but cases like this require more inferential work on the reader's part because there exists a discrete, individually dramatized narrator whose identity and relationship to the story are at issue. However, two of the characteristics of the extrafictional voice will probably be attached to the narrator: the male gender and the explicit self-identification as a writer addressing an audience.

Second, the relationships among the audience positions in the structure of narrative transmission need to be determined. In this opening the "you" seems specific enough to qualify as invoking a narratee, although it could also be taken as "one" and hence as invoking a narrating audience. In fact, the French original uses *on* (one) rather than *you* ("[d]ehors il pleut, dehors on marche sous la pluie en courbant la tête" [9]), but this does not change the rhetorical functioning of the construction in the English translation. The structure of the sentences and the lack of any transitional or relational phrase between them can suggest that the narrator and his addressee share a world or a narrating situation or both, which violates our common-sense experience that the weather can't be simultaneously rainy and sunny or does not go from rainy to sunny with no transition whatsoever. (As I noted in chapter 2, the reader does not have to mentally construct a weird world and believe that it exists in order to imagine what the narrating audience seems to be asked by the narrating voice to accept.) The extrafictional voice characteristic of "writer," conjoined with the explicit address to a "you," signals the authorial audience to pay attention to the *acts* by which this narrative is being created, rather than just to the narrative itself; an actual reader may not consciously put the effect thus, but I've had plenty of students who notice that something strange is happening with the narrating itself. A different effect would result if the opening were cast in first person ("[o]utside I walk with my head down," and so forth). No narrating audience or narratee would be explicitly present, nor would there be any clash with readers' "culture text"; the passage would no longer carry the illocutionary message "Pay attention to the narrating."

The author and audience positions enable a reader to experience this effect of attending closely to the discourse elements in order successfully to begin the novel. The third task in this particular analysis—and I stress that other narratives might require a different order of approach—is to determine how many narrative levels are present and how they relate to each other. (The precise number of levels is not so important, the crucial distinction being "one, two, or many.") This determination is crucial because of the many metalepses, such as this one:

In front of the chest, the felt slippers have cleared a large gleaming area in the dust, and another one in front of the table at the place that must be occupied by a desk chair or armchair, a stool or some kind of seat. A narrow path of gleaming floor has been made from one to the other; a second path goes from the table to the bed. Parallel to the house fronts, a little closer to the walls than to the gutter, a yellowish-gray straight path also indicates the snow-covered sidewalk. Produced by the footsteps of people now gone, the path passes between the lighted street light and the door of the last apartment house. (146)

With only the slightest signal (a new sentence, and "also" in a position that does not signal transition), the narrative has moved from what we can designate as Level One of the narrating (the "I" and the dust-filled room) to Level Two (the details of the street, where the soldier is to be found). Movements between these two levels occur throughout the book, and there is no possibility of wholly separating the two levels from each other. One of the most striking instances of this erratic and confusing movement is this:

He notices at this moment that the door is ajar: door, hallway, door, vestibule, door, then finally a lighted room, and a table with an empty glass with a circle of dark-red liquid still at the bottom, and a lame man leaning on his crutch, bending forward in a precarious balance. No. Door ajar. Hallway. Staircase. Woman running from floor to floor up the spiral staircase, her gray apron billowing about her. Door. And finally a lighted room: bed, chest, fireplace, table with a lamp on its left corner, and the lampshade casting a white circle on the ceiling. No. Above the chest is a print framed in black wood . . . No. No. No. The door is not ajar. (194)

On which level does the "No" take place as a verbal act? Do the abbreviated sentences function mimetically, directing attention to the world of the soldier, or do they function to direct attention to the narrating act itself? Probably both, but tending more toward the latter, because the scene ends up revised: "[t]he door is not ajar." The point here is not to assign each act a precise level but to recognize that the most rhetorically powerful act is the jumping between two distinct levels. An actual reader who does not recognize this act for what it is, who fails to see that something other than straight narration and description is happening here, will probably not be able to make sense either of this passage or of the novel. Furthermore, the reader must be able to read this act authorially, accepting it as an implicature crafted by Robbe-Grillet to achieve some purpose. At least this is my experience in teaching the novel to advanced undergraduates and first-year graduate students. There are always a few students who don't "get it," who feel that the author's sole purpose is to confuse them rather than meaningfully to communicate. Typically, these students also have the greatest difficulty reflecting critically on their own reading practices.

A more thorough analysis of this novel would carry out other tasks, especially identifying the functions other than narrating that the narrating voice performs (such as directing, communicating, ideological) and determining the types of focalization. But I want to jump to the final task, the goal of all this scrutiny: determining the *point* of this structure of narrative transmission and the overt narrative it structures (the soldier's attempt to deliver his package). The soldier "exists" just as materially within the painting, *The Defeat of Reichenfels*, as he does on the streets of the city he wanders, and the narrator, too, has a tangible existence. The "material" reality to which A. R.-G. refers (and perhaps the actual author as well) is one of acts as much as—perhaps more than—things. The fact of this reality also has thematic significance, developed by the inescapable tension actual readers will feel each time they must shift levels in order to follow the narrating audience, who apparently can shift with no difficulty at all. It's as if the narrating audience doesn't know that, conventionally, the boundaries of levels are impermeable, or "sacred."

Robbe-Grillet may be implicating that actual readers don't "know" that either, because we assume it unthinkingly. There are two labyrinths here. One is the city streets, hallways, and rooms through which the soldier wanders, repeatedly returning to the same places (at least he thinks they're the same) and trying new directions. The other consists of the narrator's mental meanderings as he tries to either follow or create (it's not clear which) the story about the soldier. He too encounters dead ends ("No. No. No.") and returns frequently to a few guideposts (the painting, the cracked marble on top of the chest, the box). This textual meandering also has a material reality, demonstrating that the conventional association of mimesis with "the world *of* which one tells" and diegesis with "the world *in* which one tells" is just that—a convention, an unmarked case. One plausible point, then, is the *experiencing* of both labyrinths, the direct *encountering* of conventionality, and the *recognizing* of the power of even an overtly made-up character like the soldier to elicit compassion from actual readers. I use these awkward gerundive forms intentionally to stress that the reading experiences take place through time and involve real humans with real emotions: the point of every tellable narrative is what it does to such readers.

As strange as this novel is, it does conform to the four ur-conventions. Both textual worlds can be naturalized with no great stretch of the imagination. The narrative of the soldier is mainly focalized through the soldier; because he's feverish, the occasional discontinuities and repetitions in his experience make sense mimetically. The Level One world is also psychologically plausible as a real-time record of someone's attempt to construct a narrative, internally focalized through a narrator who is trying to avoid the homodiegetic relationship to his story (hence the use of first person only at the beginning and ending, instead of locutions like "and now I describe the soldier climbing the stairs"). The metalepses make sense when read authorially, when fit into a constructive intention that includes the rhetorical purpose of foregrounding conventions of reading. Progression is created both by instabilities (within the soldier and between him and the boy, the woman, and the lame man) and tensions (occasioned by metalepses). The novel evokes heteroglossia by blocking the fulfillment of this expectation and thus calling attention to it: there is only one narrating voice for two levels, although a conventional reading might predict two different voices and would certainly predict a different voice for the doctor near the end when he enters as an intra/homodiegetic narrating presence.

There is no way to predict of any narrative that metalepsis will affect actual readers in the way I've been describing, that naturalization can be carried out as I've done for *In the Labyrinth*, or precisely how any aspect of the discourse will contribute to plot or theme. All the student of narrative can do is study the narrating acts and positions, explore their possible illocutionary aspects, place everything in the context of the ur-conventions of reading, and suggest that actual readers may react in certain ways because they will be seeking to maximize cognitive effect while keeping processing effort to a minimum. Rhetorical narratology concentrates on how the narrating happens and on which of these acts is prominent in the literary speech-act situation. The narrating act and these other illocutionary acts, rather than the story itself, most directly influence how a reader will relate to the story as well as to the whole text and the whole situation.

4

Applications of Rhetorical Narratology
to Aspects of Narrative

In the second and third chapters I provided a general approach to the analysis of narratives, concentrating on the structure of narrative transmission as defined primarily by audience positions (authorial and narrating audiences and narratees) and the voices that can be discerned or inferred (extrafictional voice, implied author, narrator, and focalizer). I have shown how relationships among these positions can be understood as offering to actual readers opportunities for identification, for ironic distance, and, in the case of a narrative that fails with a reader, for rejection. I have shown how a narrative's locutions must be understood within a context of illocutions that are constituted in the interaction between text and reader, are governed by four ur-conventions and the principle of hyperprotection, implicate messages from author to reader, and thus have a great deal to do with how a reader reacts to the narrative's ideology and "interprets" its theme. In short, I have shown how illocutionary acts can result in perlocutionary effects, as long as the situational context is one that allows the principles of relevance to operate.

My purpose in the present chapter is to refine this approach by applying it to four aspects of narrative that have especially interested narratologists over the past several decades: the relationship of plot and theme to narrative discourse, the gendering of narrating voices, the temporal structure of narratives, and the representation of both inner and voiced speech. (My exclusion of the topic of "character" may seem odd, but James Phelan, in *Reading People, Reading Plots*, has done a masterful job of placing character within a rhetorical context.) Having already touched on the first two aspects, I will begin with them.

Plot, Theme, and Narrating

Plot and theme are two of the elements of narrative most frequently discussed in introduction-to-literature textbooks, characterization being the third. They are presented as if they are intuitively obvious, as if all readers automatically recognize the conflicts that generate a plot's development and the "big ideas" about life, death, love, and so on that constitute themes. Indeed, people do seem to possess a certain competence with respect to narratives. As explained in chapter 1, plot is related to a reader's sense of causal relationships among events, to the expectation of *telos*, or designedness, hence to the expectation that the sequence of events will reflect a constructive intention. In a fictional narrative, plot (as *telos*) is expected from the beginning, but this expectation may only be fulfilled retrospectively, at the end of the narrative. Peter Brooks describes what it means to "read for the plot":

> Perhaps we would do best to speak of the *anticipation of retrospection* as our chief tool in making sense of narrative, the master trope of its strange logic. We have no doubt forgone eternal narrative ends, and even traditional nineteenth-century ends are subject to self-conscious endgames, yet still we read in a spirit of confidence, and also a state of dependence, that what remains to be read will restructure the provisional meanings of the already read. (23)

Brooks's "we" refers to contemporary readers, his point being that even though some of the roles served by narrative in earlier eras have fallen away, and even though many (late-twentieth-century, Western, highly educated) people no longer believe that "the story of humankind" has a planned or structured ending, readers still expect to experience, retrospectively, a cohesion and purpose in narrative that our individual lives lack. Brooks's phrase "strange logic" aptly captures this aspect of the experience of narrative: although we apply to narrative the same world knowledge and cultural codes that we use to navigate our daily lives, we always do so with the conscious expectation that endings will complete or resolve beginnings. Ralph Rader notes that readers feel a novel to be like our own "life world" yet also know that it is constructed so as to convey a "coherence and consummation which each of us seeks in our life worlds but never achieves" ("Emergence" 76–77). Elsewhere Rader uses the phrase "meaning-oriented direction finder" to describe this sense readers have of being able to find their way through a narrative because they know to look for a path that has already been marked, especially by the causal relationships we term *plot* ("Concept" 89).

But can this "strange logic," or this "direction finder," be rigorously described? Shlomith Rimmon-Kenan suggests that "[t]he theoretical possibility of abstracting story-form probably corresponds to the intuitive skill of users in processing stories: being able to re-tell them, to recognize variants of the same story, to identify the same story in another medium, and so on" (*Narrative Fiction* 7). Rimmon-Kenan is

drawing on one of the main premises of structuralism, a premise influenced by recent linguistics: if almost all individuals in a society, no
matter what their training or education or age or status or ethnicity or
gender, demonstrate competence in a particular area (that is, are able
to perform certain operations within that area), then the area must be
structured in some way. Most theorists believe that such structures do
exist. However, the fact that there is little agreement as to what these
structures might be raises the question of whether anything beyond
the obvious can be said about them: narratives have beginnings, mid-
dles, and endings; narratives play on the stability/instability dialectic.

It is also important to recognize that the intuitive skill displayed by
readers of narrative is limited. Readers seem better able to recall stories from narrative traditions within their own culture than from a different culture, seem to implement different cognitive strategies when
asked to summarize a story than when asked to recall a story, yet tend
to come up with the same macrostructure for a story regardless of
whether they encountered the story in a normal or in a "scrambled"
version (van Dijk and Kintsch 74–78). Robert de Beaugrande summarizes research demonstrating that readers tend to recall the "canonical" form of a narrative, but this form itself is culturally determined
("The Story" 391–92); for the story of Snow White, for instance, the
canonical form is probably the Disney version. (I first thought of limiting this claim to American audiences, but then I remembered that the
Disney version, dubbed, is also standard fare for German children. I
wouldn't be surprised if the same is true around the world.) As explained in chapter 1, I agree with Thomas Leitch that stories only exist
in the telling; neither the "theoretical possibility of abstracting story-
form" mentioned by Rimmon-Kenan nor the ability of audiences to
recognize similar stories proves that stories actually exist, separately
from their telling, in the linguistic universe. The research indicating
that the structure of stories varies from culture to culture works
against the claim that there are immanent plot structures that alone
significantly control the experience of narrative.

Even though this claim does not hold up in the face of some important evidence, both the deductive and the inductive arguments in its
favor support major elements of my rhetorical-narratological synthesis. The deductive approach—deriving narrative's organizing principles from the structures of human life and language—draws attention to the experiential distinction between plot as an element of a
narrative's mimesis and plotting as a synthetic element related to an
author's constructive intention (*telos*). While there are valid philosophical and linguistic objections to some of the concepts we use in
talking about plot, it is also true, as Wallace Martin writes (summariz-

ing an argument advanced by J. Hillis Miller), that "our conceptions of narrative and history depend on a shared set of assumptions about causality, unity, origin, and end that is characteristic of Western thought" (85). For example, even though we may not be able to specify when an event actually begins or ends, let alone specify all of the causes of an event, we do recognize beginnings, endings, and causes in a narrative, and it seems "natural" (to individuals in the Western intellectual tradition) to try to organize these according to linear, "clock" time. Each of these elements can function both mimetically and synthetically. That is, each can provide information about the world of the work, and each permits inferences about authorial intention. Readers can easily regard causality, for example, from the two distinct vantage points I've been describing: in the realm of story, one event causes another "according to the logic of verisimilitude" (everybody knows that frightening children can cause them to have bad dreams), whereas in the realm of discourse, "the structural needs of the plot" lead to certain decisions that we attribute to an author (a child's nightmare causes the child to run away from home, setting in motion a plot of searching for which readers expect one of several predictable outcomes) (Rimmon-Kenan, *Narrative Fiction* 17–18). This distinction between mimetic and synthetic functions tallies with rhetorical narratology's foundational premise that almost every instance of language use constitutes both a locution and an illocutionary act.

Pedagogically, plot is one of the easiest of the traditional categories of analysis with which to illustrate the mimetic/synthetic distinction, because questions like "What if the lawyer had physically forced Bartleby to depart his office?" invite students both to recognize the fictionality of the textual world and to apply their knowledge of their own actual world and the world Melville evokes. The main point here is that *plot* probably does not control readers' experience of narrative, does not influence narrativity except for two fundamental assumptions audiences take to the narrative situation: events will be causally linked, and situations will tend to shift between stable and unstable. *Plotting*, however, is part of readers' narrativity.

These assumptions are relevant to the inductive approach to plot, which has been mainly practiced by anthropologists and folklorists in the structuralist tradition. These researchers have cataloged elements or functions that seem common to narratives and combined them into types that might be termed *deep structures* or *monomyths*, depending on the researcher's orientation. The ancestor of this approach, and the most often cited example, is Vladimir Propp, whose *Morphology of the Folktale* is based on a study of one hundred Russian folktales. Propp established the crucial concept of "functions," which are "not simply actions but the roles actions play" in a story (Culler, *Structuralist Poetics* 209). According to Culler, Propp's approach is noteworthy because he grasped the importance of readers' intuitive sense of similarities among groups of stories and readers' ability to summarize stories (207). On the other hand, commenting on such typologies as Propp's, Chatman writes that they depend on "an understanding of cultural codes and their interplay with literary and artistic codes and codes of ordinary life," and he goes on to point out that the typological elements "only materialize when an audience enters into a contract with the author on the basis of known or learnable conventions" (*Story and Discourse* 95). For these reasons, Chatman doubts that "all narratives can be successfully grouped according to a few forms of plot-content . . . We are not ready yet for a massive assault on the question of plot macrostructure and typology" (95); I think Chatman is implying, and I agree, that any "assault" should target the known or learnable conventions.

Plot is not the defining feature of narrative; as I've shown earlier, both narrativity and fiction are established by context, and plot is a higher-order feature of narrative that depends on narrativity. The seemingly intuitive ability of audiences to recognize similarities among stories is important because it helps define basic conventions, not because it stands as evidence for anything like a Chomskyan "deep structure of narrative." As Robert de Beaugrande notes, if anything like a "story grammar" is going to be developed, it must be "fully integrated into the larger picture of communication and cognition, in which the telling and enjoying of stories is an enduring component of human activity" ("The Story" 419).

I intend rhetorical narratology to follow this recommendation, not in attempting to provide such a grammar but in providing a pragmatic meeting ground for both approaches to plot, the structuralist and the contextualist, as well as a framework naturally amenable to cognitivist studies that may in time establish a more empirical basis for some kinds of literary analysis. (In *Reading Minds*, Mark Turner argues that this basis already exists, but his position has not met with wide approval from literary theorists.) But rhetorical narratology will always insist on the greatest possible attention to context—cultural, literary-historical, and so on. Even a plot as apparently universal as the quest has not, historically, been available for use by women writers, nor have female characters in novels been able to embark on and fulfill quests the way their male counterparts have done (Du Plessis 478–79). There are no guarantees against a particular type being mistaken for a universal rule, as has happened with the quest plot, but a critical contextualism can help defend against this error of method.

Like plot, the concept of theme—"the construction of significance backward in time" (Martin 127)—must be approached contextually, with the same respect for the limitations imposed by the evidence of how people actually experience narratives. As with plot, theme is a helpful term that roughly corresponds to what speakers mean by "My point is . . ." and what audiences mean by the analogous question "What is your point?" but it does not signify a feature of language use that can be described with the same degree of precision we can realize with verb forms or other elements of sentence grammar. A pragmatic example: while most viewers of *Othello* would mark "jealousy" on a multiple-choice question asking "Which of the following is a theme of this play?" fewer than half of my sophomores in a recent introductory course used that word in a fill-in-the-blank version of the same question. What are the essential themes in *Bleak House*? I would answer that self-sacrifice is one, but how many other readers would use that phrase or a synonym? Would every thoughtful reader agree that "Bartleby" illustrates the theme of human connectedness?

Reading for theme involves an anticipation of retrospection and meaning-oriented direction finder similar to those used in reading for plot; these strategies operate somewhat intuitively during the reading experience but may be consciously marshaled at the end. Narrative progression, as discussed in chapter 2, is especially relevant to the consideration of how audiences experience theme as a rhetorical effect. Progression, generated by "instabilities between characters" that arise from situations and are "complicated and resolved through actions" and by tensions "between authors and/or narrators, on the one hand, and the authorial audience on the other" (Phelan, *Reading People* 15), can further three *functions*: mimetic, synthetic, and thematic. As Phelan shows, the progression of a narrative determines which of these functions, if any, a given attribute of a character will take on (9); I've generalized from Phelan's emphasis on character to show that most elements of a narrative can be seen as contributing to the perlocutionary effect of one or several of the functions.

Phelan also notes that thematizing is an activity that readers tend to engage in automatically, but there is no way to predict that any actual reader will grant thematic status to a certain attribute (104–05). Nor is there any way to predict how any actual reader will formulate a theme. I've explained the limitations in Scholes's *Textual Power* that result from his concentration on culturally coded pairs of oppositions: just because one sophisticated reader can read a narrative as turning on the opposition between sacred and profane does not mean that every reader—or even every sophisticated reader—will do the same. No one who has taught literature to college freshmen or sophomores will take for granted that such oppositions are intuitively obvious. The oppositions certainly can be taught, can be made part of the cultural or linguistic awareness of those "general" readers who pass through our courses each semester and thus can be incorporated into the script with which these readers approach narratives.

Although the connections between plot, theme, and narrative discourse cannot be precisely specified, the speech-act approach facilitates analysis. In general, narrative discourse serves a rhetorical function in placing an audience within the structure of narrative transmission; it does this by means of the types of functions that Genette says can be performed by a narrator (narrating, directing, communication, testimonial, ideological [*Narrative Discourse* 255–56]) as well as by means of signals from the extrafictional voice and details that can be taken as implying or implicating an authorial self. That is, all of these narrator functions, signals, implications, and potential implicatures serve, by definition, as illocutionary acts; awareness of this fact is part of readers' intuitive understanding of how narratives work. (As a reminder, when I say "intuitive," I don't mean "innate." I mean that the functions and so forth have been internalized to such a degree that they aren't ordinarily part of conscious awareness, although people can become aware of them by the phenomenon of marking.) For example, although pairs of oppositions do not automatically force themselves on a reader's awareness, the discourse of a narrative can engage in an ideological illocutionary act by calling attention to such oppositions. Encountering the phrase "in [the reader's] own life, or his own death," in the preface to *In the Labyrinth*, a reader may apply the life/death opposition in a thematic analysis. Yet the authority of this extrafictional voice does not necessarily extend into the actual narrative, in which the most prominent theme may strike readers who are familiar with the "new novel" as either fictionality or narration itself, a second layer of significance being created by the title's echo of the story of Theseus and the Minotaur. In teaching this "new novel," I have seen how easily students are confused by these apparently conflicting illocutionary acts: the *author* seems to be saying "Treat X as a theme" while the narrative suggests Y or Z. Readers can resolve this conflict by taking it as having thematic value—the conflict becomes part of an illocutionary act that does not violate the cooperative principle (cp) required by the ur-convention of authorial reading.

Poe's story "Ligeia" provides another interesting example of just how complicated is the task of linking theme to the structure of narrative transmission. The story begins with an epigraph attributed by the author to Joseph Glanvill. This epigraph, which by definition emanates from the extrafictional voice, contains the sentence, "Man doth not yield himself to the angels, nor unto death utterly, save only through the weakness of his feeble will." The narrating voice makes this sentence important by quoting it and attributing to it a "thrillingly exciting" sensation; it takes on even more power when Ligeia utters it twice in her final moments. A reader could feel justified assuming that in this story world, the power of Ligeia's will has enabled her to return to life by taking over the body of the narrator's second wife, Rowena, *and* that the possibility of such things happening within the actual world has authorial sanction. This is a typical response whenever a voice within the world of the narrative echoes something uttered by the extrafictional voice, the echo actually serving the ideological function.

On the basis of these assumptions concerning what the author seems to intend, a reader schooled by Scholes might then settle on the opposition mind/body as a theme; this distinction, so prominent in Western culture, is being foregrounded and made problematic by the story. Yet the story's narrating voice can also support a different assessment. Here are his first few sentences:

I cannot, for my soul, remember how, when, or even precisely where, I first became acquainted with the lady Ligeia. Long years have since elapsed, and my memory is feeble through much suffering. Or, perhaps, I cannot *now* bring these points to mind, because, in truth, the character of my beloved, her rare learning, her singular yet placid cast of beauty, and the thrilling and enthralling eloquence of her low musical language, made their way into my heart by paces so steadily and stealthily progressive that they have been unnoticed and unknown. Yet I believe that I met her first and most frequently in some large, old, decaying city near the Rhine. Of her family—I have surely heard her speak. That it is of a remotely ancient date cannot be doubted. Ligeia! Ligeia! Buried in studies of a nature more than all else adapted to deaden impressions of the outward world, it is by that sweet word alone—by Ligeia—that I bring before mine eyes in fancy the image of her who is no more. ("Ligeia" 262)

This intra/homodiegetic narrator expresses his lack of connection to the material world, the world of tangible reality, and demonstrates a possibly pathological embedding in the life of the mind. Thematically, the opposition virtual/actual may best fit this opening, if an opposition is even desirable; it could also be the case that this story's theme is the ability of a crazed mind to create an alternate reality so convincing that even actual readers sense its quiddity. The opening paragraph performs the narrative function, although in a roundabout and desultory way—emphasizing what he is unable to narrate. The communicating function seems missing; there are no overt locutions directed to a narratee. (However, the repeated references to what the narrator can't remember or explain could be taken as signals of the sort Prince says imply the presence of a narratee who is asking for everyday details that most readers like to have: when did you two meet? how did you meet? As I explained in chapter 3, I disagree with Prince, sharply limiting narratee signals to two types, but there's room here for more than one approach.) The ideological function is only present in the overlap between the extrafictional voice and the homodiegetic narrator that is created by the Glanvill quotation, but as I've said, that overlap can be taken as having thematic significance. The directing function is prominent in almost every clause: the narrator's expressions of limitation "mean" that this is not going to be an ordinary narrative. (These expressions also foreground tellability.) Likewise the testimonial function: this narrator has such a powerful emotional relationship to the story he is telling that he punctuates his reminiscences with a clutching-at-the-heart interjection, "Ligeia! Ligeia!" The instances of the directing, testimonial, and ideological functions serve as illocutionary acts; as the local guides to plot and theme, they are more reliable than abstract universals of the sort generated by Propp or Scholes.

Sex, Gender, and Narrating Voices

Rhetorical narratology aims for a consistent and rigorous contextualism: the structure of narrative transmission of any narrative has no significance apart from the context within which an audience takes up the narrative. An often discussed yet still not well understood element of this context is the sex and gender of voices. Like fictionality and narrativity, this element must be regarded as a function of the context, influenced but not determined by grammatical genders that may be present within a text or within extratextual material. According to Susan Sniader Lanser in her outstanding study *Fictions of Authority: Women Writers and Narrative Voice*, "female voice—a term used here simply to designate the narrator's grammatical gender—is a site of ideological tension made visible in textual practice," because "the 'author-function' that grounds Western literary authority is constructed in white, privileged-class male terms" (6). Lanser treats "female voice" not as "an 'essence' but [as] a variable subject position whose 'I' is grammatically feminine. *The particular characteristics of any 'female voice,' then, are a function of the context in which that voice operates*" (*Fictions* 12, emphasis added). Lanser hypothesizes that "gendered conventions of public voice and of narrative self-reference serve important roles in regulating women's access to discursive authority" (15). Further, "acts of representation make a more limited claim to discursive authority than extrarepresentational acts, which . . . allow the writer to engage, from 'within' the fiction, in a culture's literary, so-

cial, and intellectual debates" (17). As her title indicates, Lanser focuses on how gender influences the ability of women to construct
their authority as writers, but her points also apply to men as writers
and to women and men as readers: the grammatical gender of any
voice on the author side of the structure-of-narrative-transmission diagram (as well as the gender of narratee and narrating audience, to the
extent that these audience positions carry or imply gender markers)
can function as "a site of ideological tension."

Lanser identifies three modes of voice available to the woman
writer. A voice that engages in the culture's debates and can be characterized as heterodiegetic Lanser terms *authorial*; she points out that
"authorial voice has been so conventionally masculine that female authorship does not necessarily establish female voice," whereas an authorial voice that establishes itself clearly as female risks being "(dis)-
qualified" (18). That is, the male-gendered authorial voice constitutes
an unmarked case, with marking by female gender carrying the possibility of lessening or undercutting authority. The *personal* voice ("autodiegetic," in Genette's terminology) is the one in which the narrating voice is also the story's protagonist; Lanser considers only those
personal voices that are self-consciously narrative, excluding, for example, interior monologue (18–19). Third, Lanser identifies the *communal* voice: "a spectrum of practices that articulate either a collective voice or a collective of voices that share narrative authority" (21).
This third mode has not been studied by narratologists because it goes
against the dominant presumption in Western culture that "narration
is individual" (21). Lanser excludes from this mode both "the use of an
authorial voice that resorts to an inclusive 'we' " and "the presentation
of divergent and antithetical perspectives on the same events that
characterizes epistolary novels" (21).

These modes of voice

represent three distinct kinds of authority that women have needed to constitute in order to make their place in Western literary history: respectively, the
authority to establish alternative "worlds" and the "maxims" by which they
will operate, to construct and publicly represent female subjectivity and re-
define the "feminine," and to constitute as a discursive subject a female body
politic. (22)

Historically, according to Lanser, the authorial voice began to domi-
nate at the end of the eighteenth century, replacing the memoir and
epistolary forms; this shift signals an "emerging moral and intellectual authority for the novelist" (64). The same period saw the near-dis-
appearance of the female personal voice: "just when the single narrating subject becomes most insistently the center of narrative . . . that

subject becomes masculine" (157). Why, Lanser asks, did women authors participate in this shift? She suggests that "Romanticism offered women the lure of the universal, the escape from gender and thus from the always-problematic female body by which a woman's genius, spirituality, and freedom were denied" (157). Lanser summarizes her analysis this way: "[a]uthorial voice, with its structurally superior position and its superhuman privilege, seems to me always in danger of constructing its own hegemony, yet it can be a powerful tool for dislodging an existing authority" (278). As for the personal voice, "because its authority is more qualified," it "establishes a less certain hegemony, yet it has also the power to engulf the reader in the vision of a single consciousness" (278–79). "Unlike authorial and personal voice, whose singularity corresponds to that of conventional authorship, communal voice arrogates to an individual author the self-reinforcing pretence of multiplicity" (279).

Lanser demonstrates the lengthy historical reign of the *male, authorial, extra/heterodiegetic* voice as the locus of narrative and ideological authority within the genre of narrative fiction. The personal voice, by comparison, carries relatively little ideological weight, although other factors can greatly enhance the ideological value that a reader might attach to it. For example, Charles Dickens's male autodiegetic narrating voices, David Copperfield and Pip, probably carried with them, for Dickens's contemporary readers, all the weight of a cultural construction we can term "Charles Dickens, Novelist and Public Figure," but not so the voice of Esther Summerson in *Bleak House*. Ideological authority was (and still is) attached to the male voice, although as I've suggested earlier, Esther conveys considerable authority as a *narrator*: her coy behavior with respect to Alan Woodcourt's presence in the story is perfectly transparent, and otherwise she is scrupulously fair and complete. By giving narrative authority to Esther but withholding from her the authority to generalize about ideology, Dickens enables *both* voices to function as "sites of ideological tension." Of this novel, Lanser writes that its "dual narrative structure . . . proves the gender-genre rule: replicating the ideology of separate spheres, it sets the omniscient and implicitly male voice of the authorial narrator next to the personal voice of the female character Esther Summerson without acknowledging this duality: the alternating narratives proceed as if they were independent texts" (*Fictions* 239–40).

Hand in hand with the lengthy reign of the male-gendered voice goes the critical concentration on singular voices, whether authorial or personal. This concentration has been aided by the relative ease with which the authorial/personal distinction tallies with that of heterodiegetic/homodiegetic, the latter being somewhat subtilized but not fundamentally altered by Genette's further distinction between extra- and intradiegetic. Lanser's identification of the third mode, communal voice, usefully complicates the more common binary analysis. Such voices "are produced from intersections of social and formal possibilities," although "novelistic conventions of coherence and continuity inhibit the construction of communal narrative forms" (267). Some communal narrators

> are constructed through subtle but important departures from autodiegetic practices, for while the narrators retain the syntax of "first-person" narrative, their texts avoid the markers of individuality that characterize personal voice and thereby resist the equation of narrator and protagonist. Rather, the narrator's identity becomes communal: not only is she an authoritative mediator of the community, but the community is represented as the very source of her (textual) identity. Such a departure from conventional autodiegesis, however, implicates not only narration but plot: because the novel traditionally binds the female character in (heterosexual) conflict, novelistic teleology is challenged by articulations of communal voice. (241)

A fascinating example of this technique is Doris Lessing's *The Memoirs of a Survivor*. The novel opens thus:

> We all remember that time. It was no different for me than for others. Yet we do tell each other over and over again the particularities of the events we shared, and the repetition, the listening, is as if we are saying, "It was like that for you, too? Then that confirms it, yes, it was so, it must have been, I wasn't imagining things." (3)

This plural, communal "we" is repeated frequently, each time serving to "mediate" the unnamed community's experience of and reactions to the dramatic changes taking place in the society. The narrator does have unique experiences: she is the guardian of Emily, her neighbors are the Whites and the Mehtas, she allows herself "one real cigarette a day" (11). Yet she is not a protagonist, and she never divulges her name or her personal history. Lanser's discussion fits this novel well: heterosexual conflict is absent except in the narrator's reactions to the mating rituals she witnesses among the young people, rituals from which she, like the community whose voice she is, feels alienated.

A second technique developed in the nineteenth century is the adoption by the narrator, who remains a single voice, of "a collective *vision*, a focalizing consciousness that represents itself in a plural 'we,'" the use of which "breach[es] the conventions of narrative verisimilitude by constituting a plural perceptual consciousness" (Lanser, *Fictions* 249); Lanser's chief example is Sarah Orne Jewett's *The Country of the Pointed Firs*. Modernist novels bring to bear two additional techniques: "*simultaneous,* first-person-plural narration in a literal 'we' that allows voices to speak in unison (for example, Toni Morrison's *The Bluest Eye*), and *sequential* narration in which each voice speaks in turn so that the 'we' is produced from a series of collaborating 'I's,'" exemplified by Amy Tan's *The Joy Luck Club* (256). Lanser goes on to specify that in "simultaneous" narration "both voice and focalization are presented as communal, so that the 'we' who perceives is also the 'we' who speaks" (257). These techniques tally with an important trait of female readers as described by the research of David Bleich and Elizabeth Flynn to which I referred in chapter 2: they enter more immediately into the world of a novel. Such a correlation makes even more significant Lanser's finding that the communal voice almost exclusively occurs in narratives authored by women.

A notable exception is the narrator of William Faulkner's "A Rose for Emily." Every characteristic Lanser lists for the singular communal narrator applies, except that the narrator is *almost* certainly male and except that heterosexual conflict is at the heart of the story. Yet this exception, far from weakening Lanser's discussion of the communal voice, actually provides support. Part of what makes this story so interesting is a discourse tension resulting from the narrator's combination of authority and anonymity: because the relationship between extrafictional voice, implied author, and narrator is difficult to pin down, actual readers (notably first- and second-year college students) can't figure out where they should stand with respect to Emily, the town, and the narrator but do quickly sense that traditional sexual politics are being thematized.

Lanser opens and concludes *Fictions of Authority* by asserting the need for a "narrative poetics" that recognizes "the links between narrative and social practices" as well as for a feminist criticism that attends to "the complex interrelationship between representation and voice" (278). Robyn Warhol's *Gendered Interventions,* to which Lanser refers several times but never in a substantive way, contributes significantly to these goals. In general, Warhol asks the question "What happens to a text when the writer is *writing as* a woman?" She frames her answer within the hypothesis that "[g]ender in writing strategies arises . . . from the writer's making a series of rhetorical choices, whether or not those choices are consciously intentional" (*Gendered Interventions* 18–19). She distinguishes between the strategies of *distancing* and *engaging,* as defined by "the relations narrators try to establish between the actual reader and the 'you' in the text" (26, 28). The former is present when a narrator specifies a narratee so completely that an actual reader cannot identify with the narratee; the latter is present when the narrator "addresses a 'you' that is evidently intended to evoke recognition and identification in the person who holds the book and reads, even if the 'you' in the text resembles that person only slightly or not at all" (29).

In a later article, " 'Reader, Can You Imagine? No, You Cannot': The Narratee as Other in Harriet Jacobs's Text," Warhol takes herself to task for building her analysis on canonical texts and for terming "distancing" a male strategy, "engaging" a female strategy, but aside from this corrective, *Gendered Interventions* stands as an impressive example of the usefulness of combining traditional, structuralist narratology with feminist concerns. The only problem I would want to point out is that *Gendered Interventions* does not preserve a clear focus on the *functional* nature of the relationship among narrator, narratee, and actual reader. This is where *Fictions of Authority* is so strong, as Lanser shows how the communal voice creates the potential for a new functional relationship between audience positions (including the actual reader) and voice positions, a relationship in which the ur-convention of heteroglossia plays a major role.

Lanser also repeatedly insists that narratology needs to study older texts and techniques that may not have been of interest to the first generations of structural narratologists, as well as "new and challenging forms of narrative voice" that require "new and supple forms of narrative theory" (*Fictions* 279). Such a new form of voice is present in Jeanette Winterson's novel *Written on the Body*. My own experience with this novel exemplifies Lanser's paradigm of voices as well as her more specific comments in her recent essay "Queering Narratology." First of all, I expect the intra/homodiegetic narrator to have the same sex, not just the same gender, as the *female* author—as Lanser says, "readers routinely attribute a sex to narrators and characters," and "a narrator's sex is . . . normatively marked in autodiegetic texts" ("Queering Narratology" 252–53). However, a number of gender-specific details, *in the context of my own heterosexual bias,* caused me quickly to reverse this expectation. The novel is recounting a deep and passionate relationship with "Louise," who is clearly female (both by name and by description). Three times in the first ten pages the narrator refers to female friends or lovers: "I remembered vaguely that I had once had a girlfriend" (12), "I had a lover once, her name was Bathsheba" (16), "You will think I have been constantly in and out of married women's lumber rooms" (17). The narrator also quotes and implies a felt identification with Caliban (from Shakespeare's *The Tempest*) and poses cynical questions about the clichés of love, questions I associate with a male voice. All of these details contribute to my half-conscious decision to construct the narrator as male, even though the text gives me no name, no physical description, no third-party reference to the narrator as "he."

Slightly before the middle of the novel, however, my sex-and-gender construction is challenged by this: "I had a boyfriend once called Crazy Frank" (92). Later I encounter three more sentences that together not only destroy my construction but force on me the awareness of how easily even a trained reader can fall into a trap: "[i]t reminded me of a pair of shorts a boyfriend of mine had once worn" (143); "I had a boyfriend once, his name was Carlo" (143); "I had a boyfriend once, his name was Bruno" (152). Granted that the word "lover" is not used and that when "Carlo met Robert . . . [t]hey exchanged razorblades and cut me out" (143), the suggestion is still strong that the narrator has either a bi- or a homosexual orientation and may be either male or female. The more interesting fact is my longer-term reaction: I read the novel again thoroughly once and skimmed it several times, sure that I had missed some obvious reference, because it was so difficult to imagine a story of love and passion without attaching not just a grammatical gender but a biological sex to the story's main character. "*Written on the Body*, whatever the sex of its narrator, is a queer novel with a queer plot," as Lanser writes, "queer" meaning "sexually transgressive" and hence tending to challenge the culturally dominant binary thinking regarding sexual orientation ("Queering Narratology" 255, 251; the same points are made in Lanser's "Sexing the Narrative"). As a typical reader, I'm most comfortable when I can operate with those binary categories, but recognizing the novel's "queerness" made me aware of my preconscious tendency to attach gender and sex to narrating voices. Lanser suggests that a similar transformation can happen to narratology as a whole: "embracing questions of sex, gender, and sexuality" may "end up 'queering' narratology" ("Queering Narratology" 259), and this would be a good thing.

According to Kathe Keen, Winterson intended to "queer" readers' automatic responses in just this way. Quoting from several of Winterson's interviews, Keen argues that Winterson intended to undermine gender categories in order "to show how sexual differences within the language create a political difference that perpetuates social/cultural boundaries" (1). Keen focuses specifically on how the woman reader of *Written on the Body* is able to "vacillate between genders, avoiding entrapment by not assigning herself a place socially and culturally within the text" (8). According to Keen, "an ungendered subject invites the woman reader to identify herself with a whole subject, not a divided subject" (8). While the dynamics of identification and engagement between text and reader may differ for men and women, there is no question that this novel can lead both men and women to a greater awareness of our automatic tendency to foreground gender clues and to construct both grammatical gender and biological sex for narrating voices. In other words, although a text usually contains gender markers, *gendering* and *sexing* are functions of the interaction between text and audience, functions that highlight the Western need for attaching a social, cultural, and biological identity to every voice we encounter.

As with plot and theme, rhetorical narratology fosters a sensitivity to this aspect of narrating and thus may enhance how students are taught to read narratives. For instance, the narrator of *The Portrait of a Lady* is never given a gender, but probably not one reader in a thousand would consider that individual to be anything other than male. Might this unconscious assigning of the male gender limit how women experience the novel? Suppose a teacher were to urge the possibility of a female narrator, or, more radical still, an ungendered narrator? At the very least, students might become more sensitive to their—our—tendency automatically to draw a straight line from the extrafictional voice as well as from the primary focalizing character to the narrating voice. Are James's extra/heterodiegetic narrating voices really "*men* of the world"? Yes . . . because we construct them that way.

Temporal Structure of Narrating

Temporal relationship in narrating is one of the two most conventionalized aspects of narrating (the other being the representation of consciousness and speech, which is the subject of the next section). These conventions enable audiences to experience as "natural" what from a logical standpoint is very strange. The best example is the unmarked case of the temporal relationship between narrator and story: the "fiction" that "literary narrating involves an instantaneous action, without a temporal dimension"; this means that such narrating "is considered to have no duration" (Genette, *Narrative Discourse* 222). According to Genette, this "fiction" is both "powerful" and "unnoticed": a reader will only notice when a narrator or other voice remarks on how long it takes actually to tell something (that is, when a locution explicitly comments on the duration) or when some illocutionary act on the part of one of the narrating voices invites the reader's observation. Remarkably, no matter what the narrating voice's technical relationship to the story (auto-, homo- or heterodiegetic) or the technical level (intra- or extradiegetic) and no matter how much or how little textual space is devoted to narrating a given incident, readers will normally not attribute any temporal dimension to the narrating unless a directing, communicating, or perhaps testimonial function is present. The audience of a narrative can certainly lose patience with the pace of narration if we lack a sense of sufficient progression, for instance, but this reaction has to do with the context within which the narrative is being experienced, with the conventionalized expectations regarding point, tellability, narrativity, and so forth. It has nothing to do with the implausibility of instantaneous acts; in fact, Genette's observation emphasizes that narration, as an act, is as strange as some phenomena in the subatomic realm—it seems to take place where time does not exist.

A second time-related fiction of narrating is that any set of narrated events can be arranged into what Rimmon-Kenan terms a "'natural' chronology"—the timeline of the "immanent," "autonomous," or abstractable story (*Narrative Fiction* 7, 16). Rimmon-Kenan notes that although we may speak of an "ideal chronological order" of events, "strict succession can only be found in stories with a single [narrative] line or even with a single character"; because hardly any stories fit this description, the "ideal" is actually neither "natural" nor representative but has become a "conventional 'norm'" (16–17).

Additionally, as I noted in chapter 1, stories may not exist in the linguistic universe, apart from their instantiation in specific tellings, which are always shaped by the immediate purposes of the tellers. Suppose the first event in a sequence is a stepfather driving his disobedient stepdaughter out of the house and into a dark forest, but the narration actually begins with the girl being rescued in the forest. On what basis would the strictly chronological ordering be "ideal"? By eliminating the opening enigma (why is this girl in the forest?), the "natural" version reduces the narrative's tellability. If we believed we lived in a deterministic universe, then perhaps the strictly chronological version would be desirable, but most people today, in the Western intellectual tradition, assume that both free will and chance influence the courses our lives take.

Most narratologists agree that the best study of the structures of narrative chronology is Genette's. In the following paragraphs, I summarize his contributions but also emphasize the conventional nature of such chronology as well as the fact that the structures in and of themselves do not privilege any type as ideal or natural. As a strong contextualist, I insist that the effect of any chronological structure is determined by context rather than by relative nearness to or distance from some ideal.

Genette begins his first chapter of *Narrative Discourse*, "Order," by identifying three kinds of relationships between the two fundamental

Fig. 6. Temporal Relationships

STORY TIME		NARRATING TIME	
Order:	actual chronological order of events	Order:	"pseudotemporal" order of events as narrated
Duration:	actual length of events	Duration:	"pseudoduration" of the telling established by "length of text"
Frequency:	of actual events	Frequency:	of tellings about events

types of time in every narrative: "story time" and the time of narrating (35). For the sake of clarity, I present these relationships in tabular form (see fig. 6). About those connections having to do with order, Genette makes the same point Rimmon-Kenan does about "ideal" or "natural" chronology: such concepts "implicitly assume the existence of a kind of zero degree that would be a condition of perfect temporal correspondence between narrative and story," a correspondence, however, that "is more hypothetical than real" (*Narrative Discourse* 36). This correspondence does not constitute an unmarked case; aside from very simple stories (some folktales and children's stories, for instance), readers would probably be more surprised than not to find such an ideal chronology. Rather, the unmarked case of *order* includes clearly marked *anachronies*, or jumps in the narrating time. An event can be narrated or evoked in advance of when it occurs on the timeline (*prolepsis* or flash-forward), or it can be evoked in the context of events that occur later (*analepsis*, or flash-back) (40). Genette goes on to distinguish between "external" and "internal" versions of prolepsis and analepsis, depending on whether the anachrony reaches outside the span of time defined by the narrative up to the point of the anachrony (external) or remains inside that span (internal) (48–49).

Genette adds a number of other refinements to his system of temporal ordering, but these are the most useful. His structuralist orientation leads him to foreground the typology, but he does provide a bit of help with the question of how the anachronies function rhetorically. Analepses, especially, can serve a mimetic function, for example, by providing the background without which a character's present action would not make sense. A prolepsis may be more likely to serve a thematic function; by providing advance information, it enables and even invites a reader to generalize about the present situation that is being suspended in order to make room for the prolepsis. Thematizing tends to happen upon completion of a narrative, but by projecting into the future from the present narrating moment, a prolepsis can also stimulate this activity earlier than it might otherwise happen. Genette points out that prolepsis is relatively infrequent in the "Western narrative tradition," that it does not fit well with the nineteenth-century interest in narrative suspense or with "the traditional fiction of a narrator who must appear more or less to discover the story at the same time that he tells it," but that it finds a natural home in the " 'first-person' narrative" (67).

Both types of anachrony can enhance the mimetic effect of the *narrating* as well. Commenting on Proust, Genette writes that his "complexly structured openings, mimicking, as it were, the unavoidable *difficulty of beginning* the better to exorcise it, are seemingly part of the earliest and most lasting narrative tradition" (46). Quite likely, this tradition is so old and so strong because finding the right place to begin *is* so difficult. True, there are fairly simple tales with straightforward beginnings ("Es war einmal ein wunderschönes Puppenhaus"—this is how I remember the German version of Beatrix Potter's "The Tale of the Two Bad Mice" beginning). But another common narrating situation, at least in homodiegetic narratives, is something like that of Esther Summerson: "I have a great deal of difficulty in beginning to write my portion of these pages, for I know I am not clever" (Dickens, *Bleak House* 15). In fact, Esther begins with several paragraphs elaborating on this limitation and hinting at a strength ("[w]hen I love a person very tenderly indeed, [my "understanding"] seems to brighten") before she is able to begin her "portion" of the story. The narrator can also use the search for a beginning as the occasion for playful reflection, as does Oskar, in Günter Grass's *The Tin Drum* (published in German in 1959): "[y]ou can begin a story in the middle and create confusion by striking out boldly, backward and forward. You can be modern, put aside all mention of time and distance and, when the whole thing is done, proclaim, or let someone else proclaim, that you have finally, at the last moment, solved the space-time problem" (17).

These beginnings illustrate Genette's point about one of Proust's narratives, that the narrator needs "time to *position his voice*" (*Narrative Discourse* 46). Some narrating voices are confident enough to take control from the beginning (for example, the omniscient narrator of *Bleak House*), but others need to establish their authority and find the right place to begin. The more hesitant voice can gain *mimetic* authority by recognizing either implicitly (as does Esther) or explicitly that for the persons involved in getting a story told (I include both authors and the voices they create), story time is not nearly as easy to identify as we might like it to be.

Genette uses two phrases in discussing anachronies, "narrative economy" and "methods for circulating meaning in the novel" (56, 58), that imply a rhetorical perspective, although both come up in the context of specific discussions of Proust's techniques, and neither is defined. Together, they suggest that anachronies occur within a set of conventions shared by readers and authors. They are conventions that have to do with the relative weight or value to be assigned to elements within a narrative, with "economy," that is, in its more technical sense (the system by which resources are distributed) rather than as synonymous with "parsimony." These conventions influence how this value is distributed through the narrative—is experienced by a reader as "circulated" (not fixed) during the actual reading. Thus anachronies function in the reading experience as *illocutionary acts*. By jumping back or ahead in the story time, the narrating "says" that the moment jumped to is important; this "saying" can be supported by a narrating or extrafictional voice that explicitly draws attention to the jump and that may engage in such illocutionary functions as predicting, reporting, admitting, suggesting, and proposing. (Chatman lists these and many other illocutionary acts in *Story and Discourse* 162–63 n11.) But even without any direct address from a narrating voice to a narratee or from an extrafictional voice to the authorial audience, the jump can serve as an implicature, potentially contributing to a reader's experience of the narrative's thematic, synthetic, or mimetic dimension or several of these at once.

Genette also makes the very important point that prolepsis and analepsis "take for granted a perfectly clear temporal consciousness and unambiguous relationships among present, past, and future. . . . In fact, the very frequency of interpolations and their reciprocal entanglements often embroil matters in such a way as to leave the 'simple' reader, and even the most determined analyst, sometimes with no way out" (*Narrative Discourse* 79). Genette's language could be more precise; it's not clear how these techniques can "take for granted" anything. What he means, I believe, is that in discussing the techniques we tend to assume the existence of an unambiguous timeline, if only we can find it, but that this assumption isn't valid. Complexity can be created, to begin with, by analepses within prolepses, and vice versa, which "somewhat disturb our reassuring ideas about retrospection and anticipation" (83). This is the sort of complexity we find, for instance, in the later works of Henry James, such as this proleptic analepsis from *The Ambassadors*: "Strether was to remember afterwards further that this had had for him the effect of forming Chad's almost sole intervention" (464). A narrative can go even farther, can actually "disengage its arrangement from all dependence, even inverse dependence, on the chronological sequence of the story it tells" (Genette, *Narrative Discourse* 84). This situation Genette terms *achrony*, the most extreme demonstration of "narrative's capacity for *temporal autonomy*" (85). His example, summarized, is a section from Proust's *Combray*, in which events are grouped by "spatial proximity," "climactic identity," or "thematic kinship," groupings that defy "all chronology" (84–85).

Achrony constitutes the marked case of anachrony. Only when an audience experiences a narrative as autonomous with respect to the story's temporal dimension is the audience likely to notice in any significant way the temporal dimension itself; analepses and prolepses are so integral to our experience with narrative that by themselves they will almost never cause an audience to, for example, thematize temporality. The crucial caveat of course is "by themselves." Penelope Lively's *Moon Tiger* (1988) provides an excellent illustration of this point. The main narrating voice is that of Claudia Hampton, who in her early seventies is dying. The novel opens with Claudia's statement to a nurse, "I'm writing a history of the world," and it concludes, after her death, with an unnamed, apparently extra/heterodiegetic voice noting that Claudia's room is now "[v]oid," containing "[n]o life. . . . The world moves on. And beside the bed the radio gives the time signal and a voice starts to read the six o'clock news" (1, 208). Her memories are of course all analeptic with respect to the narrating present, but at times they incorporate internal prolepses. Reading this novel, I had no trouble establishing its time line, yet the arbitrary, conventional nature of that time line became thematized by an intersection between the extrafictional voice and the narrating voice in the references to Moon Tiger ("a green coil that slowly burns all night, repelling mosquitoes, dropping away into lengths of grey ash" [75]) as well as by Claudia's vocation (journalist and historian) juxtaposed against her explicit recognitions that time as a dimension is irrelevant: "[p]ast and present do not so much co-exist in the Nile valley as cease to have any meaning" (80), "[a]t night she looks at the sizzling stars, which cannot be the same stars that glimmer in English skies, and she feels eternal, which, far from being tranquil, is like some hideous fever" (90). While it is true that Claudia's "body records certain events" (having borne a child, had an appendectomy) and "records also a more impersonal history: it remembers Java Man and Australopithecus" (166), it is also true that these events exist in the present by virtue of having been recorded. These details, and many others, establish a context of reading within which the novel's analepses and prolepses, as well as the occasional shifts to other narrator-focalizers, such as Claudia's daughter, take on a significance both thematic and synthetic—in fact, the synthetic nature of the story's temporal relations is itself thematic.

In the Labyrinth achieves temporal autonomy not by thematizing the arbitrary and subjective characteristics of human time but by implying causal links between the narrating and the narrated while leaving out all temporal signals that would allow a reader unambiguously to establish a chronology of the narrating to match the chronology of events that can be established within the story. In what I'm terming "the story," a nameless soldier is trying to deliver a box; by analepsis we learn that this box belonged to a slain comrade; while looking for the right person to receive the box the soldier is wounded; at the end of the narrative, the same soldier (at least it seems to be the same one) dies from this wound. Aside from the analepsis revealing where the box came from, these events are narrated in their "natural" order, although many of the details are frequently repeated. On the other hand, references to a dark, dust-covered room, to a painting titled *The Defeat of Reichenfels* (151), and to a restaurant or bar can't be placed within this natural chronology but seem to occur on a different level. This phenomenon leads some readers, including me, to take the narrative of the soldier's quest as in process, as the written trace of a putative author in that dusty room looking at a painting and trying to construct a narrative about a soldier on a pointless personal mission.

These two levels can be made to cohere, but the work is all on the reader's part. No natural chronology emerges from these "trace" events except that the narrative's first paragraph refers to "outside," and in the final paragraph a narrating voice seems to be going out of a building, either literally or in the imagination:

But the image is blurred by trying to distinguish the outlines, as in the case of the inordinately delicate pattern of the wallpaper and the indeterminate edges of the gleaming paths made in the dust by the felt slippers, and, beyond the door, the dark vestibule where the umbrella is leaning against the coat rack, then, once past the entrance door, the series of long hallways, the spiral staircase, the door to the building with its stone stoop, and the whole city behind me. (272)

The first and final paragraphs can be taken as defining a chronological beginning and ending, but they would make just as much sense if they were reversed. Neither the narrative of the soldier nor this other possible narrative in any way depends on "the chronological sequence of the story it tells." Like *Written on the Body* and *Moon Tiger*, *In the Labyrinth* can have the perlocutionary effect of thematizing (in order to challenge) a conventional expectation—that events *can* be arranged along a single time line, and that if several sequences of events occur in one narrative, they can be collated on the same time line.

Variations in *duration*, as Genette explains, create an effect of rhythm as well as contribute to "emancipation from narrative temporality quite as much as transgressions of chronological order do" (*Narrative Discourse* 85). Genette lists four types of variations:

pause: NT=N, ST=0
scene: NT=ST
summary: NT<ST
ellipsis: NT=0, ST=N (95)

In this chart, ST stands for the story time (the span of minutes, hours, or years that is of interest at the moment), NT stands for narrative time (the time that is actually being spent narrating that span), and N simply stands for a quantity of time greater than zero. "The real rhythm of the novelistic canon," Genette writes, is "the alternation of nondramatic summaries . . . with dramatic scenes whose role in the action is decisive" (109–10). This rhythm created by variations in duration probably affects readers on a preconscious level as long as it stays within the rather indefinite range of the unmarked case, a mixing of several or all of these four types but with relatively more scene and pause, less summary and ellipsis. The marked cases are those that remain almost entirely with one of the variations, especially scene (readers will notice when a narrative moves unremittingly from event to event, each day receiving the same amount of text) and summary (if there is so much summary that no tension or instability is created, readers will notice that there's no progression).

These judgments of course are relative to the era, to the subgenre, and to the type of person reading the narrative. *In the Labyrinth* is so difficult to read not only because of its use of achrony but also because it contains no summary and no marked ellipses—the story may in fact jump ahead at times, but without signals such as "three days later" or a character noticing a calendar or clock, there's no way for readers to be sure that a jump has happened. *Scene* is the most prominent mode in the sections having to do with the soldier's mission, but the sections that seem to have to do with a story about the narrating itself (for instance, those that describe the dusty room or the painting) have more the effect of pauses—not pauses *from* the soldier's story (although that story is being held in suspense) but pauses during which a narrating voice reconsiders or reconceives that story, pauses in the present-tense story that is the narrating itself. Yet it must be remembered that *In the Labyrinth* cannot be read except by readers who are willing and able to put aside their expectation of a typical rhythm, readers who have some experience with the "new novel" or other postmodern fiction. While it is true that *"emancipations* from narrative temporality" are the rule rather than the exception, the effect of such emancipations can never be predicted. Because emancipations *are* so much a part of narrative's conventions, most will pass unnoticed.

Genette's discussion of *frequency*, the third temporal structure of narrative, can also be conveniently summarized in tabular form:

1N/1S	(narrating once what happens once—*singulative narrating*)
nN/nS	(narrating n times what happens n times)
nN/1S	(narrating n times what happens once—*repeating narrating*)
1N/nS	(narrating once what happens n times—*iterative narrating*)
	(*Narrative Discourse* 115–17)

Genette does not label the second type, pointing out that it "reduces to" the first (115). His labels actually use the word *narrative* rather than *narrating*, but I prefer the latter as more consistent with his description of each type and not implying a label that can be attached to the entire narrative: in fact, a narrative text can contain all three types of narrating.

Genette says that frequency's "classical" case places the iterative *"at the service* of the narrative 'as such,'* which is the singulative narrative"; Flaubert was the first novelist to free the iterative from this "service" and give the iterative passages "a wholly unusual fullness and autonomy," a development that Proust took to much greater lengths (117). The classical case is unmarked, requiring of readers an ability automatically to generalize, to take figuratively the narrative's statement that "this happened every day," to understand such a statement thus, as Genette puts it: "every day something of this kind happened, of which this is one realization among others" (122). Because *Narrative Discourse* is so extensively concerned with Proust, Genette dwells largely on the iterative, pointing out that Proust creates rhythm not with the "classical" alternation of scene and summary but with an alternation between iterative and singulative (143). As with the other aspects of narrative temporality, Genette provides quite a few more subtypes, especially of the iterative, but the three main categories of singulative, repeating, and iterative are the most helpful for students of narrative.

Concluding his discussion of frequency, Genette notes how these three aspects are often bound together tightly: "[f]or example, in traditional narrative, analepsis (an aspect of *sequence*) most often takes the form of summary (an aspect of *duration*, or of speed); summary frequently has recourse to the services of the iterative (an aspect of *frequency*); description is almost always at the same time pinpointed, durative, and iterative" (155). Furthermore, these aspects can serve any one or a combination of the mimetic, thematic, and synthetic purposes. The author might attempt to justify any of these variations (in order, duration, and frequency) as Proust does by asserting a "realistic motivation" to be faithful either to how experiences were lived, to how they are being recalled by a narrating voice, or to how they are most plausibly arranged (157). Instead of such a mimetic purpose, the variation might serve a thematic purpose—the author might be intending to revise ontology by creating or evoking a new sense of time: *"vision can also be a matter of style and technique"* (159). A third possibility is that the author might foreground the synthetic, trying to make readers conscious of the conventions themselves.

As noted, the "classical" iterative category occurs so often as to seem to be the way narratives are "naturally" constructed. "And so [Dolly] used to sit propped up in a great arm-chair," Esther writes, or "when I came home from school of a day" (Dickens, *Bleak House* 15)— the verbs and temporal adverbs evoke the sense of "every day something of this kind happened" while also conveying an impression of particular events. These iterations establish the background for the first great singulative event Esther remembers, her godmother telling her, on her birthday, that she should never have been born, to which the distraught child replies, "[W]hy is it my fault?" (17). The iterations prepare the way for this terrible revelation and for the guilt Esther seems immediately to assume; they serve both a mimetic and a thematic function, the latter by setting up the complex theme of guilt, redemption, forgiveness, and innocence. As is typical in the classical case, this singulative moment is followed by another relatively brief iterative paragraph: "to think . . . how often I repeated to the doll the story of my birthday, and confided to her that I would try . . . to repair the fault I had been born with (of which I confessedly felt guilty and yet innocent)" (18). This framing of the singulative by the iterative functions as an illocutionary act for actual readers who are reading authorially; it motivates questions about both theme and plot.

At the other end of the spectrum, *In the Labyrinth* forces thoughtful readers to consider such basic questions as what constitutes a discrete event and how much variation can exist between what appear to be two narrations of one event before the narrating becomes singulative rather than repeating. Several times the soldier stands before a door, follows a boy down a snowy street, encounters a "sham lame man." Or else the soldier has each of these experiences once and is remembering them repeatedly: each instance of memory is a single event, but the memories constitute repeating narratives. Or else a narrator is trying out different versions of several events: each instance is thus a single *narrating* event, but together they are iterative. The complex narrating situation in this novel makes certainty even more elusive, as I explain in the following section on speech representations.

As with all of rhetorical narratology's tools, these categories of frequency are not to be rigidly applied in order to answer all questions about a narrative but should be flexibly brought to bear in order to help identify textual features that are then available for closer rhetorical analysis. Again, a good example is Lively's technique in *Moon Tiger* of rendering the same moment through several focalizing characters. One such moment, quite detailed, occurs when Claudia's older brother reveals to her "the mechanics of sex." An extended quotation is necessary in order to describe the subtlety of Lively's technique; the quotation is printed as I render it here, including all ellipses, with a blank space of one line between the two versions:

He has hugged to himself, for the whole of the first week of the Christmas holidays, his superiority. And eventually, as he has always known he would, he can resist gloating no longer and out it comes, at a point where he is fed up with her, when she has been swanking insufferably.

"Anyway," he says, "I know how babies are made."

"So do I," Claudia says. But there has been an infinitesimal, a fatally betraying pause.

"Bet you don't."

"Bet I do."

"How, then?"

"I'm not going to say," says Claudia.

"Because you don't know."

She hesitates, trapped. He watches her. Which way will she jump? She shrugs, at last, wonderfully casual. "It's obvious. The man puts his—thing—into the lady's tummy button and the baby goes inside her tummy until it's big enough."

Gordon collapses in glee. He rolls about on the sofa, howling. "In her tummy button! What an absolute ass you are, Claudia! In her tummy button!"

She stands over him, scarlet not with embarrassment but with chagrin and rage. "He does! I know he does!"

Gordon stops laughing. He sits up. "Don't be such a cretin. You don't know *anything*. He puts his thing—and it's called a penis, you didn't know that either, did you?—*there* . . ." And he stabs with a finger at Claudia's crotch, pushing the stuff of her dress between her thighs. Her eyes widen—in surprise? In outrage? They stare at each other. Somewhere downstairs, out of sight, in her own world, they can hear the tranquil hum of their mother's sewing machine.

"I'm not going to tell you," she says.

"Because you don't know."

She could gladly hit him, lolling there complacent on the sofa. And anyway she does know—she's almost sure she does. She says defiantly, "I do know. He

puts this thing in the lady's tummy button." She does not add that the inadequacy of her own navel for such a performance bothers her—she assumes that
it must be going to expand when she is older.

He hurls himself around in laughter. He is speechless. Then he leans forward. "I knew you didn't know," he says. "Listen. He puts his penis—it's called
a penis, incidentally—*there* . . ." And he stabs with his finger against her dress,
between her legs.

And her anger, strangely, evaporates; eclipsed by something different, equally
forceful, baffling. Something mysterious is present, something she cannot nail
or name. She stares in wonder at her grey-flannelled brother. (26–27)

Rather than debate whether these two sections constitute singulative
or repetitive narratives, which at first seems the most obvious question, I can better understand how the sections may function rhetorically by looking at order, duration, and frequency. The category of duration leads me to note that the sentences conclude a chapter and
exemplify the classical balance between scene and summary. Ellipsis
is also present, minimally between the introductory summary and
this scene ("I went back to Miss Lavenham's, and Gordon to Winches-
ter where his housemaster, delicately approached by Mother with
murmurings about his fatherless condition, had him into his study
one evening for a chat" [26]) and radically after the scene. The sum-
mary/scene contrast is strengthened by the verb-tense shifts as well as
by the shift from Claudia's conventional autodiegetic voice to the
voice of the impersonal extra/heterodiegetic narrator. Together these
technical details serve the directing function as well as contributing to
the theme of time. As a fairly sophisticated reader, nevertheless I have
trouble locating these sections and others of similar construction
within any "natural chronology"; they disturb my desire to have
events line up chronologically.

This experience of mine is strengthened by *Moon Tiger*'s repetitive/
singulative interplay. I'm experiencing the same event—Gordon
taunting Claudia—but simultaneously I'm experiencing two different
events—Gordon's thoughts and emotions and Claudia's. On a fine-
grained level, I have to admit that the single event may not even exist
because of some differences in the spoken words: "I'm not going to
say" versus "I'm not going to tell you," "It's obvious. The man puts
his—thing—into the lady's tummy button" versus "I do know. He
puts this thing in the lady's tummy button," "He puts his thing—and
it's called a penis, you didn't know that either did you?—*there*" versus
"He puts his penis—it's called a penis incidentally—*there*." The repet-
itive/singulative distinction breaks down, but not before it draws my
attention to crucial although small features of the text. Written language must move linearly; Lively had to put one section before the

other. But I have no absolute, objective basis on which to assert even that the word *"there"* or the phrase "the lady's tummy button" was only uttered once. Even such an apparently obvious and visible difference as that between the iterative and the singulative can't be unambiguously and incontrovertibly attached to specific textual features but is invoked by context. Or, as is the case in *Moon Tiger*, evoked in order to be dismantled in the service of a theme.

Representing Speech (Inner and Voiced)

Characters' actual words and thoughts are of great interest to the narratologist because they're of such interest to actual readers. Depending on how she chooses to represent speech, the author can give readers the impression of directly encountering characters, of experiencing them through an objectivizing or a biasing filter, or of knowing no more about them than we know about strangers whose conversation we overhear on a bus. Characterization and the mimetic function are especially influenced by speech representation, but so is the reader's impression of narrating voices. Thus the representation of speech fulfills two linked functions. First, it provides an index of where the narrator and narratee are located within the narrating situation, how the narrating acts are situated with respect to the story. Second, it contributes to how actual readers experience a narrative's mimetic, thematic, and synthetic elements.

As with the temporal structuring of narrative, Genette has created the best system for discussing what he terms "the narrative of words," placing it in the context of how a narrative provides readers with information about both voiced speech and inner speech (including what is usually termed "stream of consciousness"). He distinguishes three "states" of speech, both voiced and inner; figure 7 is my synopsis of these states, with examples from *In the Labyrinth*. *Narrated speech* simply reports the contents of an utterance, using the narrator's words (*Narrative Discourse* 171). *Transposed speech* brings the reader somewhat closer to the words that were actually spoken (or thought) but at the same time "never gives the reader any guarantee—or above all any feeling—of literal fidelity to the words 'really' uttered: the narrator's presence is still too perceptible in the very syntax of the sentence for the speech to impose itself with the documentary autonomy of a quotation" (171). In this state Genette includes "free indirect speech": "the narrator takes on the speech of the character, or, if one prefers, the character speaks through the voice of the narrator," resulting in a merging of character's voice and narrator's voice (172, 174). (The term

Fig. 7. Speech States

NARRATED:	the narrator's words and syntax are used. "The soldier asked the boy where the street went."
TRANSPOSED:	the narrator's syntax is used, although some of the character's words may be included. "The soldier asked where did the street go?" A variation of transposed is *free indirect speech*, which drops the narrator's syntax from some sentences. *In the Labyrinth* sets up the embedded clause as a separate sentence: "Where did the street go?" (157)
REPORTED:	the character's actual words or thoughts are quoted using inquit signals (he thought, she said). "The soldier asked, 'Where does this street go?'" A variation of reported is *immediate*, which drops the inquit signals and thus has the effect of removing the mediating narrating voice. "Where does this street go?"

free indirect discourse, or FID, is more common; I prefer Genette's term because it transmutes more easily to inner *speech*.) The example in figure 7 makes clear by the verb form and the pronomial adjective that the question is not being rendered exactly from the perspective or with the words of the soldier, yet it also makes clear that the rendering is not simply a summary, as in the narrated-speech example.

In the third state, *reported speech*, the words actually spoken or thought are quoted (172–73). The quotation, however, does not have to occur within quotation marks. In the example, we are clearly being allowed to share the soldier's spatial and temporal perspective: it is this street right here, and we're concerned right now with where the street leads. Reported speech includes the form that is usually termed *interior monologue* but that Genette prefers to call *immediate speech*— "immediate" in the sense that no narrating voice is mediating the character's thoughts (173–74). Chatman elaborates, drawing on psychologists' distinction between verbalized mental activity (*cognition*) and nonverbalized (*perception*) (*Story and Discourse* 182). He says that interior monologue gives "direct free thought—self-reference by first person pronoun (if used), the present orientation of verb tenses, and the deletion of quotation marks" (185). It can represent either cognition or perception. The form is distinguished from "other representations of consciousness" in that the narrator is prohibited from explicitly stating "that a character is in fact thinking or perceiving. The words purport to be exactly and only those that pass through [the character's] mind, or their surrogates, if the thoughts are perceptions" (185). Genette's term *immediate speech* captures the lack of a mediating voice, as Chatman shows, but I want to make the term more descriptive by adding another adjective: immediate *inner* speech.

An attendant aspect of immediate inner speech, very important for assessing the narrating situation, is that it "preclude[s] any formal determination of the narrating instance which it constitutes" (*Narrative Discourse* 230). For a voice like the one Beckett creates in *The Unnameable* or that of Molly Bloom in the final chapter of Joyce's *Ulysses*, there is no way to assess narrative transmission. We can't say that The Unnameable's words are his (its?) written narrative or that a narrator has transcribed the monologue; we can only say that the effect is as if, and the convention is as if, we are being allowed to overhear this "stream of consciousness" (230).

Dorrit Cohn approaches the narration of mental events, including inner speech and nonverbalized perceptions, very much as does Genette. Although Genette's system is more general, Cohn's is worth describing because so many critics have found her term "psycho-narration" helpful and because Cohn frequently comments on the likely rhetorical effects of the various forms. Cohn's system may have had less impact than it could have had, however, because of a confusion between two types that I will discuss shortly. Parallel to Genette's "narrated speech," Cohn identifies *psychonarration*: "the narrator's discourse about a character's consciousness" (*Transparent Minds* 14). Of Cohn's terms, this one is most frequently used by critics, and it may also be the most powerful as a technique because it has the greatest reach in terms of subject matter. Cohn expands the definition to include discourse about the unconscious as well as about consciousness (140). Cohn also says that the stream-of-consciousness technique has frequently been misunderstood as providing a window into all levels of a character's mind; she says that actually it is "limited to the linguistic activity of the mind"—it can render *cognition* but not *perception*, in Chatman's terms. To represent the unconscious level, the novelist must provide the language rather than using the character's (56); the same is true if the novelist desires to represent perceptions, unless those perceptions are verbalized (internally) by the character. There's probably a gray area here. I think it's possible for readers to feel that not everything present in a chunk of stream-of-consciousness narrative has been consciously thought by the character but has been part of the character's preverbal awareness. I make this suggestion because the experiencing of narrative does not line up neatly within strict categories. As a general rule, however, Cohn is correct.

Paralleling Genette's *transposed speech* is Cohn's *narrated monologue*: "a character's mental discourse in the guise of the narrator's discourse" (*Transparent Minds* 14). This form reaches into the preverbal realm of mental experience (140); a character can have intuitions and sensations without verbalizing them, and the language of this form might use fragmented syntax, associations, and so forth to render for readers some sense of the experience of this realm. As with free indirect speech, which gives the effect of a merging of character's and narrator's voices, the narrated monologue superimposes those "two voices that are kept distinct in the other two forms"; it is the most complex and most flexible of the techniques available to an author for the rendering of consciousness (107). Furthermore, because of the level of the narrator's involvement, this form tends to "commit the narrator to attitudes of sympathy or irony" (117). The narrator's commitment, even if not literally expressed, can then function as an illocutionary act, implicating to a reader the desirable attitude—desirable, of course, from the perspective of the narrator but always potentially ironized by the implied author.

Brief sections of narrated monologue in several of Henry James's novels, such as *Washington Square* and *The Bostonians*, work exactly this way. In the former, the narrator notes of Dr. Sloper that "[i]t made him fairly grimace, in private, to think that a child of his should be *both ugly and overdressed*," and "he caught himself murmuring more than once that it was *a grievous pity his only child* was *a simpleton*" (13, 43—the emphasized words can be taken as Dr. Sloper's). The narrator comes across in these passages as indulgently critical of Dr. Sloper: the doctor may be guilty of bad taste in his choice of words, but after all, the daughter really is ugly, overdressed, and simple-minded. The implied author, however, can be construed as much more negative about both Sloper and the narrator. (For an extended discussion of this phenomenon, see Kearns, "Narrative Discourse.")

Cohn's *quoted monologue*, "a character's mental discourse" (*Transparent Minds* 14), is analogous to Genette's "reported [inner] speech." By definition this form is verbal ("mental discourse"), hence can only represent conscious mental phenomena (*Transparent Minds* 140). The rhetorical effect of this form depends on the overall narrating situation. In what Cohn terms "authorial" narrative (extra/heterodiegetic with external focalization), quoted monologues "tend to increase the distance that separates a narrator from his character," whereas in "figural" situations (using internal focalization), the novelist blends "the narrating and the figural voices" by means of the "omission or discreet use of inquit signals, espousal of the character's vantage point on the surrounding scene, omission of psycho-narration, syntactic ambiguity, or coloration of the narrator's language by a character's idiolect" (76). However, this description of quoted monologue in figural narrating situations sounds very similar to Cohn's description of narrated monologue; the two types may lead to the same rhetorical effect. In both there is a "blending" of the narrator's and character's perspectives, and both—not just narrated monologue—allow for "attitudes of sympathy or irony" on the narrator's part, attitudes that may influence how readers react to any or all of the other voice positions in the narrative. Thus the only clear difference seems to be that narrated monologue can reach into a character's preverbal awareness.

Because Genette's three "states" can be distinguished by syntax and diction, his system is preferable, but Cohn's analysis is valuable in pointing out that one of the most interesting effects in the narration of speech is the creation of uncertainty within the narrating situation. "Yet it is this same boy with the serious expression who had led him to the cafe run by the man who is not his father," I read in *In the Labyrinth* (Robbe-Grillet 157). The first half of this sentence, through "expression," could be either the soldier's mental discourse represented by the speech state Genette terms *immediate* (inner) speech or a narrator's report in the *transposed* form; because the novel is narrated in present tense, the syntaxes of narrator and character are for all practical purposes indistinguishable. The sentence's second half, because of the words "had led him," more likely comes from a narrator who is reporting on what the soldier remembers (the *narrated* state).

Either way I take the first half allows for the possibility that the soldier is mistaken about the boy's identity, but the two ways may yield different rhetorical effects. Reported speech can convey a fairly strong impression that the words correspond to the world represented by the text, unless such a correspondence is specifically contraindicated, and it also conveys the impression that the words are being rendered objectively, without shading by the narrating voice. If I take this small portion of the text as immediate (inner) speech, then I assume that the soldier really thought these words, and I have no obvious reason to doubt the truth of the statement that this *is* the same boy. Transposed speech can convey an attitude of sympathy or irony, with irony being more common in twentieth-century novels. If I take that same chunk of text in this way, I may sense that I'm being invited to collude with the narrator behind the soldier's back, because the soldier fails to see that this may not be the same boy. Because of other elements of this novel, especially the characterization of the soldier, such collusion actually leads me personally to an attitude of sympathetic, rather than superior or distanced, irony.

Both the example from *Washington Square* and this sentence from *In the Labyrinth* also illustrate F. K. Stanzel's point that "FID can induce in the reader a sense of ironic ambivalence or ambiguity, which has been described as the most universal sign of modernity in fiction" ("Free Indirect Discourse" 145). Stanzel's article usefully compares two approaches to transposed speech, which he terms the grammatical, represented by Ann Banfield's *Unspeakable Sentences*, and the narratological, represented by Monika Fludernik's *The Fictions of Language and the Languages of Fiction* ("Free Indirect Discourse" 148–49). The former approach, based on analysis of grammatical details such as verb forms and pronouns, does not account for what Stanzel rightly regards as "the most significant generic specificity of FID, its 'dual voice' character" (144, 150). The narratological or discourse-analysis approach preserves this trait and can demonstrate its presence in homodiegetic narratives in which a single narrator speaks "with two voices, the voice of the narrating self and the voice of the experiencing self," which "become distinguishable for the reader only when some distance in time or in mood separates them" (146).

Narratological analysis achieves this end by looking beyond the individual sentence to the larger context within which the putative transposed speech occurs ("Free Indirect Discourse" 149). Banfield's system works well enough, Stanzel notes, on the limited corpus of nineteenth- and twentieth-century heterodiegetic fictions, but not on homodiegetic (149—Stanzel's terms are "reflector mode" and "teller mode"). However, Stanzel mistakenly implies that grammatical analysis is not a very good tool. In *The Fictions of Language*, Fludernik actually puts the point more subtly than Stanzel indicates. On the one hand, she stresses the "theoretical relevance" of the "transgression," by FID, of the "otherwise neat separation line between the words of the text in the narrating process and the plot level of the fictional world" (*Fictions* 3). On the other hand, her entire book demonstrates that "[t]he various languages of fiction or narrative . . . are in fact fictions created by the infinite resources of language as literary style" (463); these "fictions" serve "discourse strategic requirements, whether these are brevity, poignancy, pithiness, verisimilitude, exaggeration, ironic over-characterization or, simply, truthful representation" (22).

Fludernik's extensive examples from oral narrative and other types show that "formal properties, namely such as those that have traditionally been called upon to distinguish between the (free) (in)direct discourse categories, are cognitively much less significant in the reading process than the manipulation of expressive signals that can claim to attract much higher readerly attention levels" (429). These signals are processed within a context of general cognitive "frames" such as actor/action/object/direction/instrument and object/state/value and of more specific "scripts" that are much more culture-dependent; this context enables a recipient to focus on relevant details, for example, those that indicate the presence of a voice (437, 447–48). Fludernik offers as an example the reader's sense of "double-voicing" in texts, for example, *Madame Bovary*: such passages "rely not on a linguistics of double voicing . . . but on the telling incompatibility between Emma's fantasies and the accepted cultural *episteme* regarding accepted standards of religiosity or the reality of love and passion" (440). Fludernik would not, however, say that the "formal properties" are irrelevant for critical analysis.

The Fictions of Language constitutes a massive defense of contextual analysis and an argument against the binary-system approach described by Stanzel. The best way to carry out this analysis is to preserve Genette's categories of speech states but to contextualize the grammatical distinctions that help to define the categories: grammatical information establishes unmarked cases, with marking occurring as a function of the structure of narrative transmission and within specific historical and cultural contexts of reading. From a strictly narratological standpoint, reported speech is directly related to mimesis and inversely related to diegesis; with narrated speech, these relationships are reversed. Lanser illustrates these various connections in a diagram adapted from Chatman.

Fig. 8. Diegesis, Mimesis, and Speech Representation

DIEGETIC DISCLOSURE
|
| ——— narrator's own discourse
| ——— psychonarration
| ——— indirect ("tagged") discourse
| ——— indirect free (narrated) discourse
| ——— direct thought, interior monologue
| ——— direct speech (monologue or dialogue)
| ——— written records (letters, journals, documents)
|
MIMETIC DISCOURSE

(*Narrative Act* 187)

This diagram establishes unmarked cases for the various speech states. All other things being equal, readers of a narrative will tend to take reported speeches (and thoughts) as really occurring within the narrative's world. They will also tend to take narrated and transposed discourse as the narrator's honest attempt to get it right, but it is the nature of these speech states to allow readers to question the narrator's credibility. These states are also more likely to serve a synthetic function, activating readers' sense of constructive intention.

Furthermore, as the examples from *In the Labyrinth* have shown and as Genette says, the theoretically distinct forms Genette outlines (and on which Lanser and Cohn elaborate) "will not be so clearly separated in the practice of texts" (*Narrative Discourse* 175). Especially in the case of transposed inner speech, it is often difficult to tell to what extent a character's thoughts are being "mediated" through a narrator. The example with which I opened this book, from *The Portrait of a Lady*, is such a one: "[t]here was a very straight path" (644). We can often recognize a sentence of transposed speech if we can change it into a first-person form simply by altering verbs, *and* if the change is plausibly something that the character would think. This sentence can be easily transformed: "Isabel thought, 'There is a very straight path'" (or perhaps "At last I have a very straight path"). Given the kind of person she is, this is a plausible thought. But "Isabel finally found herself facing a straight, definite path" is equally plausible, a transformation that emanates from a narrating voice who is summarizing Isabel's conclusion. James's sentence behaves more like one of those symmetrical designs that can be either of two shapes depending on where one focuses: a pair of faces turns into a vase turns into a pair of faces turns into a vase . . . until the viewer tires and looks away.

Transposed inner speech is most likely to exhibit this ambiguity, but the other two states can do so as well. Reported speech would seem to be clearly located within the world of the story: after all, the convention is that words within quotation marks were really spoken and that a character's immediate inner speech was really thought. However, many readers have wondered how it is that Ishmael can report characters' "soliloquies" in *Moby-Dick*, such as in chapter 123, "The Musket," when Starbuck stands outside Ahab's cabin with a musket leveled at the old man's sleeping head on the other side of the wall, or in chapter 37, "Sunset," in which Ahab is "sitting alone, and gazing out" of his cabin window. Of course the question is beside the point; *Moby-Dick* is not a realistic novel, so its narrating voice is under no obligation to explain sources or to preserve one style of presentation. Yet because so much of this novel *does* seem realistic, readers are not unreasonable in asking such questions and thereby foregrounding the discourse aspect. Likewise, if narrated speech is presented directly and without lexical or syntactical flourishes, it can come to seem an objective report of what a character actually said or felt, inviting no question about how the narrating voice might be selecting, emphasizing, or otherwise playing with readers' mimetic expectations. Any actual reader is potentially interested in both the story and the discourse of a narrative, interested in the mimetic surface (how realistic is a particular piece of spoken or inner speech?) but also in the narrating voice (how is this voice relating to me, to a narratee, and to the story?). There is no way to be sure about how a given reader will react to a given segment of speech.

As with the other topics discussed in this chapter, the history of speech representation in narration is important in establishing the conventions that shape current reading practices. Transposed speech shows the most interesting developments. Cohn's summary of the variety she calls narrated monologue cannot be improved upon. This form occurred occasionally in the eighteenth century, after which we see

> its upsurge in the nineteenth-century Realist novel, in rough correspondence with the rise of objective over obtrusive narrators, and of the inner over the outer scene; its expansion in the twentieth-century psychological novel, prompted by the unprecedented importance given to the language of consciousness . . . [The form's] evolution thus differs considerably from that of the quoted monologue and of psycho-narration: since the narrated monologue blurs the line between narration and quotation so dear to the old-fashioned authorial narrator, it makes its appearance rather late in the history of narrative genres. (*Transparent Minds* 112–13)

Cohn points out that Jane Austen was one of the pioneers in the extensive use of this form and that the later writers who worked so much with the "dramatic novel" (Flaubert, Zola, and James) "were the ones who re-introduced the subjectivity of private experience into the novel: this time not in terms of direct self-narration, but by imperceptibly integrating mental reactions into the neutral-objective report of actions, scenes, and spoken words" (113, 115).

A final point about speech representation is that it can serve, especially in the FID state, as "an ideal site within which to query authority and speaking, question traditional gender roles, and explore indeterminacies of gender" (Mezei, "Who Is Speaking Here?" 86). Mezei sees in *Emma, Howards End,* and *Mrs. Dalloway* "a struggle . . . between narrators and character-focalizers for control of the word, the text, and the reader's sympathy, a struggle paradigmatic of the conflict between conventional gender roles and of the resistance to traditional narrative authority in which a masterly male subject speaks for and over the female object of his gaze" (66). Mezei's key methodological move is to concentrate on the double-voiced quality of FID that results from the "ambiguous relation . . . between narrator and character-focalizer," a relation that allows for narratorial attitudes of both irony and sympathy toward the character-focalizer (68–69). These characteristics, in turn, put the actual reader in the position of deciding "where in all this the [actual] author stands" (72). Mezei's discussions of the three novels are not equally convincing; her references to "the reader" are monolithic, and at times she attributes, to characters, discourse that arguably emanates from a narrating voice. These flaws may stem from her belief that "FID offers a coded structure within the text to reveal authors' discomfort with conventional gender roles and forms of gender polarization" (71); I say "belief" because she fails to explain the details of this supposed code. Nevertheless, her article stands as a worthy example of the feminist narratology for which she calls in "Contextualizing Feminist Narratology."

In discussing the four topics of this chapter, I have taken the strong-contextualist position, insisting on the convention-bound nature of such questions as "What are this narrative's plot and theme?" and "Who is speaking?" and "What is the chronology of this story?" The approach of rhetorical narratology to these questions is best described as a combination of Genette's structuralism in *Narrative Discourse* and Lanser's contextualism in *Fictions of Authority*, within a framework of speech-act theory that mandates considering discourse features as illocutionary acts whose force is relatively proportional to their degree of marking and whose *relevance* results from the situational context of "experiencing a narrative." No scientific system can be developed for answering these apparently simple questions: although structuralist methodology can identify discourse features, marking is almost entirely determined by the context within which an audience receives a narrative. The role of context leads me to predict that even such highly marked narratives as *Written on the Body* and *In the Labyrinth* may come to seem unremarkable (hence will become unmarked) for a future generation of thoughtful, experienced readers, in the same way that *Washington Square* and *The Mill on the Floss* today seem so "natural." But I also expect that even these classic texts, if read with the attention usually paid to lyric poems, may turn out to contain heretofore unnoticed or unclassified discourse features.

5

Narrative Transmission, Readers' Scripts, and Illocutionary Acts

In this chapter I intend to provide an extended illustration of the primary methods and concepts I've been discussing, using two contemporary novels, *Written on the Body* (1992) by Jeanette Winterson and *Waiting for the Barbarians* (1980) by J. M. Coetzee. My purpose is to demonstrate that analyzing the structure of narrative transmission in a novel, while it cannot predict specific rhetorical effects, can identify and discriminate among textual elements that constitute illocutionary acts. Such analysis can identify at least some aspects about which an actual audience is likely to construct implicatures and, from them, to make judgments about thematic, mimetic, and synthetic elements, ultimately arriving at an interpretation of the novel. I've already used *Written on the Body* to exemplify several key points in the preceding chapters, especially the function of the ungendered narrator. Setting this novel against *Waiting for the Barbarians* and tracing how each novel may shape its readers' experiences during the actual time of reading will demonstrate once again the role of context in determining rhetorical effects. Additionally, the comparison yields some refinements in the tools of rhetorical narratology. Several of the elements discussed in the previous chapter will come up, notably theme, but the main purpose of this chapter is to explore and illustrate the rhetorical functioning of the structure of narrative transmission.

Written on the Body and *Waiting for the Barbarians* are both autodiegetic narratives. Both are relatively short, are open-ended, foreground sexual relationships, and have narrators who occasionally comment on the narrating itself. *Waiting for the Barbarians* is narrated simultaneously, *Written on the Body* retrospectively although with quite a bit of present-tense commentary. In spite of their similarities, the novels yield very different rhetorical effects. To dramatize this point I've selected the following pairs of sentences. (Ellipses are mine.)

See? Even here in this private place my syntax has fallen prey to the deceit. (*Written* 15)

Of the screaming which people afterward claim to have heard from the granary, I hear nothing. . . . what was once an outpost and then a fort on the frontier has grown into an agricultural settlement, a town of three thousand souls in which the noise of life, the noise that all these souls make on a warm summer evening, does not cease because somewhere someone is crying. (At a certain point I begin to plead my own cause.) (*Waiting* 4–5)

I can tell by now that you are wondering whether I can be trusted as a narrator. (*Written* 24)

Perhaps by the end of the winter . . . I will abandon the locutions of a civil servant with literary ambitions and begin to tell the truth. (*Waiting* 154)

I could understand how Elgin felt about his bed. Bathsheba had always insisted that we use their marital bed. . . . It was the violation of innocence I objected to, a bed should be a safe place. . . . I air my scruples now but it didn't stop me at the time. I do despise myself for that. (*Written* 83)

Where civilization entailed the corruption of barbarian virtues and the creation of a dependent people, I decided, I was opposed to civilization; and upon this resolution I based the conduct of my administration. (I say this who now keep a barbarian girl for my bed!) (*Waiting* 38)

Syntax and diction reveal the narrator of *Waiting for the Barbarians* to be the more formal, perhaps the more conventionally literary, of the two. But as locutions, the two items of each pair convey a similar mimetic characteristic: a realization that the human tendency to deceive oneself can manifest itself without conscious control (first pair), an awareness of a conscious tendency to deceive a probable or possible audience (second pair), a tendency to loathe one's self (third pair). When these sentences are placed within each novel's structure of narrative transmission, however, their differences as illocutions become apparent, as I'll show in the course of this chapter.

My discussion emphasizes the fact that the readings I offer are indeed my own; they don't emanate from some transcendental critical voice. James Phelan points out that audience-oriented criticism typically presents itself either as relatively objective and text-centered or as somewhat "confessional," with the critic "call[ing] attention to his subjectivity" ("Present Tense Narration" 232–33). Phelan leans toward the former "more traditional" practice; I lean toward the latter. My reasons, like Phelan's, are rhetorical: I want to stress the subjective and limited nature of actual applications of rhetorical narratology and honor these two novels, to acknowledge their power in a direct and personal way. The fact is, these novels selected me; their usefulness for my project followed from rather than preceded my desire to write about them. A second important fact is that I've recently taught both, although in courses that are almost polar opposites (*Waiting for the Barbarians* in sophomore general education, *Written on the Body* in senior special topics). Thus my personal responses have been influenced and somewhat validated by these reading communities, even though mine was the dominant voice in each.

I'm going to discuss my reading of each novel using present tense except when describing my prereading mindset. Each "reading" is actually a composite of several past readings; I didn't keep a log of my initial responses, nor can I ignore later responses. So I'm presenting a fictionalized, "simultaneous" narrative about each reading, the point being to thematize the usefulness of my approach. Yet I'm being as true as I can to my first readings, and I'm trying not to create an ideal reader as the protagonist of my narratives. I'm sure that this rhetoric of presentation will falter in places, for which lapses I ask my actual reader's indulgence. We're all corrupted.

As I explained in earlier portions of this book, the *narrating situation* is determined by considering whether the narrative is set up like a "real-world narrative display text." That is, does the narrating voice observe the cooperative principle (CP), or can this principle be hyperprotected, is the narrative tellable, and do the ur-conventions apply? The purpose of this display text is to stimulate in readers an imaginative, affective, and evaluative involvement leading to an interpretation. These characteristics define the unmarked case for the novel genre; any variation from them constitutes a case that is marked (noticed) by readers. The narrating situation also includes aspects of how the story is ostensibly getting told that are typically lumped under point of view. Is the narrative ostensibly spoken or written, reflective or simultaneous, crafted or spontaneous? Is the narrator a character in the story or not? A participant in the story's world or not?

The *structure of narrative transmission* is more complicated. To analyze this structure, I go beyond the narrating situation to consider the functions served by the narrating voice(s) in addition to narrating, the prominence of and the roles played by other voice positions (extrafictional voice, implied author, narratee, focalizer, authorial reader), and the extent to which the CP is preserved or violated by these voice positions. The structure of narrative transmission has an important temporal dimension: some voice and audience positions will be prominent when a reader first picks up a book, others may dominate during the body of the reading, and still others are prominent once the reading nears completion. I organize my discussion of *Waiting for the Barbarians* and *Written on the Body* according to these three main temporal divisions.

Beginnings: Extratextual Material and the Extrafictional Voice

As explained in chapter 1, rhetorical narratology emphasizes that most if not all readers approach narratives with some fairly clear expectations and procedures—"scripts"—that vary from reader to reader but have some basic similarities. These scripts are activated by the context within which a narrative is encountered and that determines the "frames of reference" that will delimit scripts. The frame for narrative consists of display text, ur-conventions (except heteroglossia), and narrativity (the essential component here being the complicating action) as required elements, and it elicits the question "Fictional or factual?" It also establishes the unmarked cases. Someone who picks up a book labeled "novel" will unthinkingly activate that script and so will expect these narrative-frame elements plus the ur-convention of heteroglossia and the experience of mediacy. This basic, shared script will not only set a reader's expectations but will order them temporally. The expectations are not part of a reader's conscious mental processes, although a reader can become conscious of them. Teun Van Dijk and Walter Kintsch point out that "the rules of linguistic processing are no more available to introspection at the text level than they are at the level of syntactic or phonological analyses" (75), but at the level of frames and scripts, these "rules" *can* be thought about.

In the following discussions and illustrations of scripts, I emphasize the temporal dimension of processing, but I'm well aware that while my language has to move along a single line, the experiences of a reader occur on many planes simultaneously. Susan Stanford Friedman develops the metaphor of spatialization to describe "a strategy for reading narrative." According to Friedman, a narrative may be conceived of as containing both a horizontal dimension—roughly, reading as narrating audience, reading for the story—and a vertical dimension, along which lie "historical, literary, and psychic intertextualities" (14, 19). These intertextualities "initiate . . . dialogic narratives 'told' by the reader in collusion with a writer who inscribes them in the text consciously or unconsciously" (19–20). While the vertical dimension as Friedman describes it may apply more to academic than to general readers, these intertextualities or others like them certainly play a role in the reading experience. I'm inclined to say that insofar as they are demonstrably present in or implicated by the narrative text, or if a reader imports them into the experience and attributes them to the author, they can be discussed as contributing to the structure of narrative transmission. Otherwise they lie outside my scope here.

In this novel-reading script, then, one of the first activities a reader will engage in is quickly and roughly to infer an extrafictional voice and an implied author on the basis of impressions gathered from the physical object itself. I term these impressions *extratextual* because they derive from material other than the text of the narrative, although they still have to do with the physical context that "contains" the narrative text (a printed book, a stage, etc.). One such impression is that both novels are contemporary. Each of my copies also contains a biographical sketch before the story actually begins, so if I read the prefatory matter I'll know in advance that Winterson is British and now lives in London, that Coetzee is a South African. Because the opening paragraphs give me no reasons not to do so, I automatically attach the same location, era, and gender to the narrating voices, although because I'm an experienced reader, I can set aside these characteristics just as easily.

A second field also provides impressions that help define for me the extrafictional voice and influence my sense of the implied author—the front and back covers. My paperback copies of both novels carry snippets of reviewers' prose on the front covers, phrases such as "the nature of the human heart" (*Written on the Body*) and "the nerve-centre of being" (*Waiting for the Barbarians*) that as a practiced reader I recognize to be freighted with evaluations: these are *serious* books that will teach me something, that may even change my life. More of the same is present on the back covers, along with the following unattributed descriptions:

For decades the Magistrate has run the affairs of a tiny frontier settlement, ignoring the impending war between the barbarians and the Empire whose servant he is. When interrogation experts arrive, however, he finds himself jolted into sympathy with their victims—until their barbarous treatment of prisoners of war finally pushes him into a quixotic act of rebellion, and thus into imprisonment as an enemy of the state.

Waiting for the Barbarians, J. M. Coetzee's second prize-winning novel, is an allegory of the war between oppressor and oppressed. It is a disturbing tour de force. The Magistrate is not simply a man living through a crisis of conscience in an obscure place in remote times; his situation is that of all men living in unbearable complicity with regimes that elevate their own survival above justice and decency.

With the same stylistic daring and emotional energy that have made her one of England's most celebrated young writers, Jeanette Winterson has written her most beguilingly seductive novel to date.

The narrator of *Written on the Body* has neither name nor gender; the beloved is a married woman. And as Winterson chronicles their consuming affair, she compels us to see love stripped of clichés and categories, as a phenomenon as visceral as blood and organs, bone and tissue—and as strange as an undiscovered continent.

Because I encountered both novels outside of any formal academic context (*Written on the Body* was recommended by a friend, and *Waiting for the Barbarians* was on the list of a reading group I participated in), I was perfectly willing to accept these descriptions as pertinent to my reading experience. In their way, they are as conventionalized as used-car ads. Each places its author in contemporary literary culture (both are important, but Winterson belongs to a later literary generation than Coetzee). Each also tells me how to categorize the book and what to expect from the reading experience: both are important and "disturbing," significant for our time but also carrying universal relevance. *Waiting for the Barbarians* is "not simply" about an individual's "crisis of conscience" but is an "allegory," while *Written on the Body* will "compel us"—all thoughtful, open-minded readers—to see something new about one of the emotions we probably thought we knew well. It's been a long time since I first read the novels, so I can't remember exactly what these descriptions led me to expect, and in any case, as I've said, such expectations are highly provisional and indefinite. But the descriptions do forecast strong, although perhaps veiled, thematic elements; they can position readers to assume that the authors think deeply and feel passionately and to be willing to apply the practice of hyperprotecting the CP. Readers probably also feel authorized to attribute to the implied author of *Waiting for the Barbarians* a strong moral and political sense, whereas the implied author of *Written on the Body* may be expected to be mainly concerned with the details of physical passion (love is "a phenomenon as visceral as blood and organs"). These expectations and reactions are very similar to what I felt; at this distance in time I can't say they're identical—but close enough.

One additional factor deserves mention about the situational context within which I began *Written on the Body*—my knowledge that Winterson is lesbian in her sexual orientation. As I explained in chapter 4, I read this novel with a fairly common heterosexual default condition: I'll take a sexual relationship as heterosexual unless told otherwise, and I'll expect to be able to attach not only a sex but a gender to each person involved in the relationship. Interestingly, my knowledge of Winterson's own orientation did not influence my construction of the implied author *or* of the narrator. I began the novel knowing that Winterson intended to dramatize sexual politics, but this purpose is so clear from the novel's opening paragraphs that I needed no external pressure. Nor could I simplistically equate author and autodiegetic narrator, partly because I know that such an equation is inconsistent with good critical-reading practice, and partly because my default assumption led me to at first read the narrator as male. By the time I encountered textual details suggesting that the narrator could be female, I was already in the habit of separating author and narrator. This non-influence of an aspect of the author's life on my reading practice *may* count as a small piece of evidence for my earlier claim that the extra-textual elements of author's gender, geographical location, and tempo-ral location are more important than other elements in how I con-struct the novel's voice positions.

Once I begin each narrative, my reading script directs me to turn my attention at least temporarily from the extrafictional voice and im-plied author to the actual narrating voice, which is my most immedi-ate guide through the fictional world. Here is each opening:

I have never seen anything like it: two little discs of glass suspended in front of his eyes in loops of wire. Is he blind? I could understand it if he wanted to hide blind eyes. But he is not blind. The discs are dark, they look opaque from the outside, but he can see through them. He tells me they are a new invention. (*Waiting* 1)

Why is the measure of love loss?

It hasn't rained for three months. The trees are prospecting underground, sending reserves of roots into the dry ground, roots like razors to open any ar-tery water-fat.

The grapes have withered on the vine. What should be plump and firm, re-sisting the touch to give itself in the mouth, is spongy and blistered. Not this year the pleasure of rolling blue grapes between finger and thumb juicing my palm with musk. Even the wasps avoid the thin brown dribble. Even the wasps this year. It was not always so. (*Written* 9)

When I make the transition from the extratextual material to the opening of each narrative, I immediately and automatically compare the narrating voice to the extrafictional voice, to determine whether I'm dealing with a marked or an unmarked case of the relationship be-tween these voices. For *Written on the Body*, the relationship is un-marked, whereas for *Waiting for the Barbarians* it is marked, a differ-ence that will have important consequences for the illocutionary effects of utterances that are otherwise similar between the two novels. Each unattributed description characterizes its author as con-cerned, thoughtful, and contemporary. These traits are consistent with the narrating voices I encounter in the openings, so I can feel fairly sure that there will not arise huge differences *in values* between each novel's narrating voice and implied author. On the other hand, the narrator of *Waiting for the Barbarians* clearly does not belong to the later twentieth century (sunglasses are "a new invention"). So for this novel an additional element of my script is activated: I recognize that an ironic reading experience may be explicitly offered by the text. I make this adjustment easily, although the extratextual material, as I said, led me to expect identity rather than difference, because as a practiced reader I know that such irony is common. An ironic reading of *Written on the Body* is not precluded by the apparent similarity between the two voices, but neither do I expect it.

The other expectation my script directs me to verify at this point in the reading is that the narrative is tellable, which I do by noticing that the first several sentences establish enigmas. *Written on the Body* raises one explicit enigma ("Why is the measure of love loss?") and one implicit (What is the connection between this dry year and the loss of love?). Both are equally present for narrating and authorial audiences, a feature that has the effect of reducing or even eliminating the potential distinction between the two audience positions; this effect means that both the authorial audience and actual readers can feel that the novel's world is identical to our own. (Rabinowitz would say, and I agree, that such identification only happens if actual readers feel that they share the particular "corruptions" of this authorial audience. Rabinowitz defines "authorial audience" as the "*corrupted* reader this particular author wrote for," a reader with specifiable "beliefs, engagements, commitments, prejudices, and stampedings of pity and terror" [*Before Reading* 26].) Also contributing to reducing this distinction is the apparent lack of distance between extrafictional and narrating voices. The opening of *Waiting for the Barbarians* raises one enigma located strictly within the *world* of the story and hence present for a narrating audience (who is "he"?), but a second is present only for an authorial audience (when and where does the story take place?).

Each beginning also preserves the CP, especially the requirement that a speaker tell everything that is necessary but no more than is relevant. "He" is identified two paragraphs later as Colonel Joll, "from the Third Bureau" (*Waiting* 2); this resolution of one enigma is probably sufficient to convince most readers that other questions will likewise be answered in due course, such as why this man wants to hide his eyes. I feel comfortable knowing that this narrator is qualified— has a sense of how to tell a story. The two enigmas of *Written on the Body* begin to be resolved immediately in the next paragraph: "I am thinking of a certain September: Wood pigeon Red Admiral Yellow Harvest Orange Night. You said, 'I love you.' Why is it that the most unoriginal thing we can say to one another is still the thing we long to hear? 'I love you' is always a quotation" (9). And here too, another enigma immediately arises: who is this "you"?

Both of these beginnings activate my script for the unmarked case of fictional narrative, as defined by speech-act theory: each demonstrates tellability; each preserves the CP by using narrators who know that they're telling stories and thus need to meet certain expectations on the part of their audiences; each enables me easily to invoke hyper-protection. For example, the anger of the narrator of *Written on the Body* and the lack of connection between that opening sentence and the following description of drought implicate that the narrator is at least distraught, perhaps internally conflicted. Each opening adheres to the ur-conventions. I can easily engage in authorial reading, because both novels quickly reveal themselves to be autodiegetic in terms of the relationship between the narrator and the world of the story and thus enable me to assume that an author has constructed this relationship for me to view from the outside. My expectation of progression is met, due to the presence of instabilities between characters (Joll and the narrator, "you" and the narrator) as well as a possible instability within the narrator of *Written on the Body*; tension may also exist between authorial and narrating audiences in *Waiting for the Barbarians*, created by the impossibility of identifying the narrator with the extrafictional voice. Likewise, both novels can be naturalized; although the temporal setting of *Waiting for the Barbarians* is not clear, nothing about the opening paragraphs of either novel causes me to doubt that I'm in the presence of a coherent, human, although perhaps hypothetical, world. I'm able automatically to apply the codes of action, character, and culture (Barthes's proairetic, semic, and referential codes): the characters, their interactions, and the contexts for their interactions are comprehensible.

Few if any readers would consciously work through the script I've just described: first shaping a sense of the extrafictional voice by studying a book's cover, title page, and so forth, then comparing this voice to that of the narrator, all while determining whether the narrating situations of these novels are like those of "real-world narrative display texts" and whether the ur-conventions hold. But the elements of this script help define the expertise that readers automatically apply in beginning a novel. Readers differ in their willingness to tolerate deviations from the codes, in their sensitivity to instabilities and tensions, and so forth, but the elements themselves are part of every reader's script—applied at different times and with different degrees of intensity, but present for and available to all. The elements help readers establish the parameters and activate the conventions—although not on a fully conscious level—that will shape the bulk of their encounter with a narrative.

To move farther along in the reading script, from the first few minutes to the hours that are spent reading the body of the narrative, is to move into less defined territory. The ability to describe this territory probably falls off in precision at a geometric rate, minute by minute. I feel somewhat like Tristram Shandy trying to narrate a single day in his life: I've written eight or ten pages and am still only a few minutes into the script. However, it is possible to be somewhat precise about how each of these novels establishes and develops discourse tensions that, as illocutionary acts, serve thematic purposes. This is the realm in which the differences in structure of narrative transmission between the two novels become most interesting, creating differences in rhetorical effect between locutions that seem similar, such as those I quoted at the beginning of this chapter.

Middles and Endings: *Waiting for the Barbarians*

Very quickly after I begin the narrative of *Waiting for the Barbarians*, my focus shifts from the extrafictional voice and the implied author to the narrating voice, because my script calls for me to locate myself as a reader in relationship to how that voice aligns itself with a narratee, the narrating audience, and the authorial audience and to identify one of those alignments as dominant in my reading process. Because the novel lacks a narratee or specified narrating audience and because the narrating voice is autodiegetic, I at first feel that I'm serving as the narrating audience, yet when I turn my critical attention to what I'm being told and not told, I find myself preferring to read authorially—*and* I believe that the novel's structure of narrative transmission is leading me to do so. To read primarily as a member of the narrating audience, I would need to feel as if I were overhearing someone's private monologue, when in fact I feel myself listening to a plea cast with an eye to history's verdict—my verdict, since I'm located roughly a century later than the ostensible temporal setting of the story.

The narrating audience, by definition, receives as "really happening" the magistrate's pleas and other self-conscious speech acts, such as setting off in quotation marks certain of his thoughts ("I think: 'There has been something staring me in the face, and still I do not see it'" [*Waiting* 155]), his doubts and reflections, as well as his actual narrating. The magistrate's first plea is to Colonel Joll on behalf of the two prisoners the colonel wants to interrogate: "I grow conscious that I am pleading" (4). Almost immediately, however, he remarks parenthetically, "At a certain point I begin to plead my own cause" (5). These self-aware statements plausibly emanate from "a civil servant with literary ambitions," as he characterizes himself near the end (154); they've been crafted for public delivery. Early on, the magistrate puts both his narrating problem and his ethical problem succinctly:

I know somewhat too much; and from this knowledge, once one has been infected, there seems to be no recovering. I ought never to have taken my lantern to see what was going on in the hut by the granary. On the other hand, there was no way, once I had picked up the lantern, for me to put it down again. The knot loops in upon itself; I cannot find the end. (21)

The narrating audience by definition takes this statement at face value and does not ask whether the magistrate is really trying to "find the end" or is trying in the right places. In particular, the narrating audience accepts the magistrate's belief that his problems began when he went out that night with his lantern, rather than taking his cue from Colonel Joll and keeping his eyes hooded. The magistrate's honesty, his admitted confusion, and his willingness to say harsh things about himself are engaging characteristics, the sort that can win the sympathy of a narrating audience.

In fact, these characteristics stand as an example of why the concept of narrating audience is theoretically necessary. The theory of speech acts assumes that all interesting human discourse is motivated by the need or desire to communicate. The magistrate needs a reason, a motivation, for remarking on his own pleading, for pointing out that he knows "somewhat too much." He never identifies the audience he expects, but he clearly expects one and is performing for their benefit, knowing that they will follow the CP and attempt to believe him and trust his narrative skill—knowing that they will share or at least accept his "corruptions."

However, the authorial audience is led to a more critical position by aspects of the structure of narrative transmission: lacunae in the magistrate's assessment of the meaning of his story, the highly wrought, literary quality of some of his language, and the nonnarrating functions served by the narrating, not to mention the magistrate's lack of reference to the history of empire building in "our" world. The narrating audience sees the magistrate honestly trying to find the end of that knot; the authorial audience, because its script includes an orientation to thematic and synthetic aspects, is going to recognize that the problem of "the knot" is implicated in the narrating itself. It will do so because of the structure of narrative transmission. Authorially, I become sensitive very quickly to tensions between the narrating-audience and authorial-audience positions. This aspect has become marked in my experience of the novel, so that my progression through the novel is not just stimulated by instabilities (between and within characters) but also by the tensions.

One of the narrative's most important yet most subtle gaps is the lack of any indication that dreams—even recurrent dreams—signify; the magistrate occasionally connects several dreams and recognizes repeated motifs, but he never wonders why he is dreaming these things or what the dreams mean. The narrating audience, by definition, shares this "corruption." The authorial audience, however, has been differently "corrupted" by twentieth-century psychology and could hardly construct a plausible intention on the part of the implied author that does not attach both mimetic and thematic significance to the dreams. Two dreams occur before the magistrate meets the barbarian girl. There is a snow-filled square in which children are building a snowcastle; also present is a girl, "perhaps not even a child," with her back toward him: "I try to imagine the face between the petals of her peaked hood but cannot" (*Waiting* 9–10). The second dream:

I sleep, wake to another round of dance-music from the square, fall asleep again, and dream of a body lying spread on its back, a wealth of pubic hair glistening liquid black and gold across the belly, up the loins, and down like an arrow into the furrow of the legs. When I stretch out a hand to brush the hair it begins to writhe. It is not hair but bees clustered densely atop one another: honey-drenched, sticky, they crawl out of the furrow and fan their wings. (13)

The magistrate dreams while he's together with the barbarian girl; he can't remember the dreams, but he wonders if "the dream of the hooded child building the snowcastle has been coming back" (48). Then later he does remember that it is this dream: "The dream has taken root. Night after night I return to the waste of the snowswept square, trudging towards the figure at its centre, reconfirming each time that the town she is building is empty of life" (53). Earlier, Star has told him that he pushed her out of bed in his sleep and told her to go away, but she has tried to lessen the potential impact of this information by also telling him that "[w]e cannot help our dreams or what we do in our sleep" (23). Her comment may be taken as defining the position of the narrating audience, but as a member of the authorial audience I know that dreams are important. Reading authorially, I assume that every detail in the novel contributes to constructive intention; this set of lapses constitutes an *implicature* that the magistrate's responsibility for the atrocities extends beyond just being a civil servant of the Empire. The strength of this implicature depends on my being able to position myself authorially and being able to hold that position consistently.

The effect would probably not be as strong had Coetzee introduced the kind of rhetorical "noise" present in *Written on the Body*—the complicated dance around the aspect of the marking of the identification between actual author and narrator. As I noted earlier, both narrators tend to deceive both themselves and their intradiegetic audiences, but in *Written on the Body* the deception has greater consequences for interpretation because the boundary between intra- and extradiegetic is more difficult to establish: if I can't say for sure that Winterson is not the narrator, then I can't wholeheartedly enter into the unwritten contract to hyperprotect the CP. Recognizing this dynamic relationship has the pedagogical benefit of helping to account for the reaction of some students that it is Winterson who is deceiving, who perhaps can't be "trusted as a narrator."

The magistrate's literary language contributes to the same rhetorical effects that the dreams do, enhancing the mimetic quality of the narrating while also implicating a thematic connection between how a person uses language and uses people. In one especially revealing passage the magistrate is attempting to understand why he is drawn to this particular girl and what role her disfigurements play in the attraction:

I am with her not for whatever raptures she may promise or yield but for other reasons, which remain as obscure to me as ever. Except that it has not escaped me that in bed in the dark the marks her torturers have left upon her, the twisted feet, the half-blind eyes, are easily forgotten. Is it then the case that it is the whole woman I want, that my pleasure in her is spoiled until those marks on her are erased and she is restored to herself; or is it the case (I am not stupid, let me say these things) that it is the marks on her which drew me to her but which, to my disappointment, I find do not go deep enough? . . . "I must be tired," I think. "Or perhaps whatever can be articulated is falsely put." My lips move, silently composing and recomposing the words. "Or perhaps it is the case that only that which has not been articulated has to be lived through." I stare at this last proposition without detecting any answering movement in myself toward assent or dissent. The words grow more and more opaque before me; soon they have lost all meaning. (*Waiting* 64–65)

Here the magistrate moves from what seems an honest attempt to investigate his motives, which climaxes in the parenthetical insertion, to acts of composing that take his focus from the girl to words that he manipulates as self-consciously as he manipulated her body. He seems to lull himself into a moral stupor with this verbal manipulation, in the same way that bathing the girl's feet causes him to sink into sleep. He fails to realize that to reformulate and stare at the proposition is to turn away from an honest inquiry into himself. Of course the words lose meaning; they're not connected with the tangible reality of his life.

Similarly, when the magistrate does commit his unquestionably heroic acts, he describes them with an eye for literary effect, almost as if he hopes the written record will exonerate his earlier complicity. Hearing a commotion while in his cell, he lets himself out, sees the prisoners being led into the square by Colonel Joll, and this time decides to act rather than to turn away. His description of his realization is telling: "I cannot save the prisoners, therefore let me save myself. Let it at the very least be said, if it ever comes to be said, if there is ever anyone in some remote future interested to know the way we lived, that in this farthest outpost of the Empire of light there existed one man who in his heart was not a barbarian" (104). This "saving" of himself exists on two realms simultaneously, the realm of action and the realm of report on the action; he saves himself both by trying to stop the abuse and by putting his action into words. The narrating audience takes the magistrate's utterances at face value, and many actual readers may do the same, because he can be so engaging as a voice—he seems alive, vital, courageous. But saving himself in order to try to secure a favorable verdict from future historians is not wholly admirable. Such, at least, is a plausible implicature that I can reach, authorially, on the basis of the language. This is not to deny that he really does prevent what would have been the most perverse abuse, Joll's attempt to have a child use a hammer on one of the prisoners; the magistrate's motives may not be entirely admirable, but the outcome is.

These tensions between narrating and authorial audiences serve a thematic function: will the magistrate ever realize that, like the Empire whose servant he has been, he is using words to block rather than engage with some of the realities of his life? Will he, that is, realize that the distinction between "barbaric" and "civilized" relates to one's private discourse as well as to public policies and actions? The barbarian girl's silences, her unwillingness to talk about being tortured, her failure to express to him her unhappiness, her sensitivity to being termed an animal—these mimetically plausible details contrast with the magistrate's verbosity in an ironic, thematically charged counterpoint.

All practiced readers probably have, as part of their script, an awareness that a narrating voice can serve nonnarrating functions and that these functions engage them with the novel's mimetic, thematic, and synthetic elements by emphasizing the basic aspects of display and tellability. In addition to narrating, the narrator can direct attention to the narrative text; communicate to the narratee; give testimony that establishes an affective, moral, or intellectual relationship to the story; and comment ideologically (in a way that seems to carry authorial authority). In *Waiting for the Barbarians*, the most important of these nonnarrating functions are the *testimonial* and the *ideological*. Because there is no narratee, the communicating function is not applicable; the directing function occurs infrequently, as in the previously quoted "My lips move, silently composing and recomposing the words."

The magistrate often "testifies to" either his own conflicting emotions or his inability to understand those emotions; much of his "pleading" falls into one of these categories. The presence of this testimonial function contributes to the book's powerful irony by sensitizing actual readers to the issues about which the magistrate pleads even while within the narrative it serves the mimetic purpose of making the narrating seem lifelike. In one important passage he seems to acknowledge his complicity, but the acknowledgment remains questioning and general:

> For I was not, as I liked to think, the indulgent pleasure-loving opposite of the cold rigid Colonel. I was the lie that Empire tells itself when times are easy, he the truth that Empire tells when harsh winds blow. Two sides of imperial rule, no more, no less. But I temporized, I looked around this obscure frontier . . . and I said to myself "Be patient, one of these days he will go away . . ." Thus I seduced myself, taking one of the many wrong turnings I have taken on a road that looks true but has delivered me into the heart of a labyrinth. (135)

Here the magistrate implies that his self-seduction only began with the arrival of Colonel Joll: "[b]ut I temporized" while waiting for him to leave. An earlier event raises questions about this explicit testimony. When he shows Colonel Joll the first two prisoners, a boy and an old man who were taken after one of the barbarians' usual stock raids, they have already been beaten. He expresses surprise at finding them thus, but why should he: the system is *his* responsibility. And perhaps the surprise was only an act for the colonel's benefit; the text allows this interpretation.

Of course it's the authorial audience who is aware of these particular half-truths, not the narrating audience; the latter accepts at face value the narrator's confessions and testimonials. Likewise, the authorial audience, not the narrating, receives the ideological function served by the magistrate's statement that "[t]he distance between myself and [the girl's] torturers, I realize, is negligible" (27). On the surface, this is an admirable admission of his failings, his complicity. Yet, authorially, I see that the extent of his complicity is lost on him. "The knot" actually extends far into the past, well before the arrival of Colonel Joll. It includes the magistrate's decision not to reside in the "attractive villa with geraniums in the windows which falls to the lot of the civil magistrate" but in the apartment near the barracks, where the "military commandant" would reside if this town had one (21). It includes his having acted on what he was told as a younger man: "[i]f there was anything to be envied in a posting to the frontier, my friends told me, it was the easy morals of the oases, the long scented summer evenings, the complaisant sloe-eyed women. For years I wore the well-fed look of a prize boar" (45). It surely also includes his having punished a young man for deserting. He refers to the young man "waiting to hear his punishment," notes that "[a]fter lecturing him I sentenced him," and reports that the young man "accepted the sentence without murmur"

(138–39). But what was the sentence? Desertion can be punished by death; is this why the magistrate comments, "I remember the uneasy shame I felt on days like that" (139)? All of these events are part of the beginning of the knot, but the memories don't move him toward an awareness of the life-long history of his complicity. As a member of the authorial audience, I feel a tension with the narrating audience, because of this longer implicated scope of the magistrate's statement about negligible distance.

The same interplay of voice and audience positions is at work in the magistrate's "long-meditated" lesson to Colonel Joll, delivered as the latter is fleeing after his expeditionary force has been decimated by the barbarians: "[t]he crime that is latent in us we must inflict on ourselves" (146). It's also present in the magistrate's statement that he arrived long ago at certain principles that he is only now violating: "[w]here civilization entailed the corruption of barbarian virtues and the creation of a dependent people, I decided, I was opposed to civilization; and upon this resolution I based the conduct of my administration. *(I say this who now keep a barbarian girl for my bed!)*" (38, emphasis added). This passage demonstrates both the testimonial and the ideological functions. The "aside" character of the parenthetical remark heightens the impression of an honest realization, while the link between dependency and corruption has the sort of thematic power that would cause most readers to attribute it to an implied author, to a constructive intention. The narrating audience is invited to believe that the magistrate's regime differed significantly from the one Colonel Joll represents. Yet the "conduct of his administration" included usurping the perquisites of military commander and using the whole town as his personal bordello, exactly the kind of corruption he says he opposed.

I claim that the ideological function is present in these passages partly because as a late-twentieth-century reader I can't imagine Coetzee intending otherwise than for me to regard the magistrate even more critically than he regards himself. A second basis is my construction of the extrafictional voice from the novel's covers and prefatory material. This is an important point. As a principled reader, I want to have some kind of objective basis for my sense that a text is calling my attention to one or another ideologically charged issue; I don't want to be guilty of forcing on the text a reading that only reflects who I am. A key basis, I argue, is the part of the material object external to the narrative; this part helps establish the situational context within which I arrive at implicatures. A novel with no cover or introductory pages, no date, no author's name might make a powerful appeal to my beliefs and values, but it would be more difficult for me to say, of a given passage, "I'm pretty sure that the author intends me to recognize her voice as speaking through this passage"—or to say this in a way that would gain the assent of other principled readers. This lack of certitude is one of the consequences, but also one of the pleasures, of the novel form, which has been continually reinventing itself. Only in the speech-act context can any certitude be found: we fundamentally assume that a novel is a narrative display text whose purpose is to stimulate an imaginative, affective, and evaluative involvement and that this purpose can be attached to a human being who created the text. As the reader of a novel (or of any other narrative that engages more than the necessary minimum of narrativity), I'm seeking a sense of transaction.

In sum, the voice and audience positions of *Waiting for the Barbarians*, as well as the extranarrative functions performed by the narrating voice, create tensions, thus contributing in two ways to my experience of progression. Synthetically, the novel's existence as a fictional narrative, a created object, is emphasized by a pattern in the narrator's omissions that I, a critical reader, can take as revealing a constructive intention on the part of the author. These omissions constitute illocutionary acts whose intended audience is authorial. They add another layer of complexity to the question of what constitutes barbaric and civilized behavior: to what extent do the magistrate's heroic actions redeem his life-long service to the Empire, his willingness to profit from what seem to be loose frontier morals, and his conflation of civil and military authority? I care about these questions as much as I do, however, more because of the novel's strong mimetic elements; the synthetic aspect involves me intellectually rather than emotionally. Most students I've worked with on this novel react more or less the way I do: they find the magistrate quite real even though they can't situate him in a specific country and decade. While we can talk about the magistrate as Everyman and his story as a parable or allegory, he makes his strongest impression as a real person. He matters as a moral being—in the same way, I might add, that the nameless soldier of *In the Labyrinth* matters.

While my desire to interpret a narrative is present throughout the reading process, it becomes most prominent in the script at the end of this process, when I ask, "What is the governing constructive intention of this story I've been involved with?" This is the time when considerations of theme come to the fore, when I expect tensions to resolve themselves, when the narrating voice's ideological, testimonial, directing, and communicating functions can have their greatest impact as illocutionary acts. Rhetorical narratology leads me to hypothesize that these functions are more likely to be noticed near the end than in the middle, especially in a novel that is not strictly plot-driven.

All good readers play the narrating-audience role for substantial portions of a narrative (becoming, as we all say, "lost in the story"), but when a reader sees that only a few pages are left, this role fades—the fictional world *will* cease to exist. Thus it's plausible that readers direct their attention more to thematic issues and distance themselves from the fictional world, although they probably don't do so consciously. The nonnarrating functions facilitate this shift, hence figure more prominently in one's end-of-novel script.

In the final paragraph of *Waiting for the Barbarians*, part of what has been dreamed becomes reality. "Inexplicably joyful," the magistrate approaches a group of children who are building a snowman in the square. They complete the snowman's face, and the magistrate comments to himself, "It strikes me that the snowman will need arms too, but I do not want to interfere" (155). Why not? Has he learned something about when to interfere and when to remain silent? As always with this narrator, there are gaps. The group has a leader, but no gender is noted, nor does he mention anyone who looks like the girl of whom he has been dreaming. Most prominent is that the magistrate makes no connection between this experience and his recurring dream. An astute reader with a good memory may recollect that one element in the dream was "reconfirming each time that the town she is building is empty of life" (53). The actual experience provides the magistrate with one answer to his old friend and sometime lover Mai, who has told him she is "terrified" of the future and who demands to know *"What is going to become of the children?"* (153). He responds that the barbarians "won't harm the children . . . They won't harm anyone" (153). If he has a basis for this statement, he doesn't make it clear; a stronger reason for optimism is implied by the contrast between his dream of children building a fort and the fact of their building a snowman, even one lacking arms. By this point it has become a convention that the magistrate won't comment, a convention that leaves room for me to resolve instabilities in a way he can't. He is still puzzled, but this concluding image conveys to me a note of optimism.

Mai's question about the children not only resonates within the story itself but functions ideologically as a communication from the implied author to the authorial audience. The question provides a test, a way to compare the "civility" of "barbarians" and servants of the Empire: I find myself asking, "Which group better nurtures children?" The image of children engaging in the relatively innocent activity of building a snowman, once Joll's force has fled, reinforces the novel's theme of the corruption of Empire. I connect it both mimetically and thematically with the moment when Joll hands a girl the hammer to use on a prisoner. I also tentatively connect it with the magistrate's actions and thoughts at the conclusion of Joll's first visit, after the old man has been killed and the boy tortured. He asks the colonel ironically, "Can we rest securely at night?" (23). This questioning of Empire is strengthened by his reflection on his own behavior as a member of a supposedly civilized group: "[t]hroughout a trying period [Colonel Joll] and I have managed to behave towards each other like civilized people. All my life I have believed in civilized behavior; on this occasion, however, I cannot deny it, the memory leaves me sick with myself" (24).

The directing and testimonial functions are also prominent in the novel's concluding pages. The magistrate decides that he should write a local history, but after composing a few sentences he realizes that he has written nothing more than a "plea." He thinks to himself, "Perhaps by the end of the winter . . . I will abandon the locutions of a civil servant with literary ambitions and begin to tell the truth" (154). The plea was this: "[w]e would have made any concession, had we only known what, to go on living here. This was paradise on earth" (154). He also wonders if the wooden slips he spent years collecting, those with the undecipherable writing, "contain a message as devious, as equivocal, as reprehensible as this" (154). These passages direct my attention to the narrating itself, inviting questions such as "How much truth is being told?" The testimonial function is also evoked: the narrator's pleading signifies his affective relationship with the story, while his concern with truth signifies both a moral and an intellectual relationship. As I explained in chapter 3, these functions attach not only to the narrator but to the narrating; their recipients can include any of the audience positions: narratee, narrating audience, and authorial audience. Occurring near the end, they are more likely to be taken by actual readers as directed to an authorial audience than they would if they occurred anywhere else, because of the shift readers make toward an interpretive mode. Similarly, readers will bring the extrafictional voice into the mix again, asking how far the South African author J. M. Coetzee, writing in the late 1970s, intended his story to reach. Is it a criticism of apartheid? Of regimes based on repression and torture? Of the confused human soul? I have no answers for these questions, aside from a general "Yes, I think so." That hesitancy seems to be appropriate for this novel—seems to be appropriate for the corrupted, authorial audience.

Middles and Endings: *Written on the Body*

Waiting for the Barbarians creates considerable tension by positioning authorial and narrating audiences differently once the novel is under way. *Written on the Body* activates the same basic narrative script but uses the communicating and directing functions to a different end, stressing the synthetic nature of the narrating while undercutting the mimetic basis of the story (but not of the narrating itself). These aspects create a fascinating contrast with *Waiting for the Barbarians*: the clearly fictional, even allegorical Colonel Joll and the other characters of Coetzee's novel have more mimetic reality than do Winterson's characters, even though the latter are located in a real city in a specific historical period.

Written on the Body, according to the cover, has an unnamed and ungendered narrator, but the cover also attributes to "Winterson" the "chronicling" and the "compelling." For this reason and also because the narrating voice is autodiegetic, I begin by assuming the conventional identity of gender between author and narrator. The cultural code, however, causes me to counteract this assumption by defining heterosexual relationships as the norm. The first physical description of "you" implies that "you" is a woman: "[y]ou turned on your back and your nipples grazed the surface of the river . . . You are creamy but for your hair your red hair that flanks you on either side" (*Written* 11). Applying the cultural code that privileges heterosexuality, I discard my first assumption, that the extrafictional voice and the narrating voice share the same gender. This adjustment is easy, still within the range of expectations that I apply to the reading of autodiegetic narratives. The adjustment also serves a thematic purpose: while I began by unthinkingly attaching the extrafictional voice's gender to the narrating voice, I'm suddenly made aware of *my* need to attach a gender. (At the risk of sounding confessional, I'm describing my initial reading accurately. Although I had previously read some of the theoretical discussions of this readerly tendency, I had not yet directly experienced the tendency, and I was surprised to find myself as controlled by my expectations as any sophomore in my critical-reading class.)

This awareness makes the question of the narrating voice's gender prominent as both a synthetic and a thematic element in *Written on the Body* and contributes to the tension I experience later in the novel. As I've pointed out in chapter 4, the narrating voice's first references to former relationships are to women: "I had once had a girlfriend," "I had a lover once, her name was Bathsheba" (12, 16). These references reinforce my impression that Winterson has simply inverted the more common identity between author and narrating voice present in an autodiegetic narrative. (Further reinforcing this impression is my sense of a masculine tone in the narrating voice. I've spoken with other men who have a similar reaction, but as yet I can offer no reason for it, and several women have told me they hear a definite *female* voice.) However, when I encounter the narrating voice's references to male lovers, my simple analysis of the narrating situation is no longer tenable. I have to recognize that *Written on the Body* is problematizing both the convention by which readers attach to the narrating voice the gender of the extrafictional voice and the assumption that a sexual or love relationship is heterosexual unless we're explicitly told otherwise.

Rhetorical narratology would explain my reaction thus: the textual fact that no gender is ever unambiguously attached to the narrating voice constitutes an implicature, a covert signal between the implied author and the authorial audience that a tension exists between the narrating and the authorial audiences. Experiencing this tension, and because I'm trying to read authorially, I must become conscious of that early step of my script in which I labeled the narrating voice and provisionally decided that in this novel I would not experience ironic tension between narrator and author. Because the narrating voice never makes an issue of its gender, the narrating audience, whose role is to take at face value everything the narrating voice says, will not remark on what, for the authorial audience, constitutes a lapse or a gap. True, the cover *told* me that the narrating voice is never assigned a gender, but this fact does not influence my experience of the tension between audiences. As a reader, I'm most attuned to voices when I begin a novel, and something that I encounter on the cover is only relevant to the initial moments of my reading, when I'm first creating extrafictional and narrating voices. At the end of a novel, when I'm operating at an interpretive level and am attempting to thematize the whole work, this cover material may again become important, especially if I haven't been able to generalize or to convince myself that I caught all of the available clues to the narrator's identity.

Just as my script causes me to remain somewhat off balance in my attempt to fix an identity for the narrator, it also causes me difficulty when I encounter *Written on the Body*'s two narratees: Louise and the unnamed "you" who receives such statements as "I can tell by now that you are wondering whether I can be trusted as a narrator" (24) and a few others having to do overtly with the narrating. These narratees contrast in their rhetorical effect. The "you" narratee implicates a narrating audience who is fairly close to authorial audience in terms of interest in how the story is being transmitted—reliably, accurately, and so forth. This is a conventional position for actual readers to be invited to share. It is somewhat unusual but still within conventional limits for a narratee to be addressed in the narrating present, to be a character in the story who is receiving a narrator's impassioned pleading. The kinds of statements directed to this narratee suggest an emotional distance. In contrast, the passages directed to Louise lay bare the narrator's pain, confusion, passion, and self-hatred. Thus *Written on the Body* textualizes two different audience positions *within* the narrative, each of which we may at least briefly identify with as members of the narrating audience.

Another important textual feature is that addresses to these two narratees are not distinguished, either from each other or from narration and description, by any orthographic or other visual means. So actual readers are likely to experience each narratee with dramatic immediacy but also likely to experience a tension when encountering each. Like most readers, I have a component in my script that calls for me to scan or survey upcoming chunks of texts in order to be prepared for shifts in the kind of discourse, but *Written on the Body* provides no visible clues to such shifts. Finding myself suddenly addressed either as "you" or as "Louise" causes me to feel engaged with, but also at times emotionally assaulted by, the narrating voice. For example, when the narrator raises that question of trustworthiness for the "you" narratee, I think to myself, "Well, yes, now that you mention it, I do wonder what axe you're grinding."

There's nothing unusual about a narrator explicitly raising doubts; such an utterance serves as a sort of inverted testimonial. Yet the distance between narrator and narratee invited by such passages is shattered by the addresses to Louise, which plunge me into the story world, as here:

I don't want to be your sport nor you to be mine. I don't want to punch you for the pleasure of it, tangling the clear lines that bind us . . . I don't want to pull you tighter than you can bear. I don't want the lines to slacken either . . .

I was sitting in the library writing this to Louise, looking at a facsimile of an illuminated manuscript, the first letter a huge L. . . . The letter was a maze. . . . I tried to fathom the path for a long time but I was caught at dead ends by beaming serpents. I gave up and shut the book, forgetting that the first word had been Love. (88, ellipses added)

There is no typographical indication that the first paragraph literally exists as an inscription within the world of the narrative, and in fact this is one of only two passages with such a mimetic basis in the narrating situation. The final sentence of the second paragraph resonates metaphorically—the looming fact of the narrator's relationship with Louise should have been Love, rather than the contorted yet comprehensible reasonings by which the narrator decides to leave her.

In addition to this thematic significance, actual readers may find a synthetic element in this pair of paragraphs that relates directly to the question of trustworthiness. My script leads me, as I've said, to expect some kind of material signal when I'm being given a different type of discourse. For instance, if the narrator is going to quote from a journal, I expect either to be told in advance, not after the fact, that such is the case or to be able to see on the page a different type of text. Once I begin wondering how competent or trustworthy this narrator is, I may also begin wondering how much of what at first seems to be the novel's objective reality "really happened." Elgin, for instance, is presented as an ungrateful son and selfish husband, but the story of his early life actually reaches me thirdhand, from Louise to narrator and from narrator to me. The synthetic element leads me to think about the narrator's possible (likely?) role as a *creator* of the story, not just a reporter.

The directing function also contributes to this effect, especially in passages (like the one about trustworthiness) that link the "you" narratee with self-conscious attention to the diegesis. The first such passage occurs when the narrator is reflecting on the institution of marriage: "I've been through a lot of marriages. Not down the aisle but always up the stairs. I began to realize I was hearing the same story every time. It went like this" (*Written* 13). There follows a brief section written as a scene in a play, with stage directions and three chunks of speech by a "naked woman" who is married; the scene ends thus: "*Cut to en suite bathroom. The lover is crying. End scene*" (15). The "story" the narrator is "hearing" is that of the "middle-aged happily married woman" who claims that she has never before been unfaithful to her husband, doesn't want to be "cruel and selfish," but can't get the lover out of her thoughts. The story also includes the detail of the wordless, nameless, ungendered lover crying. Almost immediately, another reflection occurs:

I've seen some very famous shells and blown into the hollows of many more. Where I've left cracking too severe to mend the owners have simply turned the bad part to the shade.

See? Even here in this private place my syntax has fallen prey to the deceit. It was not I who did those things; cut the knot, jemmied the lock, made off with goods not mine to take. (15)

These several pages call my attention to the narration as an artifact rather than a mimetically transparent report, and I think it's clear that they're designed to have this effect. They function as illocutionary acts on the part of the implied author as well as acts of directing on the narrator's part.

The ideological function, while not prominent in *Written on the Body*, does surface in one significant spot. Louise and the narrator have been vigorously making love, the description of which is interrupted by two present-tense paragraphs:

Articulacy of fingers, the language of the deaf and dumb, signing on the body body longing. Who taught you to write in blood on my back? Who taught you to use your hands as branding irons? You have scored your name into my shoulders, referenced me with your mark. The pads of your fingers have become printing blocks, you tap a message onto my skin, tap meaning into my body. Your morse code interferes with my heart beat. I had a steady heart before I met you, I relied upon it, it had seen active service and grown strong. Now you alter its pace with your own rhythm, you play upon me, drumming me taut.

Written on the body is a secret code only visible in certain lights; the accumulations of a lifetime gather there. In places the palimpsest is so heavily worked that the letters feel like braille. I like to keep my body rolled up away from prying eyes. Never unfold too much, tell the whole story. I didn't know that Louise would have reading hands. She has translated me into her own book. (89)

Because the novel's title is echoed here, these paragraphs carry authorial authority and perform an ideological function: this single utterance can be read as spoken by two voices simultaneously, narrating and extrafictional. This is an excellent example of a rather obvious but important point, that the ideological function, as an illocutionary act, probably has to be linked either explicitly, as here, or by inference to the extrafictional voice.

The diegetic repetition of the extradiegetic title stands as an illocutionary act pertinent to at least one theme, and it further complicates the relationship between actual readers and the narrator. Not only are readers asked to deal with the dual position of, on the one hand, being told that the narrator may be deceitful (i.e., readers are reminded of the narrative's synthetic aspect) and, on the other hand, being forced to receive passionate pleadings intended for someone else, but now Jeanette Winterson seems to be stepping in and validating the narrator. The phrase "written on the body" carries a thematic charge and lends even more importance to the novel's theme of inscription. What has been synthetic is becoming mimetic of my actual world—this is how stories are really told. This echo of the title crosses the diegetic/extradiegetic boundary and can draw actual readers into an even closer identification with the "you" in these passages—as if the author is suddenly addressing actual readers at the same instant a fictional voice addresses another fictional character. The lack of any typographical signal heightens this effect by preventing us actual readers from recognizing ahead of time the kind of discourse we'll be encountering and setting our defenses accordingly. The body is one palimpsest; the text is another, although there is nothing secret about its code.

Especially prominent as illocutionary acts are the four short sections that occur later in the novel, headed by title pages such as "The

Cells, Tissues, Systems and Cavities of the Body" and "The Skin" (113, 121) and containing subsections introduced by epigraphs that read as if from an encyclopedia or textbook. The narrating situation of these sections is clarified at the end of the section titled "The Skin": "I've been sitting in this chair by the fire, my hand on the cat, talking aloud, fool ramblings. There's a doctor's text-book fallen open on the floor. To me it's a book of spells. Skin, it says. Skin" (124–25). Like other things the narrator has read, written, or thought, this "text-book" is bleeding into the present narrative. It first impresses itself on actual readers with the immediacy of an unexpected touch, then the narrator explains how it has come to be a part of this text. Throughout the novel, the narrator is struggling with a question posed at the beginning: "[i]t's the clichés that cause the trouble. A precise emotion seeks a precise expression. If what I feel is not precise then should I call it love?" (10). The narrator is caught on the cusp of knowing and not knowing, feeling and not feeling, desiring and wanting not to desire. The entire narrative transmission dramatizes this cusp experience: the events with Louise exist in the past, but the emotions continue on in the present for the narrator, the narrating audience, and the authorial audience.

At the novel's end, the narrator has lost Louise, who has gone away to be treated for cancer and seems to have disappeared—perhaps dead, perhaps having left her husband. "Did I invent her?" the narrator asks Gail Right, who answers, "No, but you tried to. . . . She wasn't yours for the making" (189). Gail has no way of knowing this, never having met Louise, but her comment is plausible. The novel's final paragraphs leave unresolved the question of what happens to Louise and evoke one more time the tensions arising from the structure of narrative transmission:

From the kitchen door Louise's face. Paler, thinner, but her hair still mane-wide and the colour of blood. I put out my hand and felt her fingers, she took my fingers and put them to her mouth. The scar under the lip burned me. Am I stark mad? She's warm.

This is where the story starts, in this threadbare room. The walls are exploding. The windows have turned into telescopes. Moon and stars are magnified in this room. The sun hangs over the mantelpiece. I stretch out my hand and reach the corners of the world. The world is bundled up in this room. Beyond the door, where the river is, where the roads are, we shall be. We can take the world with us when we go and sling the sun under your arm. Hurry now, it's getting late. I don't know if this is a happy ending but here we are let loose in open fields. (190)

Again the authorial audience is invited to wonder whether the narrator can be trusted ("Am I stark mad?"), but some closure is achieved by the first sentence of the final paragraph, which states that, mimetically, the narrating itself has been taking place in the rented cottage to which the narrator escaped. Clichés seem to have been left behind; the language is fresh, although it does not allow readers to determine, mimetically, whether Louise really has returned. The novel's opening question, "Why is the measure of love loss?" has been set aside, not answered; what was lost has been regained, although perhaps only in the narrator's imagination.

The issue of gender has also been left behind. When I begin reading a narrative, I believe that it will be tellable and that, because it's a display text, its purpose is to involve me imaginatively, emotionally, or intellectually—ultimately, to move me toward an interpretation and toward the position occupied by the corrupted audience. A point of identity between narrating and authorial audiences is that neither is concerned about gender; both are able to think about love without worrying about the genders or sexual preferences of the lovers. Most readers probably wonder about Gail Right's preferences, but by the time the novel ends she has become a fixture both in the story and in the narrator's life, so that I no longer feel any tensions with her presence, only a final instability when she accuses the narrator of trying to "invent" Louise (189). That issue and the one of language are important now; the narrator echoes the novel's beginning by quoting Louise as having said, "It's the clichés that cause the trouble" (189). Because my script directs my attention to thematic issues at the end of the reading experience, and because I reactivate my impression of the extrafictional voice, I may conclude that gender is a cliché; trustworthiness is a cliché; scripts themselves are collections of clichés that need to be questioned.

Coda

To conclude, I want to return to the three pairs of sentences with which I began this chapter. I noted that as locutions, there was not a great deal of difference between the sentences in each pair, although the sentences from each novel suggest the different personalities of the narrators. They work differently in each novel's structure of narrative transmission, however. In the first pair, the sentence from *Written on the Body*, "Even here in this private place my syntax has fallen prey to the deceit" (15), serves a directing function strong enough to cause actual readers to feel that they, like the "you" narratee, are receiving this utterance. The question of the narrating situation is also foregrounded: how is the narrative being generated within the world of the novel, that is, where or what is this "private place"? The magistrate's parenthetical comment, "At a certain point I begin to plead my own cause" (*Waiting* 5), does not force itself on a narratee or on an actual reader; if the directing function is operating here, it is doing so only by implication. Both utterances contribute to doubts the actual reader may have about the narrators, but these doubts coalesce around different questions because of the differences in the directing function: a reader may well doubt that the magistrate is telling the whole truth when he keeps referring to his efforts to find the beginning of the knot, whereas a reader is justified in doubting the mimetic veracity of everything Louise's lover writes, except that Louise and Elgin probably did exist and that the narrator is actually writing. (A minor hint in this direction is the made-up quality of some of the names the narrator attaches to the other "boyfriends" and "lovers.")

The sentences in the second pair display the same kinds of differences, the *Written on the Body* sentence strongly exercising the directing function to create doubt, the *Waiting for the Barbarians* sentence allowing that possibility but not making it primary. In fact, this sentence may also be perceived as exercising the testimonial function. When the magistrate admits that he may not be truthful that the inhabitants of the outpost "would have made any concession . . . to go on living here" (*Waiting* 154), this admission really doesn't say that he has written a lie, nor has he presented enough information about his fellow citizens to allow readers to verify his assessment of the statement as "devious," "equivocal," and "reprehensible." Surely, for many readers, the magistrate's assessment serves as an indirect confirmation of the veracity of most of what he has written about the characters and events he has observed during the previous year, as well as yet another confirmation that in spite of his flaws, he *is* trying to understand the extent of his complicity. "Hold on," I think, "you're being too hard on yourself. True, you made mistakes and compromised yourself before Joll arrived and during his first visit, but then you did as much as any human being could, and better than most would have done, certainly better than I would have done."

In the third pair of sentences, that from *Written on the Body* is quite straightforward, carrying very little if any sense of functions other than narrating. It adds to the implicit self-portrait of the narrator as an opportunist, someone whose scruples are never strong enough to block an action that the narrator will later "despise" him- or herself for. The sentences contribute mimetically to a reader's experience but not thematically or synthetically. However, the key *Waiting for the Barbarians* sentence, the parenthetical "I say this who now keep a barbarian girl for my bed!" (38) is part of a larger pattern of synthetic elements that foreground the simultaneous narration. Each of the other quoted sentences from *Waiting for the Barbarians* contributes to this pattern as well; all three shape the key rhetorical effect of what Phelan terms "[o]ur double experience of complicity—in the events and in our activity of processing them" ("Present Tense Narration" 241). This experience, Phelan says, can help readers "move away from the effort to achieve a final, definitive evaluation of the magistrate's actions and toward the unsettling recognition of the power of complicity" ("Present Tense Narration" 242).

As an occasional member of the narrating audience, I accept without comment—I am complicitous in—the magistrate's observations regarding his emotional and moral state in the narrating present. As an occasional member of the authorial audience, especially in my script for finishing a narrative, I can recognize that some truths may remain untellable within the world of the narrative. Even though the magistrate is not able to write "the annals of an imperial outpost" but only what strikes him as "reprehensible," an actual reader playing the role of authorial audience is not obligated to rest content with this self-assessment. This section ends with one of the magistrate's many non-realizations: "I think: 'There has been something staring me in the face, and still I do not see it'" (*Waiting* 155). With respect to his ability to *write* something that satisfies him, he has not progressed beyond where he was nearly a year ago, when he sat for two days before blank paper and then set out to return the girl to her people (57–58). But authorially I easily step outside of the narrative's conceptual and ethical space. The concluding scene is not of dream-children building a fort but of actual children building a snowman. The magistrate leaves this scene "feeling stupid, like a man who lost his way long ago but presses on along a road that may lead nowhere" (156). Authorially, I take the contrast between dream and reality as having illocutionary force, hence as signifying an authorial intention at this point in the reading script. The script, as I've said, places this intention in the context of the extrafictional voice: the issue is *Coetzee's* purpose in leaving the magistrate confused and troubled.

For Phelan, this purpose is to involve actual readers in the experience of complicity. For me, the purpose is to send readers back again and again to the question of how much one can really "see." The point is that this general script raises but can't answer the question of intention. In attempting to describe how the structure of narrative transmission works in these two novels and in trying to trace my readerly reactions to that structure, I'm aware of an imperfect fit between the tools at my disposal and the task at hand. The scripts I've suggested are plausible, and they do correspond fairly well with my experiences and those of students in my classes. But they're sketchy. Similarly, while

I'm confident that it's helpful to determine the audience and voice positions, the functions, and so forth that operate in a narrative, helpful
especially for someone teaching narrative texts, I'm also aware that
any reader's experience of a narrative is several orders of magnitude
more complex than these tools can show. A third limitation of rhetorical narratology is that it will always be behind the developmental
curve of narrative forms, because these forms keep reinventing themselves. Scripts, ur-conventions, unmarked cases, and so forth—these
analytical constructions are necessarily conservative. They establish
a set of norms against which narrative, the perpetual adolescent in the
verbal universe, will always strain.

Works Cited

Abrams, M. H. *A Glossary of Literary Terms.* 6th ed. Fort Worth: Harcourt Brace Jovanovich, 1985.

Bach, Kent, and Robert M. Harnish. *Linguistic Communication and Speech Acts.* Cambridge: MIT P, 1979.

Bain, Carl E., Jerome Beaty, and J. Paul Hunter. *The Norton Introduction to Literature.* 5th ed. New York: Norton, 1991.

Bakhtin, Mikhail. *Dialogic Imagination: Four Essays.* Ed. Michael Holquist. Trans. Caryl Emerson and Michael Holquist. Austin: U of Texas P, 1981.

Bal, Mieke. *Narratology: Introduction to the Theory of Narrative.* Trans. Christine van Boheemen. Toronto: U of Toronto P, 1985.

———. "The Point of Narratology." *Poetics Today* 11 (winter 1990): 727–53.

Banfield, Ann. *Unspeakable Sentences: Narration and Representation in the Language of Fiction.* Boston: Routledge and Kegan Paul, 1982.

Barry, Jackson G. "Narratology's Centrifugal Force: A Literary Perspective on the Extensions of Narrative Theory." *Poetics Today* 11 (summer 1990): 295–307.

Barthes, Roland. "The Death of the Author." *Image—Music—Text.* By Roland Barthes. New York: Hill and Wang, 1977. 142–48.

———. "Introduction to the Structural Analysis of Narratives." *Image—Music—Text.* By Roland Barthes. New York: Hill and Wang, 1977. 79–124.

———. *S/Z.* Trans. Richard Miller. New York: Hill and Wang, 1974.

Beaugrande, Robert de. "Schemas for Literary Communication." *Literary Discourse: Aspects of Cognitive and Social Psychological Approaches.* Ed. Låszlo Hålasz. Berlin: Walter de Gruyter, 1987. 49–99.

———. "The Story of Grammars and the Grammar of Stories." *Journal of Pragmatics* 6 (1982): 383–422.

Bleich, David. "Gender Interests in Reading and Language." *Gender and Reading: Essays on Readers, Texts, and Contexts.* Ed. Elizabeth

Flynn and Patrocinio P. Schweickart. Baltimore: Johns Hopkins UP, 1986. 234–66.

Booth, Wayne C. *The Rhetoric of Fiction*. 1961. 2nd ed. Chicago: U of Chicago P, 1983.

Brooke-Rose, Christine. "Whatever Happened to Narratology?" *Poetics Today* 11 (summer 1990): 283–93.

Brooks, Peter. *Reading for the Plot: Design and Intention in Narrative*. 1984. Cambridge: Harvard UP, 1992.

Chambers, Ross. *Story and Situation: Narrative Seduction and the Power of Fiction*. Minneapolis: U of Minnesota P, 1984.

Chatman, Seymour. *Coming to Terms: The Rhetoric of Narrative in Fiction and Film*. Ithaca: Cornell UP, 1990.

——. "Narratological Empowerment." *Narrative* 1 (1993): 59–65.

——. *Reading Narrative Fiction*. New York: Macmillan, 1992.

——. "The 'Rhetoric' of 'Fiction.'" *Reading Narrative: Form, Ethics, Ideology*. Ed. James Phelan. Columbus: Ohio State UP, 1989. 40–56.

——. *Story and Discourse: Narrative Structure in Fiction and Film*. Ithaca: Cornell UP, 1978.

——. "What Can We Learn from Contextualist Narratology?" *Poetics Today* 11 (summer 1990): 309–28.

Chekhov, Anton. "Gooseberries." 1898. *To Read Literature*. Ed. Donald Hall. 3rd ed. Fort Worth: Harcourt Brace Jovanovich, 1992. 136–43.

Clemens, Samuel Langhorne. *Adventures of Huckleberry Finn*. 1885. Ed. Gerald Graff and James Phelan. Boston: Bedford Books, 1995.

Coetzee, J. M. *Waiting for the Barbarians*. 1980. New York: Penguin, 1982.

Cohan, Steven, and Linda M. Shires. *Telling Stories: A Theoretical Analysis of Narrative Fiction*. New York: Routledge, 1988.

Cohn, Dorrit. "Fictional *versus* Historical Lives: Borderlines and Borderline Cases." *Journal of Narrative Technique* 19 (1989): 3–24.

——. "Signposts of Fictionality: A Narratological Perspective." *Poetics Today* 11 (winter 1990): 775–804.

——. *Transparent Minds: Narrative Modes for Presenting Consciousness in Fiction*. Princeton: Princeton UP, 1978.

Culler, Jonathan. "Problems in the Theory of Fiction." *Diacritics* 14 (1984): 2–11.

——. *Structuralist Poetics: Structuralism, Linguistics, and the Study of Literature*. Ithaca: Cornell UP, 1975.

Davis, Lennard. *Resisting Novels: Ideology and Fiction*. New York: Methuen, 1987.

Davis, Robert Con, and Ronald Schleifer, eds. *Contemporary Literary Criticism: Literary and Cultural Studies*. 2nd ed. New York: Longman, 1989.

Davis, Steven. "Introduction." *Pragmatics: A Reader*. Ed. Steven Davis. New York: Oxford UP, 1991. 3–13.

Dickens, Charles. *Bleak House*. 1852–53. Oxford Illustrated Dickens. Oxford: Oxford UP, 1948.

———. *Our Mutual Friend*. 1864–65. Harmondsworth: Penguin, 1971.

Dillon, George. *Constructing Texts: Elements of a Theory of Composition and Style*. Bloomington: Indiana UP, 1981.

———. *Language Processing and the Reading of Literature: Toward a Model of Comprehension*. Bloomington: Indiana UP, 1978.

———. "Styles of Reading." *Poetics Today* 3 (spring 1982): 77–88.

Dolezel, Lubomir. "Fictional Worlds: Density, Gaps, and Inference." *Style* 29 (1995): 201–15.

Du Plessis, Rachel Blau. "Breaking the Sentence; Breaking the Sequence." *Writing Beyond the Ending*. By Rachel Blau du Plessis. Bloomington: Indiana UP, 1985. Repr. in *Essentials of the Theory of Fiction*. Ed. Michael J. Hoffman and Patrick D. Murphy. Durham: Duke UP, 1988. 473–92.

Eagleton, Terry. *Criticism and Ideology: A Study in Marxist Literary Theory*. Atlantic Highlands: Humanities, 1976.

———. *Literary Theory: An Introduction*. Minneapolis: U of Minnesota P, 1983.

Fish, Stanley. "How to Do Things with Austin and Searle: Speech Act Theory and Literary Criticism." *Modern Language Notes* 91 (1977): 983–1025.

Fleischman, Suzanne. *Tense and Narrativity: From Medieval Performance to Modern Fiction*. Austin: U of Texas P, 1990.

Fludernik, Monika. *The Fictions of Language and the Languages of Fiction: The Linguistic Representation of Speech and Consciousness*. London: Routledge, 1993.

———. *Towards a "Natural" Narratology*. London: Routledge, 1996.

Flynn, Elizabeth. "Gender and Reading." *Gender and Reading: Essays on Readers, Texts, and Contexts*. Ed. Elizabeth Flynn and Patrocinio P. Schweickart. Baltimore: Johns Hopkins UP, 1986. 267–88.

Fowler, Roger. *Linguistic Criticism*. Oxford: Oxford UP, 1986.

Friedman, Susan Stanford. "Spatialization: A Strategy for Reading Narrative." *Narrative* 1 (1993): 12–23.

Gelley, Alexander. *Narrative Crossings: Theory and Pragmatics of Prose Fiction*. Baltimore: Johns Hopkins UP, 1987.

Genette, Gérard. "Fictional Narrative, Factual Narrative." *Poetics Today* 11 (winter 1990): 755–74.

———. *Narrative Discourse: An Essay in Method*. Trans. Jane Lewin. Ithaca: Cornell UP, 1980.

———. *Narrative Discourse Revisited.* Trans. Jane Lewin. Ithaca: Cornell UP, 1988.

Gibson, Andrew. *Towards a Postmodern Theory of Narrative.* Edinburgh: Edinburgh UP, 1996.

Goodrich, Diana Sorenson. *The Reader and the Text: Interpretive Strategies for Latin American Literatures.* Amsterdam: Benjamins, 1986.

Grass, Günter. *The Tin Drum.* Trans. Ralph Manheim. New York: Vintage, 1990.

Grice, Paul. *Studies in the Way of Words.* Cambridge and London: Harvard UP, 1989.

Hall, Donald. *To Read Literature.* 3rd ed. Fort Worth: Harcourt Brace Jovanovich, 1992.

Hamburger, Käte. *The Logic of Literature.* 2nd ed. Trans. Marilynn J. Rose. Bloomington: Indiana UP, 1973.

Hartwell, Patrick. "Grammar, Grammars, and the Teaching of Grammar." *The Allyn and Bacon Sourcebook for College Writing Teachers.* Ed. James C. McDonald. Boston: Allyn and Bacon, 1996. 234–57. First published in *College English* 47 (1985): 105–27.

Hawthorne, Nathaniel. *The Scarlet Letter.* Ed. Ross C. Murfin. Boston: Bedford Books, 1991.

Herman, David. "Hypothetical Focalization." *Narrative* 2 (1994): 230–53.

Hoesterey, Ingeborg. "Introduction." *Neverending Stories: Toward a Critical Narratology.* Ed. Ann Fehn, Ingeborg Hoesterey, and Maria Tatar. Princeton: Princeton UP, 1992. 3–14.

Ibsch, Elrud. "The Cognitive Turn in Narratology." *Poetics Today* 11 (1990): 411–18.

Iser, Wolfgang. *The Act of Reading: A Theory of Aesthetic Response.* Baltimore: Johns Hopkins UP, 1978.

———. *The Implied Reader: Patterns of Communication from Bunyan to Beckett.* Baltimore: Johns Hopkins UP, 1975.

———. "Interaction between Text and Reader." *The Reader in the Text: Essays on Audience and Interpretation.* Ed. Susan Suleiman and Inge Crosman. Princeton: Princeton UP, 1980. 106–20.

Jahn, Manfred. "Windows of Focalization: Deconstructing and Reconstructing a Narratological Concept." *Style* 30 (1996): 241–67.

James, Henry. *The Ambassadors.* 1903. New York ed. 1907–09. London: Penguin, 1986.

———. *The Bostonians.* 1886. Harmondsworth: Penguin, 1966.

———. *The Portrait of a Lady.* 1881. Rev. ed. 1907. Oxford: Oxford UP, 1981.

———. *Washington Square*. 1880. In *Henry James: Novels 1881–1886*. New York: Library of America, 1985.

Jefferson, Ann. "Structuralism and Post-Structuralism." *Modern Literary Theory: A Comprehensive Introduction*. Ed. Ann Jefferson and David Robey. Totowa: Barnes and Noble Books, 1982. 84–112.

Kafka, Franz. *The Trial*. Trans. Willa and Edwin Muir. New York: Pantheon, 1984.

Kearns, Michael. "Henry James, Principled Realism, and the Practice of Critical Reading." *College English* 56 (1994): 766–87.

———. "Narrative Discourse and the Imperative of Sympathy in *The Bostonians*." *Henry James Review* 17 (1996): 162–81.

———. "Narrative Voices in *The Scarlet Letter*." *Nathaniel Hawthorne Review* 22 (1996): 36–52.

———. "Reading Novels: Toward a Cognitivist Rhetoric." *Rhetoric Society Quarterly* 26 (1996): 17–30.

Keen, Kathe. "Crossing Boundaries: Effacing Gender Categories in Jeanette Winterson's *Written on the Body*." Unpublished paper.

Kinneavy, James L. *A Theory of Discourse: The Aims of Discourse*. New York: Norton, 1971.

Kirszner, Laurie G., and Stephen R. Mandell. *Literature: Reading, Reacting, Writing*. 3rd ed. Fort Worth: Harcourt Brace, 1997.

Lanser, Susan Sniader. *Fictions of Authority: Women Writers and Narrative Voice*. Ithaca: Cornell UP, 1992.

———. *The Narrative Act: Point of View in Prose Fiction*. Princeton: Princeton UP, 1981.

———. "Queering Narratology." *Ambiguous Discourse: Feminist Narratology and British Women Writers*. Ed. Kathy Mezei. Chapel Hill: U of North Carolina P, 1996. 250–61.

———. "Sexing the Narrative: Propriety, Desire, and the Engendering of Narratology." *Narrative* 3 (1995): 85–94.

Leitch, Thomas M. *What Stories Are: Narrative Theory and Interpretation*. University Park: Pennsylvania State UP, 1986.

Lessing, Doris. *The Memoirs of a Survivor*. 1974. Repr. New York: Bantam, 1976.

Lively, Penelope. *Moon Tiger*. New York: Harper and Row, 1988.

Ludwig, Hans-Werner, and Werner Faulstich. *Erzählperspektive empirisch-Untersuchungen zur Rezeptionsrelevanz narrativer Strukturen*. Tübingen: Gunter Narr, 1985.

Martin, Wallace. *Recent Theories of Narrative*. Ithaca: Cornell UP, 1986.

Melville, Herman. "Bartleby the Scrivener." *The Piazza Tales and Other Prose Pieces, 1839–1860*. Ed. Harrison Hayford, Alma A. Mac-

Dougall, and G. Thomas Tanselle. Evanston and Chicago: Northwestern UP and the Newberry Library, 1987. 13–45.

Meyer, Michael. *The Compact Bedford Introduction to Literature.* 4th ed. Boston: Bedford Books, 1997.

Mezei, Kathy. "Contextualizing Feminist Narratology." *Ambiguous Discourse: Feminist Narratology and British Women Writers.* Ed. Kathy Mezei. Chapel Hill: U of North Carolina P, 1996. 1–20.

———. "Who Is Speaking Here? Free Indirect Discourse, Gender, and Authority in *Emma, Howards End,* and *Mrs. Dalloway.*" *Ambiguous Discourse: Feminist Narratology and British Women Writers.* Ed. Kathy Mezei. Chapel Hill: U of North Carolina P, 1996. 66–92.

Nelles, William. "Getting Focalization into Focus." *Poetics Today* 11 (summer 1990): 365–82.

O'Neill, Patrick. *Fictions of Discourse: Reading Narrative Theory.* Toronto: U of Toronto P, 1994.

Olsson, Ulf. "The Greatest Story Ever Told: Some Remarks on the Voice of Narratology." *Perspectives on Narratology: Papers from the Stockholm Symposium on Narratology.* Ed. Claes Wahlin. Frankfurt: Peter Lang, 1996. 81–94.

Pavel, Thomas. "Naturalizing *Molloy.*" *Understanding Narrative.* Ed. James Phelan and Peter Rabinowitz. Columbus: Ohio State UP, 1994. 178–98.

Petrey, Sandy. *Speech Acts and Literary Theory.* New York: Routledge, 1990.

Phelan, James. *Narrative as Rhetoric: Technique, Audiences, Ethics, Ideology.* Columbus: Ohio State UP, 1996.

———. "Present Tense Narration, Mimesis, the Narrative Norm, and the Positioning of the Reader in *Waiting for the Barbarians.*" *Understanding Narrative.* Ed. James Phelan and Peter Rabinowitz. Columbus: Ohio State UP, 1994. 222–45.

———. *Reading People, Reading Plots: Character, Progression, and the Interpretation of Narrative.* Chicago: U of Chicago P, 1989.

Phelan, James, and Peter J. Rabinowitz. "Understanding Narrative." *Understanding Narrative.* Ed. James Phelan and Peter Rabinowitz. Columbus: Ohio State UP, 1994. 1–15.

Poe, Edgar Allan. "The Fall of the House of Usher." 1839. *Poetry, Tales, and Selected Essays.* Library of America College Edition. New York: Penguin, 1996. 317–36.

———. "Ligeia." 1838. *Poetry, Tales, and Selected Essays.* Library of America College Edition. New York: Penguin, 1996. 262–77.

Pratt, Mary Louise. "The Ideology of Speech-Act Theory." *Centrum,* n.s. 1 (spring 1981): 5–18.

———. "Literary Cooperation and Implicature." *Essays in Modern Stylistics.* Ed. Donald Freeman. London: Methuen, 1981. 377–412.

———. *Toward a Speech Act Theory of Literary Discourse.* Bloomington: Indiana UP, 1977.

Preston, Elizabeth. "Implying Authors in *The Great Gatsby.*" *Narrative* 5 (1997): 143–64.

Prince, Gerald. *A Dictionary of Narratology.* Lincoln: U of Nebraska P, 1987. Aldershot, Great Britain: Scolar Press, 1988.

———. "Introduction to the Study of the Narratee." *Poetique*, no. 14 (1973). Repr. in *Reader-Response Criticism: From Formalism to Post-Structuralism.* Ed. Jane P. Tompkins. Baltimore: Johns Hopkins UP, 1980. 7–25.

———. "Narrative Studies and Narrative Genres." *Poetics Today* 11 (summer 1990): 271–82.

———. *Narratology: The Form and Functioning of Narrative.* Berlin: Mouton, 1982.

———. "On Narratology: Criteria, Corpus, Context." *Narrative* 3 (1995): 73–84.

———. "Remarks on Narrativity." *Perspectives on Narratology: Papers from the Stockholm Symposium on Narratology.* Ed. Claes Wahlin. Frankfurt: Peter Lang, 1996. 95–106.

Puig, Manuel. *Kiss of the Spider Woman.* Trans. Thomas Colchie. New York: Vintage, 1991.

Rabinowitz, Peter. *Before Reading: Narrative Conventions and the Politics of Interpretation.* Ithaca: Cornell UP, 1987.

———. "Truth in Fiction: A Reexamination of Audiences." *Critical Inquiry* 4 (1977): 121–41.

Rader, Ralph. "The Emergence of the Novel in England: Genre in History vs. History of Genre." *Narrative* 1 (1993): 69–83.

———. "The Concept of Genre and Eighteenth-Century Studies." *New Approaches to Eighteenth-Century Literature: Essays from the English Institute.* Ed. Phillip Harth. New York: Columbia UP, 1974. 79–115.

Reid, Ian. *Narrative Exchanges.* London: Routledge, 1992.

Richter, David H., ed. *Falling into Theory: Conflicting Views on Reading Literature.* Boston: Bedford Books, 1994.

———. *Narrative/Theory.* White Plains: Longman, 1996.

Rimmon-Kenan, Shlomith. "How the Model Neglects the Medium: Linguistics, Language, and the Crisis of Narratology." *Journal of Narrative Technique* 19 (1989): 157–66.

———. *Narrative Fiction: Contemporary Poetics.* London: Routledge, 1983.

Robbe-Grillet, Alain. *Dans le labyrinthe*. Paris: Editions de Minuit, 1959.

———. *In the Labyrinth*. Trans. Richard Howard. *Two Novels by Robbe-Grillet*. New York: Grove P, 1965.

Ronen, Ruth. *Possible Worlds in Literary Theory*. Cambridge: Cambridge UP, 1994.

Ryan, Marie-Laure. "Allegories of Immersion: Virtual Narration in Postmodern Fiction." *Style* 29 (1995): 262–87.

———. "The Modes of Narrativity and Their Visual Metaphors." *Style* 26 (1992): 368–87.

———. *Possible Worlds, Artificial Intelligence, and Narrative Theory*. Bloomington: Indiana UP, 1991.

———. "Postmodernism and the Doctrine of Panfictionality." *Narrative* 5 (1997): 165–87.

Schank, Roger C., and Robert P. Abelson. *Scripts, Plans, Goals and Understanding: An Inquiry into Human Knowledge*. Hillsdale: Erlbaum, 1977.

Scholes, Robert. "Reading Like a Man." *Men in Feminism*. Ed. Alice Jardine and Paul Smith. New York: Methuen, 1987. 204–18.

———. *Structuralism in Literature: An Introduction*. New Haven: Yale UP, 1974.

———. *Textual Power: Literary Theory and the Teaching of English*. New Haven: Yale UP, 1985.

Scholes, Robert, Nancy Comley, and Gregory Ulmer. *Text Book: An Introduction to Literary Language*. 2nd ed. New York: St. Martin's, 1995.

Schweickart, Patrocinio P. "Reading Ourselves: Toward a Feminist Theory of Reading." *Speaking of Gender*. Ed. Elaine Showalter. New York: Routledge, 1989. 17–44.

Searle, John. *Expression and Meaning: Studies in the Theory of Speech Acts*. Cambridge: Cambridge UP, 1979.

———. "The Logical Status of Fictional Discourse." *New Literary History* 6 (1974–75): 319–32. Repr. in *Expression and Meaning: Studies in the Theory of Speech Acts*. By John Searle. Cambridge: Cambridge UP, 1979. 58–75.

Shapiro, Michael. *The Sense of Grammar: Language as Semiotic*. Bloomington: Indiana UP, 1983.

Shaw, Harry E. "Loose Narrators: Display, Engagement, and the Search for a Place in History in Realist Fiction." *Narrative* 3 (1995): 95–116.

Sperber, Dan, and Dierdre Wilson. "Loose Talk." *Proceedings of the Aristotelian Society* 86 (1985–86): 153–71. Repr. in *Pragmatics: A Reader*. Ed. S. Davis. Oxford: Oxford UP, 1991. 540–49.

————. *Relevance: Communication and Cognition.* 2nd ed. Cambridge: Harvard UP, 1995.

Stanzel, F. K. "Free Indirect Discourse/Erlebte Rede—An Irritation to Grammar and Narratology." *Perspectives on Narratology: Papers from the Stockholm Symposium on Narratology.* Ed. Claes Wahlin. Frankfurt: Peter Lang, 1996. 141–53.

————. *A Theory of Narrative.* Trans. Charlotte Goedsche. London: Cambridge UP, 1984.

Toolan, Michael J. *Narrative: A Critical Linguistic Introduction.* London: Routledge, 1988.

Turner, Mark. *Reading Minds: The Study of English in the Age of Cognitive Science.* Princeton: Princeton UP, 1991.

Van Dijk, Teun A., and Walter Kintsch. "Cognitive Psychology and Discourse: Recalling and Summarizing Stories." *Current Trends in Textlinguistics.* Ed. Wolfgang U. Dressler. Berlin and New York: de Gruyter, 1977. 61–80.

Warhol, Robyn. *Gendered Interventions: Narrative Discourse in the Victorian Novel.* New Brunswick: Rutgers UP, 1989.

————. "'Reader, Can You Imagine? No, You Cannot': The Narratee as Other in Harriet Jacobs's Text." *Narrative* 3 (1995): 57–72.

Watt, Anneliese. "Burke on Narrative: The Dialectic of Temporal Embodiment and Eternal Essence." *Narrative* 6 (1998): 49–71.

Williams, James D. "Rule-Governed Approaches to Language and Composition." *Written Communication* 10 (1993): 542–68.

Wimmers, Inge Crosman. *Poetics of Reading: Approaches to the Novel.* Princeton: Princeton UP, 1988.

Winterson, Jeanette. *Written on the Body.* 1992. New York: Vintage, 1994.

Index

In the Stages series